Henry James on Italy

The Aqueduct at Ariccia, near Rome, by James Baker Pyne

HENRY JAMES ON ITALY

The harbour, Genoa

SELECTIONS FROM
ITALIAN HOURS

WEIDENFELD & NICOLSON
NEW YORK

Published by Weidenfeld & Nicolson, New York
A Division of Wheatland Corporation
841 Broadway
New York, New York 10003-4793

This edition published in Great Britain in 1988
by Barrie & Jenkins Ltd., London

Library of Congress Cataloging-in-Publication Data

James, Henry, 1843-1916.
  Henry James on Italy.

  Includes index.
  1. Italy – Description and travel – 1861-1900.
  2. James, Henry, 1843-1916 – Journeys – Italy.
  3. Authors, American – 19th century – Journeys – Italy.
  I. James, Henry, 1843-1916. Italian hours. II. Title.
  DG427.J3525 1988   914.5′049   88-10596
  ISBN 1-55584-238-0

Typeset by SX Composing Ltd
Colour separation by Colorlito, Milan
Printed in Spain by Graficas Estella, Navarra

First American Edition

10 9 8 7 6 5 4 3 2 1

Cover picture: *The Campanile and the Doge's Palace, with
St Mark's in the background* (detail) by James Holland
(Bridgeman Art Library)

CONTENTS

Italy at the end of the nineteenth century

CHAPTER I

VENICE

St. Mark's, Venice

 T IS A GREAT PLEASURE to write the word; but I am not sure there is not a certain impudence in pretending to add anything to it. Venice has been painted and described many thousands of times, and of all the cities of the world is the easiest to visit without going there. Open the first book and you will find a rhapsody about it; step into the first picture-dealer's and you will find three or four high-coloured "views" of it. There is notoriously nothing more to be said on the subject. Every one has been there, and every one has brought back a collection of photographs. There is as little mystery about the Grand Canal as about our local thoroughfare, and the name of St. Mark is as familiar as the postman's ring. It is not forbidden, however, to speak of familiar things, and I hold that for the true Venice-lover Venice is always in order. There is nothing new to be said about her certainly, but the old is better than any novelty. It would be a sad day indeed when there should be something new to say. I write these lines with the full consciousness of having no information whatever to offer. I do not pretend to enlighten the reader; I pretend only to give a fillip to his memory; and I hold any writer sufficiently justified who is himself in love with his theme.

I

Mr. Ruskin has given it up, that is very true; but only after extracting half a lifetime of pleasure and an immeasurable quantity of fame from it. We all may do the same, after it has served our turn, which it probably will not cease to do for many a year to come. Meantime it is Mr. Ruskin who beyond any one helps us to enjoy. He has indeed lately produced several aids to depression in the shape of certain little humorous – ill-humorous – pamphlets (the series of *St. Mark's Rest*) which embody his latest reflections on the subject of our city and describe the latest atrocities perpetrated there. These latter are numerous and deeply to be deplored; but to admit that they have spoiled Venice would be to admit that Venice may be spoiled – an admission pregnant, as it seems to us, with disloyalty. Fortunately one reacts against the Ruskinian contagion, and one hour of the lagoon is worth a hundred pages of demoralised prose. This queer late-coming prose of Mr. Ruskin (including the revised and condensed issue of the *Stones of Venice*, only one little volume of which has been published, or perhaps ever will be) is all to be read, though much of it appears addressed to children of tender age. It is pitched in the nursery-key, and might be supposed to emanate from an angry governess. It is, however, all suggestive, and much of it is delightfully just. There is an inconceivable want of form in it, though the author has spent his life in laying down the principles of form and scolding people for departing from them; but it throbs and flashes with the love of his subject – a love disconcerted and abjured, but which has still much of the force of inspiration. Among the many strange things that have befallen Venice, she has had the good fortune to become the object of a passion to a man of splendid genius, who has made her his own and in doing so has made her the world's. There is no better reading at Venice therefore, as I say, than Ruskin, for every true Venice-lover can separate the wheat from the chaff. The narrow theological spirit, the moralism *à tout propos*, the queer provincialities and pruderies, are mere wild weeds in a mountain of flowers. One may doubtless be very happy in Venice without reading at all – without criticising or analysing or thinking a strenuous thought. It is a city in which, I suspect, there is very little strenuous thinking, and yet it is a city in which there must be almost as much happiness as misery. The misery of Venice stands there for all the world to see; it is part of the spectacle – a thorough-going devotee of local colour might consistently say it is part of the pleasure. The Venetian people have little to call their own – little more than the bare privilege of leading their lives in the most beautiful of towns. Their habitations are decayed; their taxes heavy; their pockets light; their opportunities few. One receives an impression, however, that life presents itself to them with attractions not accounted for in this meagre train of advantages, and that they are on better terms with it than many people who have made a better bargain. They lie in the sunshine; they dabble in the sea; they wear bright rags; they fall into attitudes and harmonies; they assist at an eternal *conversazione*. It is not easy to say that one would have them other than they are, and it certainly would make an immense difference should they be better fed. The number of persons in Venice who evidently never have enough to eat is painfully large; but it would be more painful if we did not equally perceive that the rich Venetian temperament may bloom upon a dog's allowance. Nature has been kind to it, and sunshine and leisure and conversation and beautiful views form the greater part of its sustenance. It takes a great deal to make a successful American, but to make a happy Venetian takes only a handful of quick sensibility. The Italian people have at once the good and the evil fortune to be conscious of few wants; so that if the civilisation of a society is measured by the number of its needs, as seems to be the common opinion to-day, it is to be

Venetian Palazzo

feared that the children of the lagoon would make but a poor figure in a set of comparative tables. Not their misery, doubtless, but the way they elude their misery, is what pleases the sentimental tourist, who is gratified by the sight of a beautiful race that lives by the aid of its imagination. The way to enjoy Venice is to follow the example of these people and make the most of simple pleasures. Almost all the pleasures of the place are simple; this may be maintained even under the imputation of ingenious paradox. There is no simpler pleasure than looking at a fine Titian, unless it be looking at a fine Tintoret or strolling into St. Mark's – abominable the way one falls into the habit – and resting one's light-wearied eyes upon the windowless gloom; or than floating in a gondola or than hanging over a balcony or than taking one's coffee at Florian's. It is of such superficial pastimes that a Venetian day is composed, and the pleasure of the matter is in the emotions to which they minister. These are fortunately of the finest – otherwise Venice would be insufferably dull. Reading Ruskin is good; reading the old records is perhaps better; but the best thing of all is simply staying on. The only way to care for Venice as she deserves it is to give her a chance to touch you often – to linger and remain and return.

II

The danger is that you will not linger enough – a danger of which the author of these lines had known something. It is possible to dislike Venice, and to entertain the sentiment in a responsible and intelligent manner. There are travellers who think the place odious, and those who are not of this opinion often find themselves wishing that the others were only more numerous. The sentimental tourist's sole quarrel with his Venice is that he has too many competitors there. He likes to be alone; to be original; to have (to himself, at least) the air of making discoveries. The Venice of to-day is a vast museum where the little wicket that admits you is perpetually turning and creaking, and you march through the institution with a herd of fellow-gazers. There is nothing left to discover or describe, and originality of attitude is completely impossible. This is often very annoying; you can only turn your back on your impertinent playfellow and curse his want of delicacy. But this is not the fault of Venice; it is the fault of the rest of the world. The fault of Venice is that, though she is easy to admire, she is not so easy to live with as you count living in other places. After you have stayed a week and the bloom of novelty has rubbed off you wonder if you can accommodate yourself to the peculiar

Venice, by Joseph Arthur Palliser Severn

Palazzo D'Osmarin

conditions. Your old habits become impracticable and you find yourself obliged to form new ones of an undesirable and unprofitable character. You are tired of your gondola (or you think you are) and you have seen all the principal pictures and heard the names of the palaces announced a dozen times by your gondolier, who brings them out almost as impressively as if he were an English butler bawling titles into a drawing-room. You have walked several hundred times round the Piazza and bought several bushels of photographs. You have visited the antiquity-mongers whose horrible sign-boards dishonour some of the grandest vistas in the Grand Canal; you have tried the opera and found it very bad; you have bathed at the Lido and found the water flat. You have begun to have a shipboard-feeling – to regard the Piazza as an enormous saloon and the Riva degli Schiavoni as a promenade-deck. You are obstructed and encaged; your desire for space is unsatisfied; you miss your usual exercise. You try to take a walk and you fail, and meantime, as I say, you have come to regard your gondola as a sort of magnified baby's cradle. You have no desire to be rocked to sleep, though you are sufficiently kept awake by the irritation produced, as you gaze across the shallow lagoon, by the attitude of the perpetual gondolier, with his turned-out toes, his protruded chin, his absurdly unscientific stroke. The canals have a horrible smell, and the everlasting Piazza, where you have looked repeatedly at every article in every shop-window and found them all rubbish, where the young Venetians who sell bead bracelets and "panoramas" are perpetually thrusting their wares at you, where the same tightly-buttoned officers are for ever sucking the same black weeds, at the same empty tables, in front of the same cafés – the Piazza, as I say, has resolved itself into a magnificent tread-mill. This is the state of mind of those shallow inquirers who find Venice all very well for a week; and if in such a state of mind you take your departure you act with fatal rashness. The loss is your own, moreover; it is not – with all deference to your personal attractions – that of your companions who remain behind; for though there are some disagreeable things in Venice there is nothing so disagreeable as the visitors. The conditions are peculiar, but your intolerance of them evaporates before it has had time to become a prejudice. When you have called for the bill to go, pay it and remain, and you will find on the morrow that you are deeply attached to Venice. It is by living there from day to day that you feel the fulness of her charm; that you invite her exquisite influence to sink into your spirit. The creature varies like a nervous woman, whom you know only when you know all the aspects of her beauty. She has high spirits or low, she is pale or red, grey or pink, cold or warm, fresh or wan, according to the weather or the hour. She is always interesting and almost always sad; but she has a thousand occasional graces and is always liable to happy accidents. You become extraordinarily fond of these things; you count upon them; they make part of your life. Tenderly fond you become; there is something indefinable in those depths of personal acquaintance that gradually establish themselves. The place seems to personify itself, to become human and sentient and conscious of your affection. You desire to embrace it, to caress it, to possess it; and finally a soft sense of possession grows up and your visit becomes a perpetual love-affair. It is very true that if you go, as the author of these lines on a certain occasion went, about the middle of March, a certain amount of disappointment is possible. He had paid no visit for several years, and in the interval the beautiful and helpless city had suffered an increase of injury. The barbarians are in full possession and you tremble for what they may do. You are reminded from the moment of your arrival that Venice scarcely exists any more as a city at all; that she exists only as a battered peep-show and bazaar. There was a horde of savage Germans encamped in the Piazza, and they filled the Ducal Palace and the Academy with their uproar. The English and Americans came a little later. They came in good time, with a great many French, who were discreet enough to make very long repasts at the Caffè Quadri, during which they were out of the way. The months of April and May of the year 1881 were not, as a general thing, a favourable season for visiting the Ducal Palace and the Academy. The *valet-de-place* had marked them for his own and held triumphant possession of them. He celebrates his triumphs in a terrible brassy voice, which resounds all over the place, and has, whatever language he be speaking, the accent of some other idiom. During all the spring months in Venice these gentry abound in the great resorts, and they lead their helpless captives through churches and galleries in dense irresponsible groups. They infest the Piazza; they pursue you along the Riva; they hang about the bridges and the

Gondola

13

doors of the cafés. In saying just now that I was disappointed at first, I had chiefly in mind the impression that assails me to-day in the whole precinct of St. Mark's. The condition of this ancient sanctuary is surely a great scandal. The pedlars and commissioners ply their trade – often a very unclean one – at the very door of the temple; they follow you across the threshold, into the sacred dusk, and pull your sleeve, and hiss into your ear, scuffling with each other for customers. There is a great deal of dishonour about St. Mark's altogether, and if Venice, as I say, has become a great bazaar, this exquisite edifice is now the biggest booth.

III

It is treated as a booth in all ways, and if it had not somehow a great spirit of solemnity within it the traveller would soon have little warrant for regarding it as a religious affair. The restoration of the outer walls, which has lately been so much attacked and defended, is certainly a great shock. Of the necessity of the work only an expert is, I suppose, in a position to judge; but there is no doubt that, if a necessity it be, it is one that is deeply to be regretted. To no more distressing necessity have people of taste lately had to resign themselves. Wherever the hand of the restorer has been laid all semblance of beauty has vanished; which is a sad fact, considering that the external loveliness of St. Mark's has been for ages less impressive only than that of the still comparatively uninjured interior. I know not what is the measure of necessity in such a case, and it appears indeed to be a very delicate question. To-day, at any rate, that admirable harmony of faded mosaic and marble which, to the eye of the traveller emerging from the narrow streets that lead to the Piazza, filled all the further end of it with a sort of dazzling silvery presence – to-day this lovely vision is in a way to be completely reformed and indeed well-nigh abolished. The old softness and mellowness of colour – the work of the quiet centuries and of the breath of the salt sea – is giving way to large crude patches of new material which have the effect of a monstrous malady rather than of a restoration to health. They look like blotches of red and white paint and dishonourable smears of chalk on the cheeks of a noble matron. The face toward the Piazzetta is in especial the newest-looking thing conceivable – as new as a new pair of boots or as the morning's paper. We do not profess, however, to undertake a scientific quarrel with these changes; we admit that our complaint is a purely sentimental one. The march of industry in united Italy must doubtless be looked at as a whole, and one must endeavour to believe that it is through innumerable lapses of taste that this deeply interesting country is groping her way to her place among the nations. For the present, it is not to be denied, certain odd phases of the process are more visible than the result, to arrive at which it seems necessary that, as she was of old a passionate votary of the beautiful, she should to-day burn everything that she has adored. It is doubtless too soon to judge her, and there are moments when one is willing to forgive her even the restoration of St. Mark's. Inside as well there has been a considerable attempt to make the place more tidy; but the general effect, as yet, has not seriously suffered. What I chiefly remember is the straightening out of that dark and rugged old pavement – those deep undulations of primitive mosaic in which the fond spectator was thought to perceive an intended resemblance to the waves of the ocean. Whether intended or not the analogy was an image the more in a treasure-house of images; but from a considerable portion of the church it has now disappeared. Throughout the greater part indeed the pavement remains as recent generations have known it – dark, rich, cracked, uneven, spotted with porphyry and time-blackened malachite, polished by the knees of innumerable worshippers; but in other large stretches the idea imitated by the restorers is that of the ocean in a dead calm, and the model they have taken the floor of a London club-house or of a New York hotel. I think no Venetian and scarcely any Italian cares much for such differences; and when, a year ago, people in England were writing to the *Times* about the whole business and holding meetings to protest against it the dear children of the lagoon – so far as they heard or heeded the rumour – thought them partly busy-bodies and partly asses. Busy-bodies they doubtless were, but they took a good deal of disinterested trouble. It never occurs to the Venetian mind of to-day that such trouble may be worth taking; the Venetian mind vainly endeavours to conceive a state of existence in which personal questions are so insipid that people have to look for grievances in the wrongs of brick and marble. I must not, however, speak of St. Mark's as if I had the pretension of giving a description of it or as if the reader

St. Mark's Sacristy

desired one. The reader has been too well served already. It is surely the best-described building in the world. Open the *Stones of Venice*, open Théophile Gautier's *Italia*, and you will see. These writers take it very seriously, and it is only because there is another way of taking it that I venture to speak of it; the way that offers itself after you have been in Venice a couple of months, and the light is hot in the great Square, and you pass in under the pictured porticoes with a feeling of habit and friendliness and a desire for something cool and dark. There are moments, after all, when the church is comparatively quiet and empty, and when you may sit there with an easy consciousness of its beauty. From the moment, of course, that you go into any Italian church for any purpose but to say your prayers or look at the ladies, you rank yourself among the trooping barbarians I just spoke of; you treat the place as an orifice in the peep-show. Still, it is almost a spiritual function – or, at the worst, an amorous one – to feed one's eyes on the molten colour that drops from the hollow vaults and thickens the air with its richness. It is all so quiet and sad and faded and yet all so brilliant and living. The strange figures in the mosaic pictures, bending with the curve of niche and vault, stare down through the glowing dimness; the burnished gold that stands behind them catches the light on its little uneven cubes. St. Mark's owes nothing of its character to the beauty of proportion or perspective; there is nothing grandly balanced or far-arching; there are no long lines nor triumphs of the perpendicular. The church arches indeed, but arches like a dusky cavern. Beauty of surface, of tone, of detail, of things near enough to touch and kneel upon and lean against – it is from this the effect proceeds. In this sort of beauty the place is incredibly rich, and you may go there every day and find afresh some lurking pictorial nook. It is a treasury of bits, as the painters say; and there are usually three or four of the fraternity with their easels set up in uncertain equilibrium on the undulating floor. It is not easy to catch the real complexion of St. Mark's, and these laudable attempts at portraiture are apt to look either lurid or livid. But if you cannot paint the old loose-looking marble slabs, the great panels of basalt and jasper, the crucifixes of which the lonely anguish looks deeper in the vertical light, the tabernacles whose open doors disclose a dark Byzantine image spotted with dull, crooked gems – if you cannot paint these things you can at least grow fond of them. You grow fond even of the old benches of red marble, partly worn away by the breeches of many generations and attached to the base of those wide pilasters of which the precious plating, delightful in its faded brownness, with a faint grey bloom upon it, bulges and yawns a little with honourable age.

St. Mark's Square, by Edward Pritchett

Even at first, when the vexatious sense of the city of the Doges reduced to earning its living as a curiosity-shop was in its keenness, there was a great deal of entertainment to be got from lodging on Riva Schiavoni and looking out at the far-shimmering lagoon. There was entertainment indeed in simply getting into the place and observing the queer incidents of a Venetian installation. A great many persons contribute indirectly to this undertaking, and it is surprising how they spring out at you during your novitiate to remind you that they are bound up in some mysterious manner with the constitution of your little establishment. It was an interesting problem for instance to trace the subtle connection existing between the niece of the landlady and the occupancy of the fourth floor. Superficially it was none too visible, as the young lady in question was a dancer at the Fenice theatre – or when that was closed at the Rossini – and might have been supposed absorbed by her professional duties. It proved necessary, however, that she should hover about the premises in a velvet jacket and a pair of black kid gloves with one little white button; as also, that she should apply a thick coating of powder to her face, which had a charming oval and a sweet weak expression, like that of most of the Venetian maidens, who, as a general thing – it was not a peculiarity of the landlady's niece – are fond of besmearing themselves with flour. You soon recognise that it is not only the many-twinkling lagoon you behold from a habitation on the Riva; you see a little of everything Venetian. Straight across, before my windows, rose the great pink mass of San Giorgio Maggiore, which has for an ugly Palladian church a success beyond all reason. It is a success of position, of colour, of the immense detached Campanile, tipped with a tall gold angel. I know not whether it is because San Giorgio is so grandly conspicuous, with a great deal of worn, faded-looking brickwork; but for many persons the whole place has a kind of suffusion of rosiness. Asked what may be the leading colour in the Venetian concert, we should inveterately say Pink, and yet without remembering after all that this elegant hue occurs very often. It is a faint, shimmering, airy, watery pink; the bright sea-light seems to flush with it and the pale whiteish-green of lagoon and canal to drink it in. There is indeed a great deal of very evident brickwork, which is never fresh or loud in colour, but always burnt out, as it were, always exquisitely mild.

Certain little mental pictures rise before the collector of memories at the simple mention, written or spoken, of the places he has loved. When I hear, when I see, the magical name I have written above these pages, it is not of the great Square that I think, with its strange basilica and its high arcades, nor of the wide mouth of the Grand Canal, with the stately steps and the well-poised dome of the Salute; it is not of the low lagoon, nor the sweet Piazzetta, nor the dark chambers of St. Mark's. I simply see a narrow canal in the heart of the city – a patch of green water and a surface of pink wall. The gondola moves slowly; it gives a great smooth swerve, passes under a bridge, and the gondolier's cry, carried over the quiet water, makes a kind of splash in the stillness. A girl crosses the little bridge, which has an arch like a camel's back, with an old shawl on her head, which makes her characteristic and charming; you see her against the sky as you float beneath. The pink of the old wall seems to fill the whole place; it sinks even into the opaque water. Behind the wall is a garden, out of which the long arm of a white June rose – the roses of Venice are splendid – has flung itself by way of spontaneous ornament. On the other side of this small water-way is a great shabby façade of Gothic windows and balconies – balconies on which dirty clothes are hung and under which a cavernous-looking doorway opens from a low flight of slimy water-steps. It is very hot and still, the canal has a queer smell, and the whole place is enchanting.

It is poor work, however, talking about the colour of things in Venice. The fond spectator is perpetually looking at it from his window, when he is not floating about with that delightful sense of being for the moment a part of it, which any gentleman in a gondola is free to entertain. Venetian windows and balconies are a dreadful lure, and while you rest your elbows on these cushioned ledges the precious hours fly away. But in truth Venice isn't in fair weather a place for concentration of mind. The effort required for sitting down to a writing-table is heroic, and the brightest page of MS. looks dull beside the brilliancy of your *milieu*. All nature beckons you forth and murmurs to you sophistically that such hours should be devoted to collecting impressions. Afterwards, in ugly places, at un-privileged times, you can convert your

Santa Maria della Salute

impressions into prose. Fortunately for the present proser the weather wasn't always fine; the first month was wet and windy, and it was better to judge of the matter from an open casement than to respond to the advances of persuasive gondoliers. Even then however there was a constant entertainment in the view. It was all cold colour, and the steel-grey floor of the lagoon was stroked the wrong way by the wind. Then there were charming cool intervals, when the churches, the houses, the anchored fishing-boats, the whole gently-curving line of the Riva, seemed to be washed with a pearly white. Later it all turned warm — warm to the eye as well as to other senses. After the middle of May the whole place was in a glow. The sea took on a thousand shades, but they were only infinite variations of blue, and those rosy walls I just spoke of began to flush in the thick sunshine. Every patch of colour, every yard of weather-stained stucco, every glimpse of nestling garden or daub of sky above a *calle*, began to shine and sparkle — began, as the painters say, to "compose". The lagoon was streaked with odd currents, which played across it like huge smooth finger-marks. The gondolas multiplied and spotted it all over; every gondola and gondolier looking, at a distance, precisely like every other.

There is something strange and fascinating in this mysterious impersonality of the gondola. It has an identity when you are in it, but, thanks to their all being of the same size, shape and colour, and of the same deportment and gait, it has none, or as little as possible, as you see it pass before you. From my windows on the Riva there was always the same silhouette — the long, black, slender skiff, lifting its head and throwing it back a little, moving yet seeming not to move, with the grotesquely-graceful figure on the poop. This figure inclines, as may be, more to the graceful or to the grotesque — standing in the "second position" of the dancing-master, but indulging from the waist upward in a freedom of movement which that functionary would deprecate. One may say as a general thing that there is something rather awkward in the movement even of the most graceful gondolier, and something graceful in the movement of the most awkward. In the graceful men of course the grace predominates, and nothing can be finer than the large, firm way in which, from their point of vantage, they throw themselves over their tremendous oar. It has the boldness of a plunging bird and the regularity of a pendulum. Sometimes, as you see this movement in profile, in a gondola that passes you — see, as you recline on your own low cushions, the arching body of the gondolier lifted up against the sky — it has a kind of nobleness which suggests an image on a Greek frieze. The gondolier at Venice is your very good friend — if you

A Venetian Alfresco, by William Logsdail

choose him happily – and on the quality of the personage depends a good deal that of your impressions. He is a part of your daily life, your double, your shadow, your complement. Most people, I think, either like their gondolier or hate him; and if they like him, like him very much. In this case they take an interest in him after his departure; wish him to be sure of employment, speak of him as the gem of gondoliers and tell their friends to be certain to "secure" him. There is usually no difficulty in securing him; there is nothing elusive or reluctant about a gondolier. Nothing would induce me not to believe them for the most part excellent fellows, and the sentimental tourist must always have a kindness for them. More than the rest of the population, of course, they are the children of Venice; they are associated with its idiosyncrasy, with its essence, with its silence, with its melancholy.

When I say they are associated with its silence I should immediately add that they are associated also with its sound. Among themselves they are an extraordinarily talkative company. They chatter at the *traghetti*, where they always have some sharp point under discussion; they bawl across the canals; they bespeak your commands as you approach; they defy each other from afar. If you happen to have a *traghetto* under your window, you are well aware that they are a vocal race. I should go even further than I went just now, and say that the voice of the gondolier is in fact for audibility the dominant or rather the only note of Venice. There is scarcely another heard sound, and that indeed is part of the interest of the place. There is no noise there save distinctly human noise; no rumbling, no vague uproar, nor rattle of wheels and hoofs. It is all articulate and vocal and personal. One may say indeed that Venice is emphatically the city of conversation; people talk all over the place because there is nothing to interfere with its being caught by the ear. Among the populace it is a general family party. The still water carries the voice, and good Venetians exchange confidences at a distance of half a mile. It saves a world of trouble, and they don't like trouble. Their delightful garrulous language helps them to make Venetian life a long *conversazione*. This language, with its soft elisions, its odd transpositions, its kindly contempt for consonants and other disagreeables, has in it something

Canal Scene

peculiarly human and accommodating. If your gondolier had no other merit he would have the merit that he speaks Venetian. This may rank as a merit even – some people perhaps would say especially – when you don't understand what he says. But he adds to it other graces which make him an agreeable feature in your life. The price he sets on his services is touchingly small, and he has a happy art of being obsequious without being, or at least without seeming, abject. For occasional liberalities he evinces an almost lyrical gratitude. In short he has delightfully good manners, a merit which he shares for the most part with the Venetians at large. One grows very fond of these people, and the reason of one's fondness is the frankness and sweetness of their address. That of the Italian family at large has much to recommend it; but in the Venetian manner there is something peculiarly ingratiating. One feels that the race is old, that it has a long and rich civilisation in its blood, and that if it hasn't been blessed by fortune it has at least been polished by time. It hasn't a genius for stiff morality, and indeed makes few pretensions in that direction. It scruples but scantly to represent the false as the true, and has been accused of cultivating the occasion to grasp and to overreach, and of steering a crooked course – not to your and my advantage – amid the sanctities of property. It has been accused further of loving if not too well at least too often, of being in fine as little austere as possible. I am not sure it is very brave, nor struck with its being very industrious. But it has an unfailing sense of the amenities of life; the poorest Venetian is a natural man of the world. He is better company than persons of his class are apt to be among the nations of industry and virtue – where people are also sometimes perceived to lie and steal and otherwise misconduct themselves. He has a great desire to please and to be pleased.

V

In that matter at least the cold-blooded stranger begins at last to imitate him; begins to lead a life that shall be before all things easy; unless indeed he allow himself, like Mr. Ruskin, to be put out of humour by Titian and Tiepolo. The hours he spends among the pictures are his best hours in Venice, and I am ashamed to have written so much of common things when I might have been making festoons of the names of the masters. Only, when we have covered our page with such festoons what more is left to say? When one has said Carpaccio and Bellini, the Tintoret and the Veronese, one has struck a note that must be left to resound at will. Everything has been said about the mighty painters, and it is of little importance that a pilgrim the more has found them to his taste. "Went this morning to the Academy; was very much pleased with Titian's 'Assumption'." That honest phrase has doubtless been written in many a traveller's diary, and was not indiscreet on the part of its author. But it appeals little to the general reader, and we must moreover notoriously not expose our deepest feelings. Since I have mentioned Titian's "Assumption" I must say that there are some people who have been less pleased with it than the observer we have just imagined. It is one of the possible disappointments of Venice, and you may if you like take advantage of your privilege of not caring for it. It imparts a look of great richness to the side of the beautiful room of the Academy on which it hangs; but the same room contains two or three works less known to fame which are equally capable of inspiring a passion. "The 'Annunciation' struck me as coarse and superficial": that note was once made in a simple-minded tourist's book. At Venice, strange to say, Titian is altogether a disappointment; the city of his adoption is far from containing the best of him. Madrid, Paris, London, Florence, Dresden, Munich – these are the homes of his greatness.

There are other painters who have but a single home, and the greatest of these is the Tintoret. Close beside him sit Carpaccio and Bellini, who make with him the dazzling Venetian trio. The Veronese may be seen and measured in other places; he is most splendid in Venice, but he shines in Paris and in Dresden. You may walk out of the noon-day dusk of Trafalgar Square in November, and in one of the chambers of the National Gallery see the family of Darius rustling and pleading and weeping at the feet of Alexander. Alexander is a beautiful young Venetian in crimson pantaloons, and the picture sends a glow into the cold London twilight. You may sit before it for an hour and dream you are floating to the water-gate of the Ducal Palace, where a certain old beggar who has one of the handsomest heads in the world – he has sat to a hundred painters for Doges and for personages more sacred – has a prescriptive right to pretend to pull your gondola to the steps and to hold out a greasy immemorial cap. But you must go to Venice in very fact to see the other masters, who form part of your life while you are there, who illuminate your view of the universe. It is difficult to express one's relation to them; the whole Venetian art-world is so near, so familiar, so much an extension and adjunct of the spreading actual, that it seems almost invidious to say one owes more to one of them than to the other. Nowhere, not even in Holland, where the correspondence between the real aspects and the little polished canvases is so constant and so exquisite, do art and life seem so interfused and, as it were, so consanguineous. All the splendour of light and colour, all the Venetian air and the Venetian history are on the walls and ceilings of the palaces; and all the genius of the masters, all the images and visions they have left upon canvas, seem to tremble in the sunbeams and dance upon the waves. That is the perpetual interest of the place – that you live in a certain sort of knowledge as in a rosy cloud. You don't go into the churches and galleries by way of a change from the streets; you go into them because they offer you an exquisite reproduction of the things that surround you. All Venice was both model and painter, and life was so pictorial that art couldn't help becoming so. With all diminutions life is pictorial still, and this fact gives an extraordinary freshness to one's perception of the great Venetian works. You judge of them not as a connoisseur, but as a man of the world, and you enjoy them because they are so social and so true. Perhaps of all works of art that are equally great they demand least reflection on the part of the spectator – they make least of a mystery of being enjoyed. Reflection only confirms your admiration, yet is almost ashamed to show its head. These things speak so frankly and benignantly to the sense that even when they arrive at the highest style – in the Tintoret's "Presentation of the little Virgin at the Temple" – they are still more familiar.

But it is hard, as I say, to express all this, and it is painful as well to attempt it – painful because in the memory of vanished hours so filled with beauty the consciousness of present loss oppresses. Exquisite hours, enveloped in light and silence, to have known them once is to have always a terrible standard of enjoyment. Certain lovely mornings of May and June come back with an ineffaceable fairness. Venice isn't smothered in flowers at this season, in the manner of Florence and Rome; but the sea and sky themselves seem to blossom and rustle. The gondola waits at the wave-washed steps, and if you are wise you will take your place beside a discriminating companion. Such a companion in Venice should of course be of the sex that discriminates most finely. An intelligent woman who knows her Venice seems doubly intelligent, and it makes no woman's perceptions less keen to be aware that she can't help looking graceful as she is borne over the waves. The handsome Pasquale, with uplifted oar, awaits your command, knowing, in a general way, from observation of your habits, that your intention is to go to see a picture or two. It perhaps doesn't immensely matter what picture you choose: the whole affair is so charming. It is charming to wander through the light and shade of intricate canals, with perpetual architecture above you and perpetual fluidity beneath. It is charming to disembark at the polished

Ponte dei Greci

steps of a little empty *campo* – a sunny shabby square with an old well in the middle, an old church on one side and tall Venetian windows looking down. Sometimes the windows are tenantless; sometimes a lady in a faded dressing-gown leans vaguely on the sill. There is always an old man holding out his hat for coppers; there are always three or four small boys dodging possible umbrella-pokes while they precede you, in the manner of custodians, to the door of the church.

VI

The churches of Venice are rich in pictures, and many a masterpiece lurks in the unaccommodating gloom of side-chapels and sacristies. Many a noble work is perched behind the dusty candles and muslin roses of a scantily-visited altar; some of them indeed, hidden behind the altar, suffer in a darkness that can never be explored. The facilities offered you for approaching the picture in such cases are a mockery of your irritated wish. You stand at tip-toe on a three-legged stool, you climb a rickety ladder, you almost mount upon the shoulders of the *custode*. You do everything but see the picture. You see just enough to be sure it's beautiful. You catch a glimpse of a divine head, of a fig-tree against a mellow sky, but the rest is impenetrable mystery. You renounce all hope, for instance, of approaching the magnificent Cima da Conegliano in San Giovanni in Bragora; and bethinking yourself of the immaculate purity that shines in the spirit of this master, you renounce it with chagrin and pain. Behind the high altar in that church hangs a Baptism of Christ by Cima which I believe has been more or less repainted. You make the thing out in spots, you see it has a fulness of perfection. But you turn away from it with a stiff neck and promise yourself consolation in the Academy and at the Madonna dell' Orto, where two noble works by the same hand – pictures as clear as a summer twilight – present themselves in better circumstances. It may be said as a general thing that you never see the Tintoret. You admire him, you adore him, you think him the greatest of painters, but in the great majority of cases your eyes fail to deal with him. This is partly his own fault; so many of his works have turned to blackness and are positively rotting in their frames. At the Scuola di San Rocco, where there are acres of him, there is

S. Salvatore

scarcely anything at all adequately visible save the immense "Crucifixion" in the upper storey. It is true that in looking at this huge composition you look at many pictures; it has not only a multitude of figures but a wealth of episodes; and you pass from one of these to the other as if you were "doing" a gallery. Surely no single picture in the world contains more of human life; there is everything in it, including the most exquisite beauty. It is one of the greatest things of art; it is always interesting. There are works of the artist which contain touches more exquisite, revelations of beauty more radiant, but there is no other vision of so intense a reality, an execution so splendid. The interest, the impressiveness, of that whole corner of Venice, however melancholy the effect of its gorgeous and ill-lighted chambers, gives a strange importance to a visit to the Scuola. Nothing that all travellers go to see appears to suffer less from the incursions of travellers. It is one of the loneliest booths of the bazaar, and the author of these lines has always had the good fortune, which he wishes to every other traveller, of having it to himself. I think most visitors find the place rather alarming and wicked-looking. They walk about a while among the fitful figures that gleam here and there out of the great tapestry (as it were) with which the painter has hung all the walls, and then, depressed and bewildered by the portentous

Chiesa dei Greci

solemnity of these objects, by strange glimpses of unnatural scenes, by the echo of their lonely footsteps on the vast stone floors, they take a hasty departure, finding themselves again, with a sense of release from danger, a sense that the *genius loci* was a sort of mad white-washer who worked with a bad mixture, in the bright light of the *campo*, among the beggars, the orange-vendors and the passing gondolas. Solemn indeed is the place, solemn and strangely suggestive, for the simple reason that we shall scarcely find four walls elsewhere that inclose within a like area an equal quantity of genius. The air is thick with it and dense and difficult to breathe; for it was genius that was not happy, inasmuch as it lacked the art to fix itself for ever. It is not immortality that we breathe at the Scuola di San Rocco, but conscious, reluctant mortality.

View of the Piazzetta and the Doge's Palace, by Edward Pritchett

Fortunately, however, we can turn to the Ducal Palace, where everything is so brilliant and splendid that the poor dusky Tintoret is lifted in spite of himself into the concert. This deeply original building is of course the loveliest thing in Venice, and a morning's stroll there is a wonderful illumination. Cunningly select your hour – half the enjoyment of Venice is a question of dodging – and enter at about one o'clock, when the tourists have flocked off to lunch and the echoes of the charming chambers have gone to sleep among the sunbeams. There is no brighter place in Venice – by which I mean that on the whole there is none half so bright. The reflected sunshine plays up through the great windows from the glittering lagoon and shimmers and twinkles over gilded walls and ceilings. All the history of Venice, all its splendid stately past, glows around you in a strong sea-light. Every one here is magnificent, but the great Veronese is the most magnificent of all. He swims before you in a silver cloud; he thrones in an eternal morning. The deep blue sky burns behind him, streaked across with milky bars; the white colonnades sustain the richest canopies, under which the first gentlemen and ladies in the world both render homage and receive it. Their glorious garments rustle in the air of the sea and their sun-lighted faces are the very complexion of Venice. The mixture of pride and piety, of politics and religion, of art and patriotism, gives a splendid dignity to every scene. Never was a painter more nobly joyous, never did an artist take a greater delight in life, seeing it all as a kind of breezy festival and feeling it through the medium of perpetual success. He revels in the gold-framed ovals of the ceilings, multiplies himself there with the fluttering movement of an embroidered banner that tosses itself into the blue. He was the happiest of painters and produced the happiest picture in the world. "The Rape of Europa" surely deserves this title; it is impossible to look at it without aching with envy. Nowhere else in art is such a temperament revealed; never did inclination and opportunity combine to express such enjoyment. The mixture of flowers and gems and brocade, of blooming flesh and shining sea and waving groves, of youth, health, movement, desire – all this is the brightest vision that ever descended upon the soul of a painter. Happy the artist who would entertain such a vision; happy the artist who could paint it as the masterpiece I here recall is painted.

The Tintoret's visions were not so bright as that; but he had several that were radiant enough. In the room that contains the work just cited are several smaller canvases by the greatly more complex genius of the Scuola di San Rocco, which are almost simple in their loveliness, almost happy in their simplicity. They have

*Marble wall tomb in the
Church of the Frari*

kept their brightness through the centuries, and they shine with their neighbours in those golden rooms. There is a piece of painting in one of them which is one of the sweetest things in Venice and which reminds one afresh of those wild flowers of execution that bloom so profusely and so unheeded in the dark corners of all of the Tintoret's work. "Pallas chasing away Mars" is, I believe, the name that is given to the picture; and it represents in fact a young woman of noble appearance administering a gentle push to a fine young man in armour, as if to tell him to keep his distance. It is of the gentleness of this push that I speak, the charming way in which she puts out her arm, with a single bracelet on it, and rests her young hand, its rosy fingers parted, on his dark breastplate. She bends her enchanting head with the effort – a head which has all the strange fairness that the Tintoret always sees in women – and the soft, living, flesh-like glow of all these members, over which the brush has scarcely paused in its course, is as pretty an example of genius as all Venice can show. But why speak of the Tintoret when I can say nothing of the great "Paradise", which unfolds its somewhat smoky splendour and the wonder of its multitudinous circles in one of the other chambers? If it were not one of the first pictures in the world it would be about the biggest, and we must confess that the spectator gets from it at first chiefly an impression of quantity. Then he sees that this quantity is really wealth; that the dim confusion of faces is a magnificent composition, and that some of the details of this composition are extremely beautiful. It is impossible however in a retrospect of Venice to specify one's happiest hours, though as one looks backward certain ineffaceable moments start here and there into vividness. How is it possible to forget one's visits to the sacristy of the Frari, however frequent they may have been, and the great work of John Bellini which forms the treasure of that apartment?

VII

Nothing in Venice is more perfect than this, and we know of no work of art more complete. The picture is in three compartments: the Virgin sits in the central division with her child; two venerable saints, standing close together, occupy each of the others. It is impossible to imagine anything more finished or more ripe. It is one of those things that sum up the genius of a painter, the experience of a life, the teaching of a school. It seems painted with molten gems, which have only been clarified by time, and it is as solemn as it is gorgeous and as simple as it is deep. Giovanni Bellini is more or less everywhere in Venice, and wherever he is, almost certain to be first – first, I mean, in his own line: he paints little else than the Madonna and the saints; he has not Carpaccio's care for human life at large, nor the Tintoret's nor that of the Veronese. Some of his greater pictures, however, where several figures are clustered together, have a richness of sanctity that is almost profane. There is one of them on the dark side of the room at the Academy that contains Titian's "Assumption", which if we could only see it – its position is an inconceivable scandal – would evidently be one of the mightiest of so-called sacred pictures. So too is the Madonna of San Zaccaria, hung in a cold, dim, dreary place, ever so much too high, but so mild and serene, and so grandly disposed and accompanied, that the proper attitude for even the most critical amateur, as he looks at it, strikes one as the bended knee. There is another noble John Bellini, one of the very few in which there is no Virgin, at San Giovanni Crisostomo – a St. Jerome, in a red dress, sitting aloft upon the rocks and with a landscape of extraordinary purity behind him. The absence of the peculiarly erect Madonna makes it an interesting surprise among the works of the painter and gives it a somewhat less strenuous air. But it has brilliant beauty and the St. Jerome is a delightful old personage.

The same church contains another great picture for which the haunter of these places must find a shrine apart in his memory; one of the most interesting things he will have seen, if not the most brilliant. Nothing appeals more to him than three figures of Venetian ladies which occupy the foreground of a smallish canvas of Sebastian del Piombo, placed above the high altar of San Giovanni Crisostomo. Sebastian was a Venetian by birth, but few of his productions are to be seen in his native place; few indeed are to be seen anywhere. The picture represents the patron-saint of the church, accompanied by other saints and by the worldly votaries I have mentioned. These ladies stand together on the left, holding in their hands little white caskets; two of them are in profile, but the foremost turns her face to the spectator. This face and figure are almost unique among the beautiful things of Venice, and they leave the susceptible observer with the impression of having made, or rather having missed, a strange, a dangerous, but a most valuable, acquaintance. The lady, who is superbly handsome, is the typical Venetian of the sixteenth century, and she remains for the mind the perfect flower of that society. Never was there a greater air of breeding, a deeper expression of tranquil superiority. She walks a goddess – as if she trod without sinking the waves of the Adriatic. It is impossible to conceive a more perfect expression of the aristocratic spirit either in its pride or in its benignity. This magnificent creature is so strong and secure that she is gentle, and so quiet that in comparison all minor assumptions of calmness suggest only a vulgar alarm. But for all this there are depths of possible disorder in her light-coloured eye.

I had meant however to say nothing about her, for it's not right to speak of Sebastian when one hasn't found room for Carpaccio. These visions come to one, and one can neither hold them nor brush them aside. Memories of Carpaccio, the magnificent, the delightful – it's not for want of such visitations, but only for want of space, that I haven't said of him what I would. There is little enough need of it for Carpaccio's sake, his fame being brighter to-day – thanks to the generous lamp Mr. Ruskin has held up to it – than it has ever been. Yet there is something ridiculous in talking of Venice without making him almost the refrain. He and the Tintoret are the two great realists, and it is hard to say which is the more human, the more various. The Tintoret had the mightier temperament, but Carpaccio, who had the advantage of more newness and more responsibility, sailed nearer to perfection. Here and there he quite touches it, as in the enchanting picture, at the Academy, of St. Ursula asleep in her little white bed, in her high clean room, where the angel visits her at dawn; or in the noble St. Jerome in his study at S. Giorgio Schiavoni. This latter work is a pearl of sentiment, and I may add without being fantastic a ruby of colour. It unites the most masterly finish with a kind of universal largeness of feeling, and he who has it well in his memory will never hear the name of Carpaccio without a throb of almost personal affection. Such indeed is the feeling that descends upon you in that wonderful little chapel of St. George of the Slaves, where this most personal and sociable of artists has expressed all the sweetness of his imagination. The place is small and incommodious, the pictures are out of sight and ill-lighted, the custodian is rapacious, the visitors are mutually intolerable, but the shabby little chapel is a palace of art. Mr. Ruskin has written a pamphlet about it which is a real aid to enjoyment, though I can't but think the generous artist, with his keen senses and his just feeling, would have suffered to hear his eulogist declare that one of his other productions – in the Museo Civico of Palazzo Correr, a delightful portrait of two Venetian ladies with pet animals – is the "finest picture in the world". It has no need of that to be thought admirable; and what more can a painter desire?

May in Venice is better than April, but June is best of all. Then the days are hot, but not too hot, and the nights are more beautiful than the days. Then Venice is rosier than ever in the morning and more golden than ever as the day descends. She seems to expand and evaporate, to multiply all her reflections and iridescences. Then the life of her people and the strangeness of her constitution become a perpetual comedy, or at least a perpetual drama. Then the gondola is your sole habitation, and you spend days between sea and sky. You go to the Lido, though the Lido has been spoiled. When I first saw it, in 1869, it was a very natural place, and there was but a rough lane across the little island from the landing-place to the beach. There was a bathing-place in those days, and a restaurant, which was very bad, but where in the warm evenings your dinner didn't much matter as you sat letting it cool on the wooden terrace that stretched out into the sea. To-day the Lido is a part of united Italy and has been made the victim of villainous improvements. A little cockney village has sprung up on its rural bosom and a third-rate boulevard leads from Santa Elisabetta to the Adriatic. There are bitumen walks and gas-lamps, lodging-houses, shops and a *teatro diurno*. The bathing-establishment is bigger than before, and the restaurant as well; but it is a compensation perhaps that the cuisine is no better. Such as it is, however, you won't scorn occasionally to partake of it on the breezy platform under which bathers dart and splash, and which looks out to where the fishing-boats, with sails of orange and crimson, wander along the darkening horizon. The beach at the Lido is still lonely and beautiful, and you can easily walk away from the cockney village. The return to Venice in the sunset is classical and indispensable, and those who at that glowing hour have floated toward the towers that rise out of the lagoon will not easily part with the impression. But you indulge in larger excursions – you go to Burano and Torcello, to Malamocco and Chioggia. Torcello, like the Lido, has been improved; the deeply interesting little cathedral of the eighth century, which stood there on the edge of the sea, as touching in its ruin, with its grassy threshold and its primitive mosaics, as the bleached bones of a human skeleton washed ashore by the tide, has now been restored

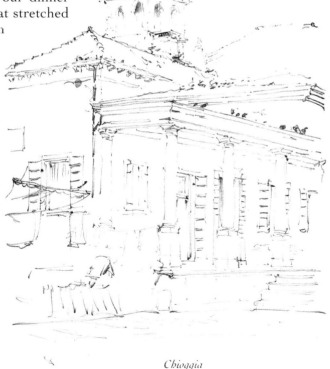

Chioggia

33

and made cheerful, and the charm of the place, its strange and suggestive desolation, has well-nigh departed.

It will still serve you as a pretext, however, for a day on the lagoon, especially as you will disembark at Burano and admire the wonderful fisher-folk, whose good looks – and bad manners, I am sorry to say – can scarcely be exaggerated. Burano is celebrated for the beauty of its women and the rapacity of its children, and it is a fact that though some of the ladies are rather bold about it every one of them shows you a handsome face. The children assail you for coppers, and in their desire to be satisfied pursue your gondola into the sea. Chioggia is a larger Burano, and you carry away from either place a half-sad, half-cynical, but altogether pictorial impression; the impression of bright-coloured hovels, of bathing in stagnant canals, of young girls with faces of a delicate shape and a susceptible expression, with splendid heads of hair and complexions smeared with powder, faded yellow shawls that hang like old Greek draperies, and little wooden shoes that click as they go up and down the steps of the convex bridges; of brown-cheeked matrons with lustrous tresses and high tempers, massive throats encased with gold beads, and eyes that meet your own with a certain traditional defiance. The men throughout the islands of Venice are almost as handsome as the women; I have never seen so many good-looking rascals. At Burano and Chioggia they sit mending their nets, or lounge at the street corners, where conversation is always high-pitched, or clamour to you to take a boat; and everywhere they decorate the scene with their splendid colour – cheeks and throats as richly brown as the sails of their fishing-smacks – their sea-faded tatters which are always a "costume", their soft Venetian jargon, and the gallantry with which they wear their hats, an article that nowhere sits so well as on a mass of dense Venetian curls. If you are happy you will find yourself, after a June day in Venice (about ten o'clock), on a balcony that overhangs the Grand Canal, with your elbows on the broad ledge, a cigarette in your teeth and a little good company beside you. The gondolas pass beneath, the watery surface gleams here and there from their lamps, some of which are coloured lanterns that move mysteriously in the darkness. There are some evenings in June when there are too many gondolas, too many lanterns, too many serenades in front of the hotels. The serenading in particular is overdone; but on such a balcony as I speak of you needn't suffer from it, for in the apartment behind you – an accessible refuge – there is more good company, there are more cigarettes. If you are wise you will step back there presently.

1882.

CHAPTER II
THE GRAND CANAL

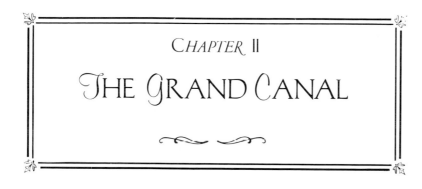

Narrow canal, Venice

HE HONOUR OF REPRESENTING the plan and the place at their best might perhaps appear, in the City of St. Mark, properly to belong to the splendid square which bears the patron's name and which is the centre of Venetian life so far (this is pretty well all the way indeed) as Venetian life is a matter of strolling and chaffering, of gossiping and gaping, of circulating without a purpose, and of staring – too often with a foolish one – through the shop-windows of dealers whose hospitality makes their doorsteps dramatic, at the very vulgarest rubbish in all the modern market. If the Grand Canal, however, is not quite technically a "street", the perverted Piazza is perhaps even less normal; and I hasten to add that I am glad not to find myself studying my subject under the international arcades, or yet (I will go the length of saying) in the solemn presence of the church. For indeed in that case I foresee I should become still more confoundingly conscious of the stumbling-block that inevitably, even with his first few words, crops up in the path of the lover of Venice who rashly addresses himself to expression. "Venetian life" is a mere literary convention, though it be an indispensable figure. The words have played an effective part in the literature of sensibility; they constituted thirty years ago the title of Mr. Howell's delightful volume of impressions; but in using them to-day one owes some frank amends to one's own lucidity. Let me carefully premise therefore that so often as they shall again drop from my pen, so often shall I beg to be regarded as systematically superficial.

Venetian life, in the large old sense, has long since come to an end, and the essential present character of the most melancholy of cities resides simply in its being the most beautiful of tombs. Nowhere else has the past been laid to rest with such tenderness, such a sadness of resignation and remembrance. Nowhere else is the present so alien, so discontinuous, so like a crowd in a cemetery without garlands for the graves. It has no flowers in its hands, but, as a compensation perhaps – and the thing is doubtless more to the point – it has money and little red books. The everlasting shuffle of these irresponsible visitors in the Piazza is contemporary Venetian life. Everything else is only a reverberation of that. The vast mausoleum has a turnstile at the door, and a functionary in a shabby uniform lets you in, as per tariff, to see how dead it is. From this *constatation*, this cold curiosity, proceed all the industry, the prosperity, the vitality of the place. The shopkeepers and gondoliers, the beggars and the models, depend upon it for a living; they are the custodians and the ushers of the great museum – they are even themselves to a certain extent the objects of exhibition. It is in the wide vestibule of the square that the polyglot pilgrims gather most densely; Piazza San Marco is the lobby of the opera in the intervals of the performance. The present fortune of Venice, the lamentable difference, is most easily measured there, and that is why, in the effort to resist our pessimism, we must turn away both from the purchasers and from the vendors of *ricordi*. The *ricordi* that we prefer are gathered best where the gondola glides – best of all on the noble waterway that begins in its glory at the Salute and ends in its abasement at the railway station. It is, however, the cockneyfied Piazzetta (forgive me, shade of St. Theodore – has not a brand new café begun to glare there, electrically, this very year?) that introduces us most directly to the great picture by which the Grand Canal works its first spell, and to which a thousand artists, not always with a talent apiece, have paid their tribute. We pass into the Piazzetta to look down the great throat, as it were, of Venice, and the vision must console us for turning our back on St. Mark's.

We have been treated to it again and again, of course, even if we have never stirred from home; but that is only a reason the more for catching at any freshness that may be left in the world of photography. It is in Venice above all that we hear the small buzz of this vulgarising voice of the familiar; yet perhaps it is in Venice too that the picturesque fact has best mastered the pious secret of how to wait for us. Even the classic Salute waits like some great lady on the threshold of her saloon. She is more ample and serene, more seated at her door, than all the copyists have told us, with her domes and scrolls, her scolloped buttresses and statues forming a pompous crown, and her wide steps disposed on the ground like the train of a robe. This fine air of the woman of the world is carried out by the well-bred assurance with which she looks in the direction of her old-fashioned Byzantine neighbour; and the juxtaposition of two churches so distinguished and so different, each splendid in its sort, is a sufficient mark of the scale and range of Venice. However, we ourselves are looking away from St. Mark's – we must blind our eyes to that dazzle; without it indeed there are brightnesses and fascinations enough. We see them in abundance even while we look away from the shady steps of the Salute. These steps are cool in the morning, yet I don't know that I can justify my excessive fondness for them any better than I can explain a hundred of the other vague infatuations with which Venice sophisticates the spirit. Under such an influence fortunately one needn't explain – it keeps account of nothing but perceptions and affections. It is from the Salute steps perhaps, of a summer morning, that this view of the open mouth of the city is most brilliantly amusing. The whole thing composes as if composition

The Dogana

37

were the chief end of human institutions. The charming architectural promontory of the Dogana stretches out the most graceful of arms, balancing in its hand the gilded globe on which revolves the delightful satirical figure of a little weathercock of a woman. This Fortune, this Navigation, or whatever she is called – she surely needs no name – catches the wind in the bit of drapery of which she has divested her rotary bronze loveliness. On the other side of the Canal twinkles and glitters the long row of the happy palaces which are mainly expensive hotels. There is a little of everything everywhere, in the bright Venetian air, but to these houses belongs especially the appearance of sitting, across the water, at the receipt of custom, of watching in their hypocritical loveliness for the stranger and the victim. I call them happy, because even their sordid uses and their vulgar signs melt somehow, with their vague sea-stained pinks and drabs, into that strange gaiety of light and colour which is made up of the reflection of superannuated things. The atmosphere plays over them like a laugh, they are of the essence of the sad old joke. They are almost as charming from other places as they are from their own balconies, and share fully in that universal privilege of Venetian objects which consists of being both the picture and the point of view.

This double character, which is particularly strong in the Grand Canal, adds a difficulty to any control of one's notes. The Grand Canal may be practically, as an impression, the cushioned balcony of a high and well-loved palace – the memory of irresistible evenings, of the sociable elbow, of endless lingering and looking; or it may evoke the restlessness of a fresh curiosity, of methodical inquiry, in a gondola piled with references. There are no references, I ought to mention, in the present remarks, which sacrifice to accident, not to completeness. A rhapsody on Venice is always in order, but I think the catalogues are finished. I should not attempt to write here the names of all the palaces, even if the number of those I find myself able to remember in the immense array were less insignificant. There are many I delight in that I don't know, or at least don't keep, apart. Then there are the bad reasons for preference that are better than the good, and all the sweet bribery of association and recollection. These

San Giorgio

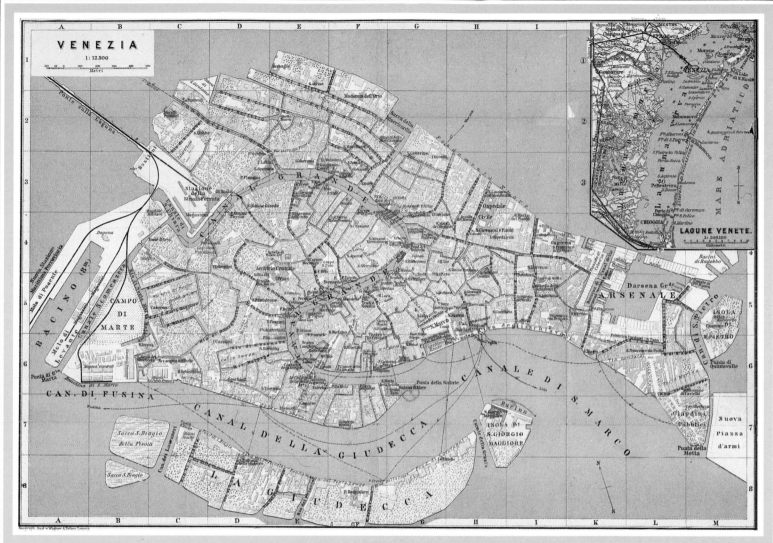

Map of Venice from Bædeker's Italy *(1892)*

things, as one stands on the Salute steps, are so many delicate fingers to pick straight out of the row a dear little featureless house which, with its pale green shutters, looks straight across at the great door and through the very keyhole, as it were, of the church, and which I needn't call by a name – a pleasant American name – that every one in Venice, these many years, has had on grateful lips. It is the very friendliest house in all the wide world, and it has, as it deserves to have, the most beautiful position. It is a real *porto di mare*, as the gondoliers say – a port within a port; it sees everything that comes and goes, and takes it all in with practised eyes. Not a tint or a hint of the immense iridescence is lost upon it, and there are days of exquisite colour on which it may fancy itself the heart of the wonderful prism. We wave to it from the Salute steps, which we must decidedly leave if we wish to get on, a grateful hand across the water, and turn into the big white church of Longhena – an empty shaft beneath a perfunctory dome – where an American family and a German party, huddled in a corner upon a pair of benches, are gazing, with a conscientiousness worthy of a better cause, at nothing in particular.

For there is nothing particular in this cold and conventional temple to gaze at save the great Tintoretto of the sacristy, to which we quickly pay our respects, and which we are glad to have for ten minutes to ourselves. The picture, though full of beauty, is not the finest of the master's; but it serves again as well as another to transport – there is no other word – those of his lovers for whom, in far-away days when Venice was an early rapture, this strange and mystifying painter was almost the supreme revelation. The plastic arts may have less to say to us than in the hungry years of youth, and the celebrated picture in general be more of a blank; but more than the others any fine Tintoret still carries us back, calling up not only the rich particular vision but the freshness of the old wonder. Many things come and go, but this great artist remains for us in Venice a part of the company of the mind. The others are there in their obvious glory, but he is the only one for whom the imagination, in our expressive modern phrase, sits up. "The Marriage in Cana", at the Salute, has all his characteristic and fascinating unexpectedness – the sacrifice of the figure of our Lord, who is reduced to the mere final point of a clever perspective, and the free, joyous presentation of all the other elements of the feast. Why, in spite of this queer one-sidedness, does the picture give us no impression of a lack of what the critics call reverence? For no other reason that I can think of than because it happens to be the work of its author, in whose very mistakes there is a singular wisdom. Mr. Ruskin has spoken with sufficient eloquence of the serious loveliness of the row of heads of the women on the right, who talk to each other as they sit at the foreshortened banquet. There could be no better example of the roving independence of the painter's vision, a real spirit of adventure for which his subject was always a cluster of accidents; not an obvious order, but a sort of peopled and agitated chapter of life, in which the figures are submissive pictorial notes. These notes are all there in their beauty and heterogeneity, and if the abundance is of a kind to make the principle of selection seem in comparison timid, yet the sense of "composition" in the spectator – if it happens to exist – reaches out to the painter in peculiar sympathy. Dull must be the spirit of the worker tormented in any field of art with that particular question who is not moved to recognise in the eternal problem the high fellowship of Tintoretto.

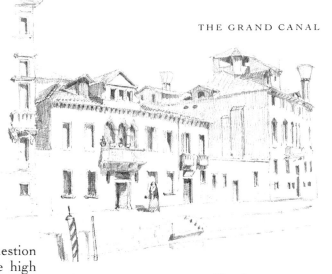

Waterfront

If the long reach from this point to the deplorable iron bridge which discharges the pedestrian at the Academy – or, more comprehensively, to the painted and gilded Gothic of the noble Palazzo Foscari – is too much of a curve to be seen at any one point as a whole, it represents the better the arched neck, as it were, of the undulating serpent of which the Canalazzo has the likeness. We pass a dozen historic houses, we note in our passage a hundred component "bits", with the baffled sketcher's sense, and with what would doubtless be, save for our intensely Venetian fatalism, the baffled sketcher's temper. It is the early palaces, of course, and also, to be fair, some of the late, if we could take them one by one, that give the Canal the best of its grand air. The fairest are often cheek by jowl with the foulest, and there are few, alas, so fair as to have been completely protected by their beauty. The ages and the generations have worked their will on them, and the wind and the weather have had much to say; but disfigured and dishonoured as they are, with the bruises of their marbles and the patience of their ruin, there is nothing like them in the world, and the long succession of their faded, conscious faces makes of the quiet water-way they overhang a *promenade historique* of which the lesson, however often we read it, gives, in the depth of its interest, an incomparable dignity to Venice. We read it in the Romanesque arches, crooked to-day in their very curves, of the early middle-age, in the exquisite individual

A View of the Grand Canal, by Carlo Ferrari

Gothic of the splendid time, and in the cornices and columns of a decadence almost as proud. These things at present are almost equally touching in their good faith; they have each in their degree so effectually parted with their pride. They have lived on as they could and lasted as they might, and we hold them to no account of their infirmities, for even those of them whose blank eyes to-day meet criticism with most submission are far less vulgar than the uses we have mainly managed to put them to. We have botched them and patched them and covered them with sordid signs; we have restored and improved them with a merciless taste, and the best of them we have made over to the pedlars. Some of the most striking objects in the finest vistas at present are the huge advertisements of the curiosity-shops.

The antiquity-mongers in Venice have all the courage of their opinion, and it is easy to see how well they know they can confound you with an unanswerable question. What is the whole place but a curiosity-shop, and what are you here for yourself but to pick up odds and ends? "We pick them up *for* you," say these honest Jews, whose prices are marked in dollars, "and who shall blame us if, the flowers being pretty well plucked, we add an artificial rose or two to the composition of the bouquet?" They take care in a word that there be plenty of relics, and their establishments are huge and active. They administer the antidote to pedantry, and you can complain of them only if you never cross their thresholds. If you take this step you are lost, for you have parted with the correctness of your attitude. Venice becomes frankly from such a moment the big depressing dazzling joke in which after all our sense of her contradictions sinks to rest – the grimace of an over-strained philosophy. It's rather a comfort, for the curiosity-shops are amusing. You have bad moments indeed as you stand in their halls of humbug and, in the intervals of haggling, hear through the high windows the soft plash of the sea on the old water-steps, for you think with anger of the noble homes that are laid waste in such scenes, of the delicate lives that must have been, that might still be, led there. You reconstruct the admirable house according to your own needs; leaning on a back balcony, you drop your eyes into one of the little green gardens with which, for the most part, such establishments are exasperatingly blessed, and end by feeling it a shame that you yourself are not in possession. (I take for granted, of course, that as you go and come you are, in imagination, perpetually lodging yourself and setting up your gods; for if this innocent pastime, this borrowing of the mind, be not your favourite sport there is a flaw in the appeal that Venice makes to you.) There may be happy cases in which your envy is tempered, or perhaps I should rather say intensified, by real participation. If you have had the good fortune to enjoy the hospitality of an old Venetian home and to lead your life a little in the painted chambers that still echo with one of the historic names, you have entered by the shortest step into the inner spirit of the place. If it didn't savour of treachery to private kindness I should like to speak frankly of one of these delightful, even though alienated, structures, to refer to it as a splendid example of the old palatial type. But I can only do so in passing, with a hundred precautions, and, lifting the curtain at the edge, drop a commemorative word on the success with which, in this particularly happy instance, the cosmopolite habit, the modern sympathy, the intelligent, flexible attitude, the latest fruit of time, adjust themselves to the great gilded, relinquished shell and try to fill it out. A Venetian palace that has not too grossly suffered and that is not overwhelming by its mass makes almost any life graceful that may be led in it. With cultivated and generous contemporary ways it reveals a pre-established harmony. As you live in it day after day its beauty and its interest sink more deeply into your spirit; it has its moods and its hours and its mystic voices and its shifting expressions. If in the absence of its masters you have happened to have it to yourself for twenty-four hours you will never forget the charm of its haunted stillness, late on the summer afternoon for instance, when the call of playing children comes in behind from the campo, nor the way the old ghosts seemed to pass on tip-toe on the marble floors. It gives you practically the essence of the matter that we are considering, for beneath the high balconies Venice comes and goes, and the particular stretch you command contains all the characteristics. Everything has its turn, from the heavy barges of merchandise, pushed by long poles and the patient shoulder, to the floating pavilions of the great serenades, and you may study at your leisure the admirable Venetian arts of managing a boat and organising a spectacle. Of the beautiful free stroke with which the gondola, especially when there are two oars, is impelled, you never, in the Venetian scene, grow weary; it is always in the picture, and the large profiled action that lets the standing rowers throw themselves forward to a constant recovery has the double value of being, at the fag-end of greatness, the only energetic note. The people from the hotels, are always afloat, and, at the hotel pace, the solitary gondolier (like the solitary horseman of the

Venetian Boat

old-fashioned novel) is, I confess, a somewhat melancholy figure. Perched on his poop without a mate, he re-enacts perpetually, in high relief, with his toes turned out, the comedy of his odd and charming movement. He always has a little the look of an absent-minded nursery-maid pushing her small charges in a perambulator.

But why should I risk too free a comparison, where this picturesque and amiable class are concerned? I delight in their sun-burnt complexions and their childish dialect; I know them only by their merits, and I am grossly prejudiced in their favour. They are interesting and touching, and alike in their virtues and their defects human nature is simplified as with a big effective brush. Affecting above all is their dependence on the stranger, the whimsical stranger who swims out of their ken, yet whom Providence sometimes restores. The best of them at any rate are in their line great artists. On the swarming feast-days, on the strange feast-night of the Redentore, their steering is a miracle of ease. The master-hands, the celebrities and winners of prizes – you may see them on the private gondolas in spotless white, with brilliant sashes and ribbons, and often with very handsome persons – take the right of way with a pardonable insolence. They penetrate the crush of boats with an authority of their own. The crush of boats, the universal sociable bumping and squeezing, is great when, on the summer nights, the ladies shriek with alarm, the city pays the fiddlers and the illuminated barges, scattering music and song, lead a long train down the Canal. The barges used to be rowed in rhythmic strokes, but now they are towed by the steamer. The coloured lamps, the vocalists before the hotels are not to my sense the greatest seduction of Venice; but it would be an uncandid sketch of the Canalazzo that shouldn't touch them with indulgence. Taking one nuisance with another, they are probably the prettiest in the world, and if they have in general more magic for the new arrival than for the old Venice-lover, they in any case, at their best,

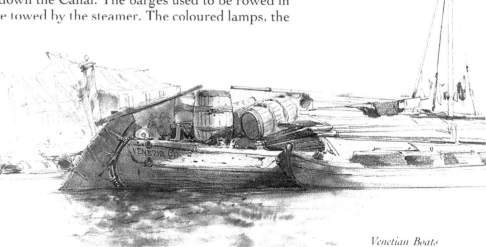

Venetian Boats

45

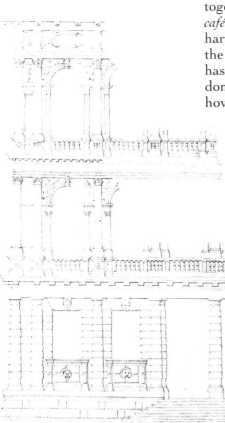

The Palazzo Rezzonico

keep up the immemorial tradition. The Venetians have had from the beginning of time the pride of their processions and spectacles, and it's a wonder how with empty pockets they still make a clever show. The Carnival is dead, but these are the scraps of its inheritance. Vauxhall on the water is of course more Vauxhall than ever, with the good fortune of home-made music and of a mirror that reduplicates and multiplies. The feast of the Redeemer – the great popular feast of the year – is a wonderful Venetian Vauxhall. All Venice on this occasion takes to the boats for the night and loads them with lamps and provisions. Wedged together in a mass it sups and sings; every boat is a floating arbour, a private *café-concert*. Of all Christian commemorations it is the most ingenuously and harmlessly pagan. Toward morning the passengers repair to the Lido, where, as the sun rises, they plunge, still sociably, into the sea. The night of the Redentore has been described, but it would be interesting to have an account, from the domestic point of view, of its usual morrow. It is mainly an affair of the Giudecca, however, which is bridged over from the Zattere to the great church. The pontoons are laid together during the day – it is all done with extraordinary celerity and art – and the bridge is prolonged across the Canalazzo (to Santa Maria Zobenigo), which is my only warrant for glancing at the occasion. We glance at it from our palace windows; lengthening our necks a little, as we look up toward the Salute, we see all Venice, on the July afternoon, so serried as to move slowly, pour across the temporary footway. It is a flock of very good children, and the bridged Canal is their toy. All Venice on such occasions is gentle and friendly; not even all Venice pushes any one into the water.

But from the same high windows we catch without any stretching of the neck a still more indispensable note in the picture, a famous pretender eating the bread of bitterness. This repast is served in the open air, on a neat little terrace, by attendants in livery, and there is no indiscretion in our seeing that the pretender dines. Ever since the table d'hôte in "Candide" Venice has been the refuge of monarchs in want of thrones – she wouldn't know herself without her *rois en exil*. The exile is agreeable and soothing, the gondola lets them down gently. Its movement is an anodyne, its silence a philtre, and little by little it rocks all ambitions to sleep. The proscript has plenty of leisure to write his proclamations and even his memoirs, and I believe he has organs in which they are published; but the only noise he makes in the world is the harmless splash of his oars. He comes and goes

The Grand Canal, by Rafael Perez Senet

along the Canalazzo, and he might be much worse employed. He is but one of the interesting objects it presents, however, and I am by no means sure that he is the most striking. He has a rival, if not in the iron bridge, which, alas, is within our range, at least – to take an immediate example – in the Montecuculi Palace. Far-descended and weary, but beautiful in its crooked old age, with its lovely proportions, its delicate round arches, its carvings and its disks of marble, is the haunted Montecuculi. Those who have a kindness for Venetian gossip like to remember that it was once for a few months the property of Robert Browning, who, however, never lived in it, and who died in the splendid Rezzonico, the residence of his son and a wonderful cosmopolite "document", which, as it presents itself, in an admirable position, but a short way further down the Canal, we can almost see, in spite of the curve, from the window at which we stand. This great seventeenth-century pile, throwing itself upon the water with a peculiar florid assurance, a certain upward toss of its cornice which gives it the air of a rearing sea-horse, decorates immensely – and within, as well as without – the wide angle that it commands.

There is a more formal greatness in the high square Gothic Foscari, just below it, one of the noblest creations of the fifteenth century, a masterpiece of symmetry and majesty. Dedicated to-day to official uses – it is the property of the State – it looks conscious of the consideration it enjoys, and is one of the few great houses within our range whose old age strikes us as robust and painless. It is visibly "kept up"; perhaps it is kept up too much; perhaps I am wrong in thinking so well of it. These doubts and fears course rapidly through my mind – I am easily their victim when it is a question of architecture – as they are apt to do to-day, in Italy, almost anywhere, in the

Foscari and Balbi Palaces

presence of the beautiful, of the desecrated or the neglected. We feel at such moments as if the eye of Mr. Ruskin were upon us; we grow nervous and lose our confidence. This makes me inevitably, in talking of Venice, seek a pusillanimous safety in the trivial and the obvious. I am on firm ground in rejoicing in the little garden directly opposite our windows – it is another proof that they really show us everything – and in feeling that the gardens of Venice would deserve a page to themselves. They are infinitely more numerous than the arriving stranger can suppose; they nestle with a charm all their own in the complications of most back-views. Some of them are exquisite, many are large, and even the scrappiest have an artful understanding, in the interest of colour, with the waterways that edge their foundations. On the small canals, in the hunt for amusement, they are the prettiest surprises of all. The tangle of plants and flowers crowds over the battered walls, the greenness makes an arrangement with the rosy sordid brick. Of all the reflected and liquefied things in Venice, and the number of these is countless, I think the lapping water loves them most. They are numerous on the Canalazzo, but wherever they occur they give a brush to the picture and in particular, it is easy to guess, give a sweetness to the house. Then the elements are complete – the trio of air and water and of things that grow. Venice without them would be too much a matter of the tides and the stones. Even the little trellises of the *traghetti* count charmingly as reminders, amid so much artifice, of the woodland nature of man. The vine-leaves, trained on horizontal poles, make a roof of chequered shade for the gondoliers and ferrymen, who doze there according to opportunity, or chatter or hail the approaching "fare". There is no "hum" in Venice, so that their voices travel far; they enter your windows and mingle even with your dreams. I beg the reader to believe that if I had time to go into everything, I would go into the *traghetti*, which have their manners and their morals, and which used to have their piety. This piety was always a *madonnina*, the protectress of the passage – a quaint figure of the virgin with the red spark of a lamp at her feet. The lamps appear for the most part to have gone out, and the images doubtless have been sold for *bric-a-brac*. The ferrymen, for aught I know, are converted to Nihilism – a faith consistent happily with a good stroke of business. One of the figures has been left, however – the Madonnetta which gives its name to a *traghetto* near the Rialto. But this sweet survivor is a carven stone inserted ages ago in the corner of an old palace and doubtless difficult of removal. *Pazienza*, the day will come when so marketable a relic will also be extracted from its socket and purchased by the devouring American. I leave that expression, on second thought, standing; but I repent of it when I remember that it is a devouring American – a lady long resident in Venice and whose kindnesses all Venetians, as well as her country-people, know, who has rekindled some of the extinguished tapers, setting up especially the big brave Gothic shrine, of painted and gilded wood, which, on the top of its stout *palo*, sheds its influence on the place of passage opposite the Salute.

If I may not go into those of the palaces this devious discourse has left behind, much less may I enter the great galleries of the Academy, which rears its blank wall, surmounted by the lion of St. Mark, well within sight of the windows at which we are still lingering. This wondrous temple of Venetian art – for all it promises little from without – overhangs, in a manner, the Grand Canal, but if we were so much as to cross its threshold we should wander beyond recall. It contains, in some of the most magnificent halls – where the ceilings have all the glory with which the imagination of Venice alone could over-arch a room – some of the noblest pictures in the world; and whether or not we go back to them on any particular occasion for another look, it is always a comfort to know that they are there, as the sense of them on the spot is a part of the furniture of the mind – the sense of them close at hand, behind every wall and under every cover, like the inevitable reverse of a medal, of the side exposed to the air that reflects, intensifies, completes the scene. In other words, as it was the inevitable destiny of Venice to be painted, and painted with passion, so the wide world of picture becomes, as we live there, and however much we go about our affairs, the constant habitation of our thoughts. The truth is, we are in it so uninterruptedly, at home and abroad, that there is scarcely a pressure upon us to seek it in one place more than in another. Choose your standpoint at random and trust the picture to come to you. This is manifestly why I have not, I find myself conscious, said more about the features of the Canalazzo which occupy the reach between the Salute and the position we have so obstinately taken up. It is still there before us, however, and the delightful little Palazzo Dario, intimately familiar to English and American travellers, picks itself out in the foreshortened brightness. The Dario is covered with the loveliest little marble plates and sculptured circles; it is made up of exquisite pieces – as if there had been only enough to make it small – so that it looks, in its extreme antiquity, a good deal like a house of cards that hold together by a tenure it would be fatal to touch. An old Venetian house dies hard indeed, and I should add that this delicate thing, with submission in every feature, continues to resist the contact of generations of lodgers. It is let out in floors (it used to be let as a whole) and in how many eager hands – for it is in great requisition – under how many fleeting dispensations have we not known and loved it? People are always writing in advance to secure it, as they are to secure the Jenkins's gondolier, and as the gondola passes we see strange faces at the windows – though it's ten to one we recognise them – and the millionth artist coming forth with his traps at the water-gate. The poor little patient Dario is one of the most flourishing booths at the fair.

The faces at the window look out at the great Sansovino – the splendid pile that is now occupied by the Prefect. I feel decidedly that I don't object as I ought to the palaces of the sixteenth and seventeenth centuries. Their pretensions impose upon me, and the imagination peoples them more freely than it can people the interiors of the prime. Was not moreover this masterpiece of Sansovino once occupied by the Venetian post-office, and thereby intimately connected with an ineffaceable first impression of the author of these remarks? He had arrived, wondering, palpitating, twenty-three years ago, after nightfall, and, the first thing on the morrow, had repaired to the post-office for his letters. They had been waiting a long time and were full of delayed interest, and he returned with them to the gondola and floated slowly down the Canal. The mixture, the rapture, the wonderful temple of the *poste restante*, the beautiful strangeness, all humanised by good news – the memory of this abides with him still, so that there always proceeds from the splendid water-front I speak of a certain secret appeal, something that seems to have been uttered first in the sonorous chambers of youth. Of course this association falls to the ground – or rather splashes into the water – if I am the victim of a confusion. *Was* the edifice in question twenty-three years ago the post-office, which has occupied since, for many a day, very much humbler quarters? I am afraid to take the proper steps for finding out, least I should learn that during these years I have misdirected my emotion. A better reason for the sentiment, at any rate, is that such a great house has surely, in the high beauty of its tiers, a refinement of its own. They make one think of colosseums and aqueducts and bridges, and they constitute doubtless, in Venice, the most pardonable specimen of the imitative. I have even a timid kindness for the

Ancient Library (Sansovino's)

51

Palazzo Pesaro

huge Pesaro, far down the Canal, whose main reproach, more even than the coarseness of its forms, is its swaggering size, its want of consideration for the general picture, which the early examples so reverently respect. The Pesaro is as far out of the frame as a modern hotel, and the Cornaro, close to it, oversteps almost equally the modesty of art. One more thing they and their kindred do, I must add, for which, unfortunately, we can patronise them less. They make even the most elaborate material civilisation of the present day seem woefully shrunken and *bourgeois*, for they simply – I allude to the biggest palaces – can't be lived in as they were intended to be. The modern tenant may take in all the magazines, but he bends not the bow of Achilles. He occupies the place, but he doesn't fill it, and he has guests from the neighbouring inns with ulsters and Baedekers. We are far at the Pesaro, by the way, from our attaching window, and we take advantage of it to go in rather a melancholy mood to the end. The long straight vista from the Foscari to the Rialto, the great middle stretch of the Canal, contains, as the phrase is, a hundred objects of interest, but it contains most the bright oddity of its general Deluge air. In all these centuries it has never got over its resemblance to a flooded city; for some reason or other it is the only part of Venice in which the houses look as if the waters had overtaken them. Everywhere else they reckon with them – have chosen them; here alone the lapping seaway seems to confess itself an accident.

There are persons who hold this long, gay, shabby, spotty perspective, in which, with its immense field of confused reflection, the houses have infinite variety, the dullest expanse in Venice. It was not dull, we imagine, for Lord Byron, who lived in the midmost of the three Mocenigo palaces, where the writing-table is still shown at which he gave the rein to his passions. For other observers it is sufficiently enlivened by so delightful a creation as the Palazzo Loredan, once a masterpiece and at present the Municipio, not to speak of a variety of other immemorial bits whose beauty still has a degree of freshness. Some of the most touching relics of early Venice are here – for it was here she precariously clustered – peeping out of a submersion more pitiless than the sea. As we approach the Rialto indeed the picture falls off and a comparative commonness suffuses it. There is a wide paved walk on either side of the Canal, on which the waterman – and who in Venice is not a waterman? – is prone to seek repose. I speek of the summer days – it is the summer Venice that is the visible Venice. The big tarry barges are drawn up at the *fondamenta*, and the bare-legged boatmen, in faded blue cotton, lie asleep on the hot stones. If there were no colour anywhere else there would be enough in their tanned personalities. Half the low doorways open into the warm interior of waterside drinking-shops, and here and there, on the quay, beneath the bush that overhangs the door, there are rickety tables and chairs. Where in Venice is there not the amusement of character and of detail? The tone in this part is very vivid, and is largely that of the brown plebeian faces looking out of the patchy miscellaneous houses – the faces of fat undressed women and of other simple folk who are not aware that they enjoy, from balconies once doubtless patrician, a view the knowing ones of the earth come thousands of miles to envy them. The effect is enhanced by the tattered clothes hung to dry in the windows, by the sun-faded rags that flutter from the polished balustrades – these are ivory-smooth with time; and the whole scene profits by the general law that renders decadence and ruin in Venice more brilliant than any prosperity. Decay is in this extraordinary place golden in tint and misery *couleur de rose*. The gondolas of the correct people are unmitigated sable, but the poor market-boats from the islands are kaleidoscopic.

The Bridge of the Rialto is a name to conjure with, but, honestly speaking, it is scarcely the gem of the composition. There are of course two ways of taking it – from the water or from the upper passage, where its small shops and booths abound in Venetian character; but it mainly counts as a feature of the Canal when seen from the gondola or even from the awful *vaporetto*. The great curve of its single arch is much to be commended, especially when, coming from the direction of the railway-station, you see it framed with its sharp compass-line the perfect picture, the reach of the Canal on the other side. But the backs of the little shops make from the water a graceless collective hump, and the inside view is the diverting one. The big arch of the bridge – like the arches of all the bridges – is the waterman's friend in

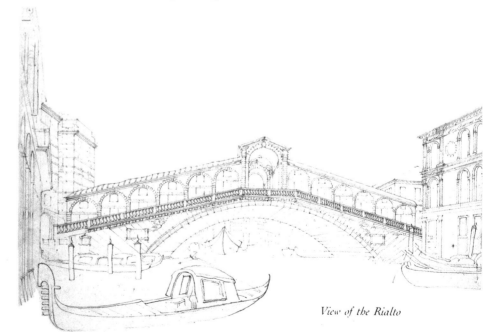

View of the Rialto

Campiello delle Mosche, by F. L. Ruben

wet weather. The gondolas, when it rains, huddle beside the peopled barges, and the young ladies from the hotels, vaguely fidgeting, complain of the communication of insect life. Here indeed is a little of everything, and the jewellers of this celebrated precinct – they have their immemorial row – make almost as fine a show as the fruiterers. It is a universal market, and a fine place to study Venetian types. The produce of the islands is discharged there, and the fishmongers announce their presence. All one's senses indeed are vigorously attacked; the whole place is violently hot and bright, all odorous and noisy. The churning of the screw of the *vaporetto* mingles with the other sounds – not indeed that this offensive note is confined to one part of the Canal. But just here the little piers of the resented steamer are particularly near together, and it seems somehow to be always kicking up the water. As we go further down we see it stopping exactly beneath the glorious windows of the Ca' d'Oro. It has chosen its position well, and who shall gainsay it for having put itself under the protection of the most romantic façade in Europe? The companionship of these objects is a symbol; it expresses supremely the present and the future of Venice. Perfect, in its prime, was the marble Ca' d'Oro, with the noble recesses of its *loggie*, but even then it probably never "met a want", like the successful *vaporetto*. If, however, we are not to go into the Museo Civico – the old Museo Correr, which rears a staring renovated front far down on the left, near the station, so also we must keep out of the great vexed question of steam on the Canalazzo, just as a while since we prudently kept out of the Accademia. These are expensive and complicated excursions. It is obvious that if the *vaporetti* have contributed to the ruin of the gondoliers, already hard pressed by fate, and to that of the palaces, whose foundations their waves undermine, and that if they have robbed the Grand Canal of the supreme distinction of its tranquillity, so on the other hand they have placed "rapid transit", in the New York phrase, in everybody's reach, and enabled everybody – save indeed those who wouldn't for the world – to rush about Venice as furiously as people rush about New York. The suitability of this consummation needn't be pointed out.

Even we ourselves, in the irresistible contagion, are going so fast now that we have only time to note in how clever and costly a fashion the Museo Civico, the old Fondaco dei Turchi, has been reconstructed and restored. It is a glare of white marble without, and a series of showy majestic halls within, where a thousand curious mementos and relics of old Venice are gathered and classified. Of its miscellaneous treasures I fear I may perhaps frivolously prefer the series of its remarkable living Longhis, an illustration of manners more copious than the celebrated Carpaccio, the two ladies with their little animals and their long sticks. Wonderful indeed to-day are the museums of Italy, where the renovations and the *belle ordonnance* speak of funds apparently unlimited, in spite of the fact that the numerous custodians frankly look starved. What is the pecuniary source of all this civic magnificence – it is shown in a hundred other ways – and how do the Italian cities manage to acquit themselves of expenses that would be formidable to communities richer and doubtless less æsthetic? Who pays the bills for the expressive statues alone, the general exuberance of sculpture, with which every *piazzetta* of almost every village is patriotically decorated? Let us not seek an answer to the puzzling question, but observe instead that we are passing the mouth of the populous Canareggio, next widest of the water-ways, where the race of Shylock abides, and at the corner of which the big colourless church of San Geremia stands gracefully enough on guard. The Canareggio, with its wide lateral footways and humpbacked bridges, makes on the feast of St. John an admirable noisy, tawdry theatre for one of the prettiest and the most infantile of the Venetian processions.

The rest of the course is a reduced magnificence, in spite of interesting bits, of the battered pomp of the Pesaro and the Cornaro, of the recurrent memories of royalty in exile which cluster about the Palazzo Vendramin Calergi, once the residence of the Comte de Chambord and still that of his half-brother, in spite too of the big Papadopoli gardens, opposite the station, the largest private grounds in Venice, but of which Venice in general mainly gets the benefit in the usual form of irrepressible greenery climbing over walls and nodding at water. The rococo church of the Scalzi is here, all marble and malachite, all a cold, hard glitter and a costly, curly ugliness, and here too, opposite, on the top of its high steps, is San Simeone Profeta, I won't say immortalised, but unblushingly misrepresented, by the perfidious Canaletto. I shall not stay to unravel the mystery of this prosaic painter's malpractices; he falsified without fancy, and as he apparently transposed at will the objects he reproduced, one is never sure of the particular view that may have constituted his

Ca d'Oro

subject. It would look exactly like such and such a place if almost everything were not different. San Simeone Profeta apears to hang there upon the wall; but it is on the wrong side of the Canal and the other elements quite fail to correspond. One's confusion is the greater because one doesn't know that everything may not really have changed, even beyond all probability – though it's only in America that churches cross the street or the river – and the mixture of the recognisable and the different makes the ambiguity maddening, all the more that the painter is almost as attaching as he is bad. Thanks at any rate to the white church, domed and porticoed, on the top of its steps, the traveller emerging for the first time upon the terrace of the railway-station seems to have a Canaletto before him. He speedily discovers indeed even in the presence of this scene of the final accents of the Canalazzo – there is a charm in the old pink warehouses on the hot *fondamenta* – that he has something much better. He looks up and down at the gathered gondolas; he has his surprise after all, his little first Venetian thrill; and as the terrace of the station ushers in these things we shall say no harm of it, though it is not lovely. It is the beginning of his experience, but it is the end of the Grand Canal.

1892.

Paese con Nuvole, by P. Joris

CHAPTER III
ITALY REVISITED

Florence

I

 WAITED IN PARIS until after the elections for the new Chamber (they took place on the 14th of October); as only after one had learned that the famous attempt of Marshal MacMahon and his ministers to drive the French nation to the polls like a flock of huddling sheep, each with the white ticket of an official candidate round his neck, had not achieved the success which the energy of the process might have promised – only then it was possible to draw a long breath and deprive the republican party of such support as might have been conveyed in one's sympathetic presence. Seriously speaking too, the weather had been enchanting –

there were Italian fancies to be gathered without leaving the banks of the Seine. Day after day the air was filled with golden light, and even those chalkish vistas of the Parisian *beaux quartiers* assumed the iridescent tints of autumn. Autumn-weather in Europe is often such a very sorry affair that a fair-minded American will have it on his conscience to call attention to a rainless and radiant October.

The echoes of the electoral strife kept me company for a while after starting upon that abbreviated journey to Turin which, as you leave Paris at night, in a train unprovided with encouragements to slumber, is a singular mixture of the odious and the charming. The charming indeed I think prevails; for the dark half of the journey is the least interesting. The morning light ushers you into the romantic gorges of the Jura, and after a big bowl of *café au lait* at Culoz you may compose yourself comfortably for the climax of your spectacle. The day before leaving Paris I met a French friend who had just returned from a visit to a Tuscan country-seat where he had been watching the vintage. "Italy," he said, "is more lovely than words can tell, and France, steeped in this electoral turmoil, seems no better than a bear-garden." The part of the bear-garden through which you travel as you approach the Mont-Cenis seemed to me that day very beautiful. The autumn colouring, thanks to the absence of rain, had been vivid and crisp, and the vines that swung their low garlands between the mulberries round about Chambéry looked like long festoons of coral and amber. The frontier station of Modane, on the further side of the Mont-Cenis Tunnel, is a very ill-regulated place; but even the most irritable of tourists, meeting it on his way southward, will be disposed to consider it good-naturedly. There is far too much bustling and scrambling, and the facilities afforded you for the obligatory process of ripping open your luggage before the officers of the Italian custom-house are much scantier than should be; but for myself there is something that deprecates irritation in the

Near Mont-Cenis

shabby green and grey uniforms of all the Italian officials who stand loafing about and watching the northern invaders scramble back into marching order. Wearing an administrative uniform doesn't necessarily spoil a man's temper, as in France one is sometimes led to believe; for these excellent under-paid Italians carry theirs as lightly as possible, and their answers to your inquiries don't in the least bristle with rapiers, buttons and cockades. After leaving Modane you slide straight downhill into the Italy of your desire; from which point the road edges, after the grand manner, along those great precipices that stand shoulder to shoulder, in a prodigious perpendicular file, till they finally admit you to a distant glimpse of the ancient capital of Piedmont.

Turin is no city of a name to conjure with, and I pay an extravagant tribute to subjective emotion in speaking of it as ancient. But if the place is less bravely peninsular than Florence and Rome, at least it is more in the scenic tradition than New York and Paris; and while I paced the great arcades and looked at the fourth-rate shop windows I didn't scruple to cultivate a shameless optimism. Relatively speaking, Turin touches a chord; but there is after all no reason in a large collection of shabbily-stuccoed houses, disposed in a rigidly rectangular manner, for passing a day of deep, still gaiety. The only reason, I am afraid, is the old superstition of Italy – that property in the very look of the written word, the evocation of a myriad images, that makes any lover of the arts take Italian satisfactions on easier terms than any others. The written word stands for something that eternally tricks us; we juggle to our credulity even with such inferior apparatus as is offered to our hand at Turin. I roamed all the morning under the tall porticoes, thinking it sufficient joy to take note of the soft, warm air, of that local colour of things that is at once so broken and so harmonious, and of the comings and goings, the physiognomy and manners, of the excellent Turinese. I

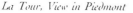

La Tour, View in Piedmont

61

Tower of St. Jean, Turin

had opened the old book again; the old charm was in the style; I was in a more delightful world. I saw nothing surpassingly beautiful or curious; but your true taster of the most seasoned of dishes finds well-nigh the whole mixture in any mouthful. Above all on the threshold of Italy he knows again the solid and perfectly definable pleasure of finding himself among the traditions of the grand style in architecture. It must be said that we have still to go there to recover the sense of the domiciliary mass. In northern cities there are beautiful houses, picturesque and curious houses; sculptured gables that hang over the street, charming bay-windows, hooded doorways, elegant proportions, a profusion of delicate ornament; but a good specimen of an old Italian palazzo has a nobleness that is all its own. We laugh at Italian "palaces", at their peeling paint, their nudity, their dreariness; but they have the great palatial quality – elevation and extent. They make of smaller things the apparent abode of pigmies; they round their great arches and interspace their huge windows with a proud indifference to the cost of materials. These grand proportions – the colossal basements, the doorways that seem meant for cathedrals, the far away cornices – impart by contrast a humble and *bourgeois* expression to interiors founded on the sacrifice of the whole to the part, and in which the air of grandeur depends largely on the help of the upholsterer. At Turin my first feeling was really one of renewed shame for our meaner architectural manners. If the Italians at bottom despise the rest of mankind and regard them as barbarians, disinherited of the tradition of form, the idea proceeds largely, no doubt, from our living in comparative mole-hills. They alone were really to build their civilisation.

An impression which on coming back to Italy I find even stronger than when it was first received is that of the contrast between the fecundity of the great artistic period and the vulgarity there of the genius of to-day. The first few hours spent on Italian soil are sufficient to renew it, and the question I allude to is, historically speaking, one of the oddest. That the people who but three hundred years ago had the best taste in the world should now have the worst; that having produced the noblest, loveliest, costliest works, they should now be given up to the manufacture of objects at once ugly and paltry; that the race of which Michael Angelo and Raphael, Leonardo and Titian were characteristic should have no other title to distinction than third-rate *genre* pictures and catchpenny statues – all this is a frequent perplexity to the observer of actual Italian life. The flower of "great" art in these latter years ceased to bloom very powerfully anywhere; but nowhere does it seem so drooping and withered as in the shadow of the immortal embodiments of the old Italian genius. You go into a church or a gallery and feast your fancy upon a splendid picture or an exquisite piece of sculpture, and on issuing from the door that has admitted you to the beautiful past are confronted with something that has the effect of a very bad joke. The aspect of your lodging – the carpets, the curtains, the upholstery in general, with their crude and violent colouring and their vulgar material – the trumpery things in the shops, the extreme bad taste of the dress of the women, the cheapness and baseness of every attempt at decoration in the cafés and railway-stations, the hopeless frivolity of everything that pretends to be a work of art – all this modern crudity runs riot over relics of the great period.

We can do a thing for the first time but once; it is but once for all that we can have a pleasure in its freshness. This is a law not on the whole, I think, to be regretted, for we sometimes learn to know things better by not enjoying them too much. It is certain, however, at the same time, that a visitor who has worked off the immediate ferment for this inexhaustibly interesting country has by no means entirely drained the cup. After thinking of Italy as historical and artistic it will do him no great harm to think of her for a while as panting both for a future and for a balance at the bank; aspirations supposedly much at variance with the Byronic, the Ruskinian, the artistic, poetic, æsthetic manner of considering our eternally attaching peninsula. He may grant – I don't say it is absolutely necessary – that its actual aspects and economics are ugly, prosaic, provokingly out of relation to the diary and the album; it is nevertheless true that, at the point things have come to, modern Italy in a manner imposes herself. I hadn't been many hours in the country before that truth assailed me; and I may add that, the first irritation past, I found myself able to accept it. For, if we think, nothing is more easy to understand than an honest ire on the part of the young Italy of to-day at being looked at by all the world as a kind of soluble pigment. Young Italy, preoccupied with its economical and political future, must be heartily tired of being admired for its eyelashes and its pose. In one of Thackeray's novels occurs a mention of a young artist who sent to the Royal Academy a picture representing "A Contadino dancing with a Trasteverina at the door of a Locanda, to the music of a Pifferaro." It is in this attitude and with these conventional accessories that the world has hitherto seen fit to represent young Italy, and one doesn't wonder that if the youth has any spirit he should at last begin to resent our insufferable æsthetic patronage. He has established a line of tram-cars in Rome, from the Porta del Popolo to the Ponte Molle, and it is on one of these democratic vehicles that I seem to see him taking his triumphant course down the vista of the future. I won't pretend to rejoice with him any more than I really do; I won't pretend, as the sentimental tourists say about it all, as if it were the setting of an intaglio or the border of a Roman scarf, to "like" it. Like it or not, as we may, it is evidently destined to be; I see a new Italy in the future which in many important respects will equal, if not surpass, the most enterprising sections of our native land. Perhaps by that time Chicago and San Francisco will have acquired a pose, and their sons and daughters will dance at the doors of *locande*.

However this may be, the accomplished schism between the old order and the new is the promptest moral of a fresh visit to this ever-suggestive part of the world. The old has become more and more a museum, preserved and perpetuated in the midst of the new, but without any further relation to it – it must be admitted indeed that such a relation is considerable – than that of the stock on his shelves to the shopkeeper, or of the Siren of the South to the showman who stands before his booth. More than once, as we move about nowadays in the Italian cities, there seems to pass before our eyes a vision of the coming years. It represents to our satisfaction an Italy united and prosperous, but altogether scientific and commercial. The Italy indeed that we sentimentalise and romance about was an ardently mercantile country; though I suppose it loved not its ledgers less, but its frescoes and altar-pieces more. Scattered through this paradise regained of trade – this country of a thousand ports – we see a large number of beautiful buildings in which an endless series of dusky pictures are darkening, dampening, fading, failing, through the years. By the doors of the beautiful buildings are little turnstiles at which there sit a great many uniformed men to whom the visitor pays a tenpenny fee. Inside, in the vaulted and frescoed chambers, the art of Italy lies buried as in a thousand mausoleums. It is well taken care of; it is constantly copied; sometimes it is "restored" – as in the case of that beautiful boy-figure of Andrea del Sarto at Florence, which may be seen at the gallery of the Uffizi with its honourable duskiness quite peeled off and heaven knows what raw, bleeding cuticle laid bare. One evening lately, near the same Florence, in the soft twilight, I took a stroll among those encircling hills on which the massive villas are mingled with the vaporous olives. Presently I arrived where three roads met at a wayside shrine, in which, before some pious daub of an old-time Madonna, a little votive lamp glimmered through the evening air. The hour, the atmosphere, the place, the twinkling taper, the sentiment of the observer, the thought that some one had been rescued here from an assassin or from some other peril and had set up a little grateful altar in consequence, against the yellow-plastered wall of a tangled *podere*; all this led me to approach the shrine with a reverent, an emotional step. I drew near it, but after a few steps I paused. I became aware of an incongruous odour; it seemed to me that the evening air was charged with a perfume which, although to a certain extent familiar, had not hitherto associated itself with rustic frescoes and wayside altars. I wondered, I gently sniffed, and the question so put left me no doubt. The odour was that of petroleum; the votive taper was nourished with the essence of Pennsylvania. I confess that I burst out laughing, and a picturesque contadino, wending his homeward way in the dusk, stared at me as if I were an iconoclast. He noticed the petroleum only, I imagine, to snuff it fondly up; but to me the thing served as a symbol of the Italy of the future. There is a horse-car from the Porta del Popolo to the Ponte Molle, and the Tuscan shrines are fed with kerosene.

II

If it's very well meanwhile to come to Turin first it's better still to go to Genoa afterwards. Genoa is the tightest topographic tangle in the world, which even a second visit helps you little to straighten out. In the wonderful crooked, twisting, climbing, soaring, burrowing Genoese alleys the traveller is really up to his neck in the old Italian sketchability. The pride of the place, I believe, is a port of great capacity, and the bequest of the late Duke of Galliera, who left four millions of dollars for the purpose of improving and enlarging it, will doubtless do much toward converting it into one of the great commercial stations of Europe. But as, after leaving my hotel the afternoon I arrived, I wandered for a long time at hazard through the tortuous byways of the city, I said to myself, not without an accent of private triumph, that here at last was something it would be almost impossible to modernise. I had found my hotel, in the first place, extremely entertaining – the Croce di Malta, as it is called, established in a gigantic palace on the edge of the swarming and not over-clean harbour. It was the biggest house I had ever entered – the basement alone would have contained a dozen American caravansaries. I met an American gentleman in the vestibule who (as he had indeed a perfect right to be) was annoyed by its troublesome dimensions – one was a quarter of an hour ascending out of the basement – and desired to know if it were a "fair sample" of the Genoese inns. It appeared an excellent specimen of Genoese architecture generally; so far as I observed there were few houses perceptibly smaller than this Titanic tavern. I lunched in a dusky ballroom whose ceiling was vaulted, frescoed and gilded with the fatal facility of a couple of centuries ago, and which looked out upon another ancient house-front, equally huge and equally battered, separated from it only by a little wedge of dusky space – one of the principal streets, I believe, of Genoa – whence out of dim abysses the population sent up to the windows (I had to crane out very far to see it) a perpetual clattering, shuffling, chaffering sound. Issuing forth presently into this crevice of a street I found myself up to my neck in that element of the rich and strange – as to visible and reproducible "effect", I mean – for the love of which one revisits Italy. It offered itself indeed in a variety of colours, some of which were not remarkable for their freshness or purity. But their combined charm was not to be resisted, and the picture glowed with the rankly human side of southern low-life.

Genoa, as I have hinted, is the crookedest and most incoherent of cities; tossed about on the sides and crests of a dozen hills, it is seamed with gullies and ravines that bristle with those innumerable palaces for which we have heard from our earliest years that the place is celebrated. These great structures, with their mottled and faded complexions, lift their big ornamental cornices to a tremendous height in the air, where, in a certain indescribably forlorn and desolate fashion, overtopping each other, they seem to reflect the twinkle and glitter of the warm Mediterranean. Down about the basements, in the close crepuscular alleys, the people are for ever moving to and fro or standing in their cavernous doorways and their dusky, crowded shops, calling, chattering, laughing, lamenting, living their lives in the conversational Italian fashion. I had for a long time had no such vision of possible social pressure. I hadn't for a long time seen people elbowing

Port of Genoa

66

I Coronari di S. Carlo ai Catinari, by L. Serra

each other so closely or swarming so thickly out of populous hives. A traveller is often moved to ask himself whether it has been worth while to leave his home – whatever his home may have been – only to encounter new forms of human suffering, only to be reminded that toil and privation, hunger and sorrow and sordid effort, are the portion of the mass of mankind. To travel is, as it were, to go to the play, to attend a spectacle; and there is something heartless in stepping forth into foreign streets to feast on "character" when character consists simply of the slightly different costume in which labour and want present themselves. These reflections were forced upon me as I strolled as through a twilight patched with colour and charged with stale smells; but after a time they ceased to bear me company. The reason of this, I think, is because – at least to foreign eyes – the sum of Italian misery is, on the whole, less than the sum of the Italian knowledge of life. That people should thank you, with a smile of striking sweetness, for the gift of twopence, is a proof, certainly, of extreme and constant destitution; but (keeping in mind the sweetness) it also attests an enviable ability not to be depressed by circumstances. I know that this may possibly be great nonsense; that half the time we are acclaiming the fine quality of the Italian smile the creature so constituted for physiognomic radiance may be in a sullen frenzy of impatience and pain. Our observation in any foreign land is extremely superficial, and our remarks are happily not addressed to the inhabitants themselves, who would be sure to exclaim upon the impudence of the fancy-picture.

The other day I visited a very picturesque old city upon a mountain-top, where, in the course of my wanderings, I arrived at an old disused gate in the ancient town-wall. The gate hadn't been absolutely forfeited; but the recent completion of a modern road down the mountain led most vehicles away to another egress. The grass-grown pavement, which wound into the plain by a hundred graceful twists and plunges, was now given up to ragged contadini and their donkeys, and to such wayfarers as were not alarmed at the disrepair into which it had fallen. I stood in the shadow of the tall old gateway admiring the scene, looking to right and left at the wonderful walls of the little town, perched on the edge of a shaggy precipice; at the circling mountains over against them; at the road dipping downward among the chestnuts and olives. There was no one within sight but a young man who slowly trudged upward with his coat slung over his shoulder and his hat upon his ear in the manner of a cavalier in an opera. Like an operatic performer too he sang as he came; the spectacle, generally, was operatic, and as his vocal flourishes reached my ear I said to myself that in Italy accident was always romantic and that such a figure had been exactly what was wanted to set off the landscape. It suggested in a high degree that knowledge of life for which I just now commended the Italians. I was turning back under the old gateway when the young man overtook me and, suspending his song, asked me if I could favour him with a match to light the hoarded remnant of a cigar. This request led, as I took my way again to the inn, to my falling into talk with him. He was a native of the ancient city, and answered freely all my inquiries as to its manners and customs and its note of public opinion. But the point of my anecdote is that he presently acknowledged himself a brooding young radical and communist, filled with hatred of the present Italian government, raging with discontent and crude political passion, professing a ridiculous hope that Italy would soon have, as France had had, her "'89", and declaring that he for his part would willingly lend a hand to chop off the heads of the king and the royal family. He was an unhappy, underfed, unemployed young man, who took a hard, grim view of everything and was operatic only quite in spite of himself. This made it very absurd of me to have looked at him simply as a graceful ornament to the prospect, an harmonious little figure in the middle distance. "Damn the prospect, damn the middle distance!" would have been all *his* philosophy. Yet but for the accident of my having gossiped with him I should have made him do service, in memory, as an example of sensuous optimism!

I am bound to say however that I believe a great deal of the sensuous optimism observable in the Genoese alleys and beneath the low, crowded arcades along the port was very real. Here every one was magnificently sunburnt, and there were plenty of those queer types, mahogany-coloured, bare-chested mariners with

The Lantern and Part of the Arsenal, Genoa

69

Genoa, by Ippolito Caffi

earrings and crimson girdles, that seem to people a southern seaport with the chorus of "Masaniello". But it is not fair to speak as if at Genoa there were nothing but low-life to be seen, for the place is the residence of some of the grandest people in the world. Nor are all the palaces ranged upon dusky alleys; the handsomest and most impressive form a splendid series on each side of a couple of very proper streets, in which there is plenty of room for a coach-and-four to approach the big doorways. Many of these doorways are open, revealing great marble staircases with couchant lions for balustrades and ceremonious courts surrounded by walls of sun-softened yellow. One of the great piles in the array is coloured a goodly red and contains in particular the grand people I just now spoke of. They live indeed on the third floor; but here they have suites of wonderful painted and gilded chambers, in which foreshortened frescoes also cover the vaulted ceilings and florid mouldings emboss the ample walls. These distinguished tenants bear the name of Vandyck, thought they are members of the noble family of Brignole-Sale, one of whose children – the Duchess of Galliera has lately given proof of nobleness in presenting the gallery of the red palace to the city of Genoa.

III

On leaving Genoa I repaired to Spezia, chiefly with a view of accomplishing a sentimental pilgrimage, which I in fact achieved in the most agreeable conditions. The Gulf of Spezia is now the headquarters of the Italian fleet, and there were several big iron-plated frigates riding at anchor in front of the town. The streets were filled with lads in blue flannel, who were receiving instruction at a schoolship in the harbour, and in the evening – there was a brilliant moon – the little breakwater which stretched out into the Mediterranean offered a scene of recreation to innumerable such persons. But this fact is from the point of view of the cherisher of quaintness of little account, for since it has become prosperous Spezia has grown ugly. The place is filled with long, dull stretches of dead wall and great raw expanses of artificial land. It wears that look of monstrous, of more than far-western newness which distinguishes all the creations of the young Italian State. Nor did I find any great compensation in an immense inn of recent birth, an establishment seated on the edge of the sea in anticipation of a *passeggiata* which is to come that way some five years hence, the region being in the meantime of the most primitive formation. The inn was filled with grave English people who looked respectable and bored, and there was of course a Church of England service in the gaudily-frescoed parlour. Neither was it the drive to Porto Venere that chiefly pleased me – a drive among vines and olives, over the hills and beside the Mediterranean, to a queer little crumbling village on a headland, as sweetly desolate and superannuated as the name it bears. There is a ruined church near the village, which occupies the site (according to tradition) of an ancient temple of Venus; and if Venus ever revisits her desecrated shrines she must sometimes pause a moment in that sunny stillness and listen to the murmur of the tideless sea at the base of the narrow promontory. If Venus sometimes comes there Apollo surely does as much; for close to the temple is a gateway surmounted by an inscription in Italian and English, which admits you to a curious, and it must be confessed rather cockneyfied, cave among the rocks. It was here, says the inscription, that the great Byron, swimmer and poet, "defied the waves of the Ligurian sea." The fact is interesting, though not supremely so; for Byron was always defying something, and if a slab had been put up wherever this performance came off these commemorative tablets would be in many parts of Europe as thick as milestones.

No; the great merit of Spezia, to my eye, is that I engaged a boat there of a lovely October afternoon and had myself rowed across the gulf – it took about an hour and a half – to the little bay of Lerici, which opens out of it. This bay of Lerici is charming; the bosky grey-green hills close it in, and on either side of the entrance, perched on a bold headland, a wonderful old crumbling castle keeps ineffectual guard. The place is classic to all English travellers, for in the middle of the curving shore is the now desolate little villa in which Shelley spent the last months of his short life. He was living at Lerici when he started on that short southern cruise from which he never returned. The house he occupied is strangely shabby and as sad as you may choose to find it. It stands directly upon the beach, with scarred and battered walls and a loggia of several arches opening to a little terrace with a rugged parapet, which, when the wind blows, must be drenched with the salt spray. The place is very lonely – all overwearied with sun and breeze and

LERICI

La Spezia

brine – very close to nature, as it was Shelley's passion to be. I can fancy a great lyric poet sitting on the terrace of a warm evening and feeling very far from England in the early years of the century. In that place, and with his genius, he would as a matter of course have heard in the voice of nature a sweetness which only the lyric movement could translate. It is a place where an English-speaking pilgrim himself may very honestly think thoughts and feel moved to lyric utterance. But I must content myself with saying in halting prose that I remember few episodes of Italian travel more sympathetic, as they have it here, than that perfect autumn afternoon; the half-hour's station on the little battered terrace of the villa; the climb to the singularly felicitous old castle that hangs above Lerici; the meditative lounge, in the fading light, on the vine-decked platform that looked out toward the sunset and the darkening mountains and, far below, upon the quiet sea, beyond which the pale-faced tragic villa stared up at the brightening moon.

Near Lerici

IV

I had never known Florence more herself, or in other words more attaching, than I found her for a week in that brilliant October. She sat in the sunshine beside her yellow river like the little treasure-city she has always seemed, without commerce, without other industry than the manufacture of mosaic paperweights and alabaster Cupids, without actuality or energy or earnestness or any of those rugged virtues which in most cases are deemed indispensable for civic cohesion; with nothing but the little unaugmented stock of her mediæval memories, her tender-coloured mountains, her churches and palaces, pictures and statues. There were very few strangers; one's detested fellow-pilgrim was infrequent; the native population itself seemed scanty; the sound of wheels in the streets was but occasional; by eight o'clock at night, apparently, every one had gone to bed, and the musing wanderer, still wandering and still musing, had the place to himself – had the thick shadow-masses of the great palaces, and the shafts of moonlight striking the polygonal paving-stones, and the empty bridges, and the silvered yellow of the Arno, and the stillness broken only by a homeward step, a step accompanied by a snatch of song from a warm Italian voice. My room at the inn looked out on the river and was flooded all day with sunshine. There was an absurd orange-coloured paper on the walls; the Arno, of a hue not altogether different, flowed beneath; and on the other side of it rose a line of sallow houses, of extreme antiquity, crumbling and mouldering, bulging and protruding over the stream. (I seem to speak of their fronts; but what I saw was their shabby backs, which were exposed to the cheerful flicker of the river, while the fronts stood for ever in the deep damp shadow of a narrow mediæval street.) All this brightness and yellowness was a perpetual delight; it was part of that indefinable charming colour which Florence always seems to wear as you look up and down at it from the river, and from the bridges and quays. This is a kind of grave radiance – a harmony of high tints – which I scarce know how to describe. There are yellow walls and green blinds and red roofs, there are intervals of brilliant brown and natural-looking blue; but the picture is not spotty nor gaudy, thanks to the distribution of the colours in large and comfortable masses, and to the washing-over of the scene by some happy softness of sunshine. The river-front of Florence is in short a delightful composition. Part of its charm comes of course from the generous aspect of those high-based Tuscan palaces which a renewal of acquaintance with them has again commended to me as the most dignified dwellings in the world. Nothing can be finer than that look of giving up the whole immense ground-floor to simple purposes of vestibule and staircase, of court and high-arched entrance; as if this were all but a massive pedestal for the real

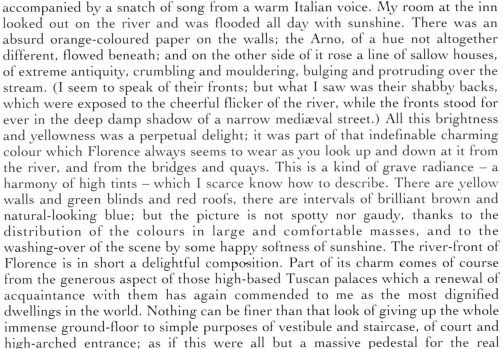

habitation and people weren't properly housed unless, to begin with, they should be lifted fifty feet above the pavement. The great blocks of the basement; the great intervals, horizontally and vertically, from window to window (telling of the height and breadth of the rooms within); the armorial shield hung forward at one of the angles; the wide-brimmed roof, overshadowing the narrow street; the rich old browns and yellows of the walls: these definite elements put themselves together with admirable art.

Take a Tuscan pile of this type out of its oblique situation in the town; call it no longer a palace, but a villa; set it down by a terrace on one of the hills that encircle Florence, place a row of high-waisted cypresses beside it, give it a grassy courtyard and a view of the Florentine towers and the valley

Porta al Prato, Florence

of the Arno, and you will think it perhaps even more worthy of your esteem. It was a Sunday noon, and brilliantly warm, when I again arrived; and after I had looked from my windows awhile at the quietly-basking river-front I have spoken of I took my way across one of the bridges and then out of one of the gates – that immensely tall Roman Gate in which the space from the top of the arch to the cornice (except that there is scarcely a cornice, it is all a plain massive piece of wall) is as great, or seems to be, as that from the ground to the former point. Then I climbed a steep and winding way – much of it a little dull if one likes, being bounded by mottled, mossy garden-walls – to a villa on a hill-top, where I found various things that touched me with almost too fine a point. Seeing them again, often, for a week, both by sunlight and moonshine, I never quite learned not to covet them; not to feel that not being a part of them was somehow to miss an exquisite chance. What a tranquil, contented life it seemed, with romantic beauty as a part of its daily texture! – the sunny terrace, with its tangled *podere* beneath it; the bright grey olives against the bright blue sky; the long, serene, horizontal lines of other villas, flanked by their upward cypresses, disposed upon the neighbouring hills; the richest little city in the world in a softly-scooped hollow at one's feet, and beyond it the most appealing of views, the most majestic, yet the most familiar. Within the villa was a great love of art and a painting-room full of felicitous work, so that if human life there confessed to quietness, the quietness was mostly but that of the intent act. A beautiful occupation in that beautiful position, what could possibly be better? That is what I spoke just now of envying – a way of life that doesn't wince at such refinements of peace and ease. When labour self-charmed presents itself in a dull or an ugly place we esteem it, we admire it, but we scarce feel it to be ideal of good fortune. When, however, its votaries move as figures in an ancient, noble landscape, and their walks and contemplations are like a turning of the leaves of history, we seem to have before us an admirable case of virtue made easy; meaning here by virtue contentment and concentration, a real appreciation of the rare, the exquisite though composite, medium of life. You needn't want a rush or a crush when the scene itself, the mere scene, shares with you such a wealth of consciousness.

It is true indeed that I might after a certain time grow weary of a regular afternoon stroll among the Florentine lanes; of sitting on low parapets, in intervals of flower-topped wall, and looking across at Fiesole or down the rich-hued valley of the Arno; of pausing at the open gates of villas and wondering at the height of cypresses and the depth of loggias; of walking home in the fading light and noting on a dozen westward-looking surfaces the glow of the opposite sunset. But for a week or so all this was delightful. The villas are innumerable, and if you're an aching alien half the talk is about villas. This one has a story; that one has another; they all look as if they had stories – none in truth predominantly gay. Most of them are offered to rent (many of them for sale) at prices unnaturally low; you may have a tower and a garden, a chapel and an expanse of thirty windows, for five hundred dollars a year. In imagination you hire three or four; you take possession and settle and stay. Your sense of the fineness of the finest is of something very grave and stately; your sense of the bravery of two or three of the best something quite tragic and sinister. From what does this latter impression come? You gather it as you stand there in the early dusk, with your eyes on the long, pale-brown façade, the enormous windows, the iron cages fastened to the lower ones. Part of the brooding expression of these great houses comes, even when they have not fallen into decay, from their look of having outlived their original use. Their extraordinary largeness and massiveness are a satire on their present fate. They weren't built with such a thickness of wall and depth of embrasure, such a solidity of staircase and superfluity of stone, simply to afford an economical winter residence to English and American families. I don't know whether it was the appearance of these stony old villas, which seemed so dumbly conscious of a change of manners, that threw a tinge of melancholy over the general prospect; certain it is that, having always found this note as of a myriad old sadnesses in solution in the view of Florence, it seemed to me now particularly strong. "Lovely, lovely, but it makes me 'blue'," the sensitive stranger couldn't but murmur to himself as, in the later afternoon, he looked at the landscape from over one of the low parapets, and then, with his hands in his pockets, turned away indoors to candles and dinner.

V

Below, in the city, through all frequentation of streets and churches and museums, it was impossible not to have a good deal of the same feeling; but here the impression was more easy to analyse. It came from a sense of the perfect separateness of all the great productions of the Renaissance from the present and the future of the place, from the actual life and manners, the native ideal. I have already spoken of the way in which the vast aggregation of beautiful works of art in the Italian cities strikes the visitor nowadays – so far as present Italy is concerned – as the mere stock-in-trade of an impecunious but thrifty people. It is this spiritual solitude, this conscious disconnection of the great works of architecture and sculpture that deposits a certain weight upon the heart; when we see a great tradition broken we feel something of the pain with which we hear a stifled cry. But regret is one thing and resentment is another. Seeing one morning, in a shop-window, the series of *Mornings in Florence* published a few years since by Mr. Ruskin, I made haste to enter and purchase these amusing little books, some passages of which I remembered formerly to have read. I couldn't turn over many pages without observing that the "separateness" of the new and old which I just mentioned had produced in their author the liveliest irritation. With the more acute phases of this condition it was difficult to sympathise, for the simple reason, it seems to me, that it savours of arrogance to demand of any people, as a right of one's own, that they shall be artistic. "Be artistic yourselves!" is the very natural reply that young Italy has at hand for English critics and censors. When a people produces beautiful statues and pictures it gives us something more than is set down in the bond, and we must thank it for its generosity; and when it stops producing them or caring for them we may cease thanking, but we hardly have a right to begin and rail. The wreck of Florence, says Mr. Ruskin, "is now too ghastly and heart-breaking to any human soul that remembers the days of old"; and these desperate words are an allusion to the fact that the little square in front of the cathedral, at the foot of Giotto's Tower, with the grand Baptistery on the other side, is now the resort of a number of hackney-coaches and omnibuses. This fact is doubtless lamentable, and it would be a hundred times more agreeable to see among people who have been made the heirs of so priceless a work of art as the sublime campanile some such feeling about it as would keep it free even from the danger of defilement. A cab-stand is a very ugly and dirty thing, and Giotto's Tower should have nothing in common with such conveniences. But there is more than one way of taking such things, and the sensitive stranger who has been walking about for a week with his mind full of the sweetness and suggestiveness of a hundred Florentine places may feel at last in looking into Mr. Ruskin's little tracts that, discord for discord, there isn't much to choose between the importunity of the author's personal ill-humour and the incongruity of horse-pails and bundles of hay. And one may say this without being at all partisan of the doctrine of the inevitableness of new desecrations. For my own part, I believe there are few things in this line that the new Italian spirit

Marble Lion, Palazzo Vecchio

isn't capable of, and not many indeed that we aren't destined to see. Pictures and buildings won't be completely destroyed, because in that case the *forestieri*, scatterers of cash, would cease to arrive and the turn-stiles at the doors of the old palaces and convents, with the little patented slit for absorbing your half-franc, would grow quite rusty, would stiffen with disuse. But it's safe to say that the new Italy growing into an old Italy again will continue to take her elbow-room wherever she may find it.

I am almost ashamed to say what I did with Mr. Ruskin's little books. I put them into my pocket and betook myself to Santa Maria Novella. There I sat down and, after I had looked about for a while at the beautiful church, drew them forth one by one and read the greater part of them. Occupying one's self with light literature in a great religious edifice is perhaps as bad a piece of profanation as any of those rude dealings which Mr. Ruskin justly deplores; but a traveller has to make the most of odd moments, and I was waiting for a friend in whose company I was to go and look at Giotto's beautiful frescoes in the cloister of the church. My friend was a long time coming, so that I had an hour with Mr. Ruskin, whom I called just now a light *littérateur* because in these little Mornings in Florence he is for ever making his readers laugh. I remembered of course where I was, and in spite of my latent hilarity felt I had rarely got such a snubbing. I had really been enjoying the good old city of Florence, but I now learned from Mr. Ruskin that this was a scandalous waste of charity. I should have gone about with an imprecation on my lips, I should have worn a face three yards long. I had taken great pleasure in certain frescoes by Ghirlandaio in the choir of that very church; but it appeared from one of the little books that these frescoes were as naught. I had much admired Santa Croce and had thought the Duomo a very noble affair; but I had now the most positive assurance I knew nothing about them. After a while, if it was only ill-humour that was needed for doing honour to the city of the Medici, I felt that I had risen to a proper level; only now it was Mr. Ruskin himself I had lost patience with, not the stupid Brunelleschi, not the vulgar Ghirlandaio. Indeed I lost patience altogether, and asked myself by what right this informal votary of form pretended to run riot through a poor charmed *flâneur's* quiet contemplations, his attachment to the noblest of pleasures, his enjoyment of the loveliest of cities. The little books seemed invidious and insane, and it was only when I remembered that I had been under no obligation to buy them that I checked myself in repenting of having done so.

Then at last my friend arrived and we passed together out of the church and,

Ponte Vecchio, by Antonietta Brandeis

through the first cloister beside it, into a smaller enclosure where we stood a while to look at the tomb of the Marchesa Strozzi-Ridolfi, upon which the great Giotto has painted four superb little pictures. It was easy to see the pictures were superb; but I drew forth one of my little books again, for I had observed that Mr. Ruskin spoke of them. Hereupon I recovered my tolerance; for what could be better in this case, I asked myself, than Mr. Ruskin's remarks? They are in fact excellent and charming – full of appreciation of the deep and simple beauty of the great painter's work. I read them aloud to my companion; but my companion was rather, as the phrase is, "put off" by them. One of the frescoes – it is a picture of the birth of the Virgin – contains a figure coming through a door. "Of ornament," I quote, "there is only the entirely simple outline of the vase which the servant carries; of colour two or three masses of sober red and pure white, with brown and grey. That is all," Mr. Ruskin continues. "And if you are pleased with this you can see Florence. But if not, by all means amuse yourself there, if you find it amusing, as long as you like; you can never see it." *You can never see it.* This seemed to my friend insufferable, and I had to shuffle away the book again, so that we might look at the fresco with the unruffled geniality it deserves. We agreed afterwards, when in a more convenient place I read aloud a good many more passages from the precious tracts, that there are a great many ways of seeing Florence, as there are of seeing most beautiful and interesting things, and that it is very dry and pedantic to say that the happy vision depends upon our squaring our toes with a certain particular chalk-mark. We see Florence wherever and whenever we enjoy it, and for enjoying it we find a great many more pretexts than Mr. Ruskin seems inclined to allow. My friend and I convinced ourselves also, however, that the little books were an excellent purchase, on account of the great charm and felicity of much of their incidental criticism; to say nothing, as I hinted just now, of their being extremely amusing. Nothing in fact is more comical than the familiar asperity of the author's style and the pedagogic fashion in which he pushes and pulls his unhappy pupils about, jerking their heads toward this, rapping their knuckles for that, sending them to stand in corners and giving them Scripture texts to copy. But it is neither the felicities nor the aberrations of detail, in Mr. Ruskin's writings, that are the main affair for most readers; it is the general tone that, as I have said, puts them off or draws them on. For many persons he will never bear the test of being read in this rich old Italy, where art, so long as it really lived at all, was spontaneous, joyous, irresponsible. If the reader is in daily contact with those beautiful Florentine works which do still, in a way, force themselves into notice through the vulgarity and cruelty of modern profanation, it will seem to him that this commentator's comment is pitched in the strangest falsetto key. "One may read a hundred pages of this sort of thing," said my friend, "without ever dreaming that he is talking about *art*. You can say nothing worse about him than that." Which is perfectly true. Art is the one corner of human life in which we may take our ease. To justify our presence there the only thing demanded of us is that we shall have felt the representational impulse. In other connections our impulses are conditioned and embarrassed; we are allowed to have only so many as are consistent with those of our neighbours; with their convenience and well-being, with their convictions and prejudices, their rules and regulations. Art means an escape from all this. Wherever her shining standard floats the need for apology and compromise is over; there it is enough simply that we please or are pleased. There the tree is judged only by its fruits. If these are sweet the tree is justified – and not less so the consumer.

One may read a great many pages of Mr. Ruskin without getting a hint of this delightful truth; a hint of the not unimportant fact that art after all is made for us and not we for art. This idea that the value of a work is in the amount of illusion it yields is conspicuous by its absence. And as for Mr. Ruskin's world's being a place – his world of art – where we may take life easily, woe to the luckless mortal who enters it with any such disposition. Instead of a garden of delight, he finds a sort of assize court in perpetual session. Instead of a place in which human responsibilities are lightened and suspended, he finds a region governed by a kind of Draconic legislation. His responsibilities indeed are tenfold increased; the gulf between truth and error is for ever yawning at his feet; the pains and penalties of this same error are advertised, in apocalyptic terminology, upon a thousand sign-posts; and the rash intruder soon begins to look back with infinite longing to the lost paradise of the artless. There can be no greater want of tact in dealing with those things with which men attempt to ornament life than to be perpetually talking about "error". A truce to all rigidities is the law of the place; the only thing absolute there is that some force and some charm have worked. The grim old bearer of the scales excuses herself; she feels this not to be her province. Differences here are not

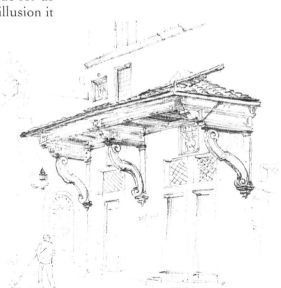

Porch behind Choir of Or San Michele

81

iniquity and righteousness; they are simply variations of temperament, kinds of curiosity. We are not under theological government.

VI

It was very charming, in the bright, warm days, to wander from one corner of Florence to another, paying one's respects again to remembered masterpieces. It was pleasant also to find that memory had played no tricks and that the rarest things of an earlier year were as rare as ever. To enumerate these felicities would take a great deal of space; for I never had been more struck with the mere quantity of brilliant Florentine work. Even giving up the Duomo and Santa Croce to Mr. Ruskin as very ill-arranged edifices, the list of the Florentine treasures is almost inexhaustible. Those long outer galleries of the Uffizi had never beguiled me more; sometimes there were not more than two or three figures standing there, Baedeker in hand, to break the charming perspective. One side of this upstairs portico, it will be remembered, is entirely composed of glass; a continuity of old-fashioned windows, draped with white curtains of rather primitive fashion, which hang there till they acquire a perceptible tone. The light, passing through them, is softly filtered and diffused; it rests mildly upon the old marbles – chiefly antique Roman busts – which stand in the narrow intervals of the casements. It is projected upon the numerous pictures that cover the opposite wall and that are not by any means, as a general thing, the gems of the great collection; it imparts a faded brightness to the old ornamental arabesques upon the painted wooden ceiling, and it makes a great soft shining upon the marble floor, in which, as you look up and down, you see the strolling tourists and the motionless copyists almost reflected. I don't know why I should find all this very pleasant, but in fact, I have seldom gone into the Uffizi without walking the length of this third-storey cloister, between the (for the most part) third-rate canvases and panels and the faded cotton curtains. Why is it that in Italy we see a charm in things in regard to which in other countries we always take vulgarity for granted? If in the city of New York a great museum of the arts were to be provided, by way of decoration, with a species of verandah inclosed on one side by a series of small-paned windows draped in dirty linen, and furnished on the other with an array of pictorial feebleness, the place being surmounted by a thinly-painted wooden roof, strongly suggestive of summer heat, of winter cold, of frequent leakage, those amateurs

Marble Pulpit, S. Croce

who had had the advantage of foreign travel would be at small pains to conceal their contempt.

Contemptible or respectable, to the judicial mind, this quaint old loggia of the Uffizi admitted me into twenty chambers where I found as great a number of ancient favourites. I don't know that I had a warmer greeting for any old friend than for Andrea del Sarto, that most touching of painters who is not one of the first. But it was on the other side of the Arno that I found him in force, in those dusky drawing-rooms of the Pitti Palace to which you take your way along the tortuous tunnel that wanders through the houses of Florence and is supported by the little goldsmiths' booths on the Ponte Vecchio. In the rich insufficient light of these beautiful rooms, where, to look at the pictures, you sit in damask chairs and rest your elbows on tables of malachite, the elegant Andrea becomes deeply effective. Before long he has drawn you close. But the great pleasure, after all, was to revisit the earlier masters, in those specimens of them chiefly that bloom so unfadingly on the big plain walls of the Academy. Fra Angelico and Filippo Lippi, Botticelli and Lorenzo di Credi are the clearest, the sweetest and best of all painters; as I sat for an hour in their company, in the cold great hall of the institution I have mentioned – there are shabby rafters above and an immense expanse of brick tiles below, and many bad pictures as well as good – it seemed to me more than ever that if one really had to choose one couldn't do better than choose here. You may rest at your ease at the Academy, in this big first room – at the upper end especially, on the left – because more than many other places it savours of old Florence. More for instance, in reality, than the Bargello, though the Bargello makes great pretensions. Beautiful and masterful though the Bargello is, it smells too strongly of restoration, and, much of old Italy as still lurks in its furbished and renovated chambers, it speaks even more distinctly of the ill-mannered young kingdom that has – as "unavoidably" as you please – lifted down a hundred delicate works of sculpture from the convent-walls where their pious authors placed them. If the early Tuscan painters are exquisite I can think of no praise pure enough for the sculptors of the same period, Donatello and Luca della Robbia, Matteo Civitale and Mina da Fiesole, who, as I refreshed my memory of them, seemed to me to leave absolutely nothing to be desired in the way of straightness of inspiration and grace of invention. The Bargello is full of early Tuscan sculpture, most of the pieces of which have come from suppressed religious houses; and even if the visitor be an ardent liberal he is uncomfortably conscious of the rather brutal

ORVIETO

Marble Font, Orvieto Cathedral

process by which it has been collected. One can hardly envy young Italy the number of odious things she has had to do.

The railway journey from Florence to Rome has been altered both for the better and for the worse; for the better in that it has been shortened by a couple of hours; for the worse inasmuch as when about half the distance has been traversed the train deflects to the west and leaves the beautiful old cities of Assisi, Perugia, Terni, Narni, unvisited. Of old it was possible to call at these places, in a manner, from the window of the train; even if you didn't stop, as you probably couldn't, every time you passed, the immensely interesting way in which, like a loosened belt on an aged and shrunken person, their ample walls held them easily together was something well worth noting. Now, however, for compensation, the express train to Rome stops at Orvieto, and in consequence. . . . In consequence what? What is the result of the stop of an express train at Orvieto? As I glibly wrote that sentence I suddenly paused, aware of the queer stuff I was uttering. That an express train would graze the base of the horrid purple mountain from the apex of which this dark old Catholic city uplifts the glittering front of its cathedral – that might have been foretold by a keen observer of contemporary manners. But that it would really have the grossness to hang about is a fact over which, as he records it, an inveterate, a perverse cherisher of the sense of the past order, the order still largely prevailing at the time of his first visit to Italy, may well make what is vulgarly called an ado. The train does stop at Orvieto, not very long, it is true, but long enough to let you out. The same phenomenon takes place on the following day, when, having visited the city, you get in again. I availed myself without scruple of both of these occasions, having formerly neglected to drive to the place in a post-chaise. But frankly, the railway-station being in the plain and the town on the summit of an extraordinary hill, you have time to forget the puffing indiscretion while you wind upwards to the city-gate. The position of Orvieto is superb – worthy of the "middle distance" of an eighteenth-century landscape. But, as every one knows, the splendid Cathedral is the proper attraction of the spot, which, indeed, save for this fine monument and for its craggy and crumbling ramparts, is a meanly arranged and, as Italian cities go, not particularly impressive little town. I spent a beautiful Sunday there and took in the charming church. I gave it my best attention, though on the whole I fear I found it inferior to its fame. A high concert of colour, however, is the densely carved front, richly covered with radiant mosaics. The old white marble of the sculptured portions is as softly yellow as ancient ivory; the large exceedingly bright pictures above them flashed and twinkled in the glorious weather. Very striking and interesting the theological frescoes of Luca Signorelli, though I have seen compositions of this general order that appealed to me more. Characteristically fresh, finally, the clear-faced saints and seraphs, in robes of pink and azure, whom Fra Angelico has painted upon the ceiling of the great chapel, along with a noble sitting figure – more expressive of movement than most of the creations of this pictorial peace-maker – of Christ in judgement. Yet the interest of the cathedral of Orvieto is mainly not the visible result, but the historical process that lies behind it; those three hundred years of the applied devotion of a people of which an American scholar has written an admirable account.

1877

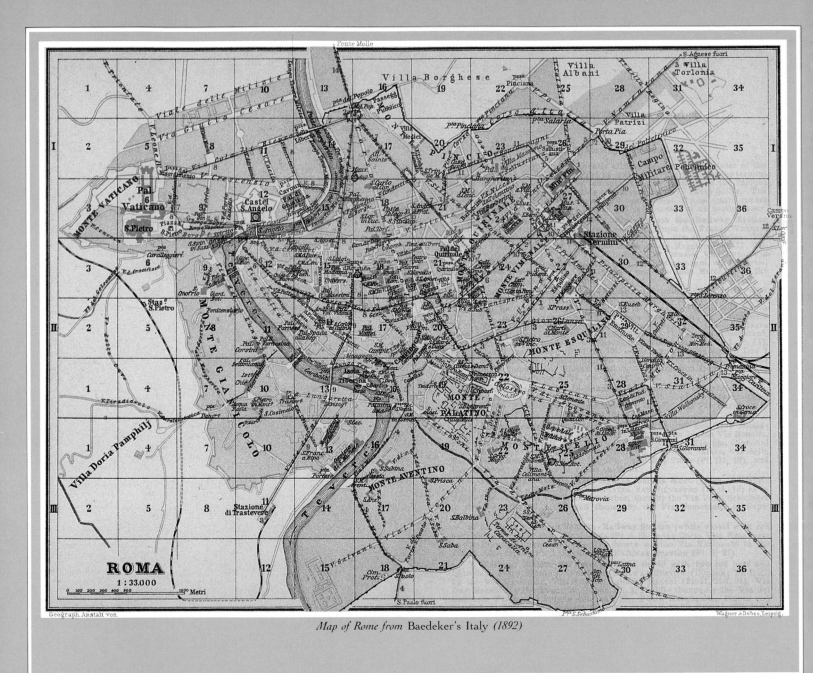

Map of Rome from Baedeker's Italy *(1892)*

CHAPTER IV

A ROMAN HOLIDAY

St. John Lateran, Rome

T IS CERTAINLY SWEET to be merry at the right moment; but the right moment hardly seems to me the ten days of the Roman Carnival. It was my rather cynical suspicion perhaps that they wouldn't keep to my imagination the brilliant promise of legend; but I have been justified by the event and have been decidedly less conscious of the festal influences of the season than of the inalienable gravity of the place. There was a time when the Carnival was a serious matter – that is a heartily joyous one; but, thanks to the seven-league boots the kingdom of Italy has lately donned for the march of progress in quite other directions, the fashion of public revelry has fallen woefully out of step. The state of mind and manners under which the Carnival was kept in generous good faith I doubt if an American can exactly conceive: he can only say to himself that for a month in the year there must have been things – things considerably of humiliation – it was comfortable to forget. But now that Italy is made the Carnival is unmade; and we are not especially tempted to envy the attitude of a population who have lost their relish for play and not yet acquired to any striking extent an enthusiasm for work. The spectacle on the Corso has seemed to me, on the whole, an illustration of that great breach with the past of which Catholic Christendom felt the somewhat muffled shock in September 1870. A traveller acquainted with the fully papal Rome, coming back any time during the past winter, must have immediately noticed that something momentous had happened – something hostile to the elements of picture and colour and "style". My first warning was that ten minutes after my arrival I found myself face to face with a newspaper stand. The impossibility in the other days of having anything in the journalistic line but the *Osservatore Romano* and the *Voce della Verità* used to seem to me much connected with the extraordinary leisure of thought and stillness of mind to which the place admitted you. But now the slender piping of the Voice of Truth is stifled by the raucous note of eventide vendors of the *Capitale*, the *Libertà* and the *Fanfulla*; and Rome reading unexpurgated news is another Rome indeed. For every subscriber to the *Libertà* there may well be an antique masker and reveller less. As striking a sign of the new régime is the extraordinary increase of population. The Corso was always a well-filled street, but now it's a perpetual crush. I never cease to wonder where the new-comers are lodged, and how such spotless flowers of fashion as the gentlemen who stare at the carriages can bloom in the atmosphere of those *camere mobiliate* of which I have had glimpses. This, however, is their own question, and bravely enough they meet it. They proclaimed somehow, to the first freshness of my wonder, as I say, that by force of numbers Rome had been secularised. An Italian dandy is a figure visually to reckon with, but these goodly throngs of them scarce offered compensation for the absent monsignori, treading the streets in their purple

Piazza S. Bernardo, Rome

stockings and followed by the solemn servants who returned on their behalf the bows of the meaner sort; for the mourning gear of the cardinals' coaches that formerly glittered with scarlet and swung with the weight of the footmen clinging behind; for the certainty that you'll not, by the best of traveller's luck, meet the Pope sitting deep in the shadow of his great chariot with uplifted fingers like some inaccessible idol in his shrine. You may meet the King indeed, who is as ugly, as imposingly ugly, as some idols, though not so inaccessible. The other day as I passed the Quirinal he drove up in a low carriage with a single attendant; and a group of men and women who had been waiting near the gate rushed at him with a number of folded papers. The carriage slackened pace and he pocketed their offerings with a business-like air – that of a good-natured man accepting hand-bills at a street-corner. Here was a monarch at his palace gate receiving petitions from his subjects – being adjured to right their wrongs. The scene ought to have thrilled me, but somehow it had no more intensity than a woodcut in an illustrated newspaper. Homely I should call it at most; admirably so, certainly, for there were lately few sovereigns standing, I believe, with whom their people enjoyed these filial hand-to-hand relations. The King this year, however, has had as little to do with the Carnival as the Pope, and the innkeepers and Americans have marked it for their own.

It was advertised to begin at half-past two o'clock of a certain Saturday, and punctually at the stroke of the hour, from my room across a wide court, I heard a sudden multiplication of sounds and confusion of tongues in the Corso. I was writing to a friend for whom I cared more than for any mere romp; but as the minutes elapsed and the hubbub deepened curiosity got the better of affection, and I remembered that I was really within eye-shot of an affair the fame of which had ministered to the day-dreams of my infancy. I used to have a scrap-book with a coloured print of the starting of the bedizened wild horses, and the use of a library rich in keepsakes and annuals with a frontispiece commonly of a masked lady in a balcony, the heroine of a delightful tale further on. Agitated by these tender memories I descended into the street; but I confess I looked in vain for a masked lady who might serve as a frontispiece, in vain for any object whatever that might adorn a tale. Masked and muffled ladies there were in abundance; but their masks were of ugly wire, perfectly resembling the little covers placed upon strong cheese in German hotels, and their drapery was a shabby water-proof with the hood pulled over their chignons. They were armed with great tin scoops or funnels, with which they solemnly shovelled lime and flour out of bushel-baskets and down on the heads of the people in the street. They were packed into balconies all the way along the straight vista of the Corso, in which their calcareous shower maintained a dense, gritty, unpalatable fog. The crowd was compact in the street, and the Americans in it were tossing back confetti out of great satchels hung round their necks. It was quite the "you're another" sort of repartee, and less seasoned than I had hoped with the airy mockery tradition hangs about this festival. The scene was striking, in a word; but somehow not as I had dreamed of its being. I stood regardful, I suppose, but with a peculiarly tempting blankness of visage, for in a moment I received half a bushel of flour on my too-philosophic head. Decidedly it was an ignoble form of humour. I shook my ears like an emergent diver, and had a sudden vision of how still and sunny and solemn, how peculiarly and undisturbedly themselves, how secure from any intrusion less sympathetic than one's own, certain outlying parts of Rome must just then be. The Carnival had received its death-blow in my imagination; and it has been ever since but a thin and dusky ghost of pleasure that has flitted at intervals in and out of my consciousness.

I turned my back accordingly on the Corso and wandered away to the grass-grown quarters delightfully free even from the possibility of a fellow-countryman. And so having set myself an example I have been keeping Carnival by strolling perversely along the silent circumference of Rome. I have doubtless lost a great deal. The Princess Margaret has occupied a balcony opposite the open space which leads into Via Condotti and, I believe, like the discreet princess she is, has dealt in no missiles but bonbons, bouquets and white doves. I would have waited half an hour any day to see the Princess Margaret hold a dove on her forefinger; but I never chanced to notice any preparation for that effect. And yet do what you will you can't really elude the Carnival. As the days elapse it filters down into the manners of the common people, and before the week is over the very beggars at the church-doors seem to have gone to the expense of a domino. When you meet these specimens of dingy drollery capering about in dusky back-streets at all hours of the day and night, meet them flitting out of black doorways between the greasy groups that cluster about Roman thresholds, you feel that a love of "pranks", the more vivid the better, must from far back have been implanted in the Roman temperament with a strong hand. An unsophisticated American is wonderstruck at the number of persons, of every age and various

Backstreet in Rome

conditions, whom it costs nothing in the nature of an ingenuous blush to walk up and down the streets in the costume of a theatrical supernumerary. Fathers of families do it at the head of an admiring progeniture; aunts and uncles and grandmothers do it; all the family does it, with varying splendour but with the same good conscience. "A pack of babies!" the doubtless too self-conscious alien pronounces it for its pains, and tries to imagine himself strutting along Broadway in a battered tin helmet and a pair of yellow tights. Our vices are certainly different; it takes those of the innocent sort to be so ridiculous. A self-consciousness lapsing so easily, in fine, strikes me as so near a relation to amenity, urbanity and general gracefulness that, for myself, I should be sorry to lay a tax on it, lest these other commodities should also cease to come to market.

I was rewarded, when I had turned away with my ears full of flour, by a glimpse of an intenser life than the dingy foolery of the Corso. I walked down by the back streets to the steps mounting to the Capitol – that long inclined plane, rather, broken at every two paces, which is the unfailing disappointment, I believe, of tourists primed for retrospective raptures. Certainly the Capitol seen from this side isn't commanding. The hill is so low, the ascent so narrow, Michael Angelo's architecture in the quadrangle at the top so meagre, the whole place somehow so much more of a mole-hill than a mountain, that for the first ten minutes of your standing there Roman history seems suddenly to have sunk through a trap-door. It emerges however on the other side, in the Forum; and here meanwhile, if you get no sense of the sublime, you get gradually a sense of exquisite composition. Nowhere in Rome is more colour, more charm, more sport for the eye. The mild incline, during the winter months, is always covered with lounging sunseekers, and especially with those more constantly obvious members of the Roman population – beggars, soldiers, monks and tourists. The beggars and peasants lie kicking their heels along that grandest of loafing-places the great steps of the Ara Cœli. The dwarfish look of the Capitol is intensified, I think, by the neighbourhood of this huge blank staircase, mouldering away in disuse, the weeds thick in its crevices, and climbing to the rudely solemn façade of the church. The sunshine glares on this great unfinished wall only to light up its featureless despair, its expression of conscious, irremediable incompleteness. Sometimes, massing its rusty screen against the deep blue sky, with the little cross and the sculptured porch casting a clear-cut shadow on the bricks, it seems to have even more than a Roman desolation, it confusedly suggests Spain and Africa – lands with no latent *risorgimenti*, with absolutely nothing but a fatal past. The legendary wolf of Rome has lately been accommodated with a little artificial grotto, among the cacti and the palms, in the fantastic triangular garden squeezed between the steps of the church and the ascent to the Capitol, where she holds a perpetual levee and "draws" apparently as powerfully as the Pope himself. Above, in the piazzetta before the stuccoed palace which rises so jauntily on a basement of thrice its magnitude, are more loungers and knitters in the sun, seated round the massively inscribed base of the statue of Marcus Aurelius. Hawthorne has perfectly expressed the attitude of this admirable figure in saying that it extends its arm with "a command which is in itself a benediction." I doubt if any statue of king or captain in the public places of the world has more to commend it to the general heart. Irrecoverable simplicity – residing so in irrecoverable Style – has no sturdier representative. Here is an impression that the sculptors of the last three hundred years have been laboriously trying to reproduce; but contrasted with this mild old monarch their prancing horsemen suggest a succession of riding-masters taking out young ladies' schools. The admirably human character of the figure survives the rusty decomposition of the bronze and the slight "debasement" of the art; and one may call it singular that in the capital of Christendom the portrait most suggestive of a Christian conscience is that of a pagan emperor.

You recover in some degree your stifled hopes of sublimity as you pass beyond the palace and take your choice of either curving slope to descend into the Forum. Then you see that the little stuccoed edifice is but a modern excrescence on the mighty cliff of a primitive construction, whose great squares of porous tufa, as they underlie each other, seem to resolve themselves back into the colossal cohesion of unhewn rock. There are prodigious strangenesses in the union of this airy and comparatively fresh-faced superstructure and these deep-plunging, hoary foundations; and few things in Rome are more entertaining to the eye than to measure the long plumb-line which drops from the inhabited windows of the palace, with their little over-peeping balconies, their muslin curtains and their bird-cages, down to the rugged constructional work of the Republic. In the Forum proper the sublime is eclipsed again, though the late extension of the excavations gives a chance for it.

Nothing in Rome helps your fancy to a more vigorous backward flight than to lounge on a sunny day over the railing which guards the great central researches. It "says" more things to you than you can repeat to see the past, the ancient world, as you stand there, bodily turned up with the spade and transformed from an immaterial inaccessible fact of time into a matter of soils and surfaces. The pleasure is the same – in kind – as what you enjoy at Pompeii, and the pain the same. It wasn't here, however, that I found my compensation for forfeiting the spectacle on the Corso, but in a little church at the end of the narrow byway which diverges up the Palatine from just beside the Arch of Titus. This byway leads you between high walls, then takes a bend and introduces you to a long row of rusty, dusty little pictures of the stations of the cross. Beyond these stands a small church with a front so modest that you hardly recognise it till you see the leather curtain. I never see a leather curtain without lifting it; it is sure to cover a constituted *scene* of some sort – good, bad or indifferent. The scene this time was meagre – whitewash and tarnished candlesticks and mouldy muslin flowers being its principal features. I shouldn't have remained if I hadn't been struck with the attitude of the single worshipper – a young priest kneeling before one of the side altars, who, as I entered, lifted his head and gave me a sidelong look so charged with the languor of devotion that he immediately became an object of interest. He was visiting each of the altars in turn and kissing the balustrade beneath them. He was alone in the church, and indeed in the whole region. There were no beggars even at the door; they were plying their trade on the skirts of the Carnival. In the entirely deserted place he alone knelt for religion, and as I sat respectfully by it seemed to me I could hear in the perfect silence the far-away uproar of the maskers. It was my late impression of these frivolous people, I suppose, joined with the extraordinary gravity of the young priest's face – his pious fatigue, his droning prayer and his isolation – that gave me just then and there a supreme vision of the religious passion, its privations and resignations and exhaustions and its terribly small share of amusement. He was young and strong and evidently of not too refined a fibre to enjoy the Carnival; but, planted there with his face pale with fasting and his knees stiff with praying, he seemed so stern a satire on it and on the crazy thousands who were preferring it to *his* way, that I half expected to see some heavenly portent out of a monastic legend come down and confirm his choice. Yet I confess that though I wasn't enamoured of the Carnival myself his seemed a grim preference and this

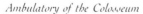

Ambulatory of the Colosseum

forswearing of the world a terrible game – a gaining one only if your zeal never falters; a hard fight when it does. In such an hour, to a stout young fellow like the hero of my anecdote, the smell of incense must seem horribly stale and the muslim flowers and gilt candlesticks to figure no great bribe. And it wouldn't have helped him much to think that not so very far away, just beyond the Forum, in the Corso, there was sport for the million, and for nothing. I doubt on the other hand whether my young priest had thought of this. He had made himself a temple out of the very elements of his innocence, and his prayers followed each other too fast for the tempter to slip in a whisper. And so, as I say, I found a solider fact of human nature than the love of *coriandoli*.

One of course never passes the Colosseum without paying it one's respects – without going in under one of the hundred portals and crossing the long oval and sitting down awhile, generally at the foot of the cross in the centre. I always feel, as I do so, as if I were seated in the depths of some Alpine valley. The upper portions of the side toward the Esquiline look as remote and lonely as an Alpine ridge, and you raise your eyes to their rugged sky-line, drinking in the sun and silvered by the blue air, with much the same feeling with which you would take in a grey cliff on which an eagle might lodge. This roughly mountainous quality of the great ruin is its chief interest; beauty of detail has pretty well vanished, especially since the high-growing wild-flowers have been plucked away by the new government, whose functionaries, surely, at certain points of their task, must have felt as if they shared the dreadful trade of those who gather samphire. Even if you are on your way to the Lateran you won't grudge the twenty minutes it will take you, on leaving the Colosseum, to turn away under the Arch of Constantine, whose noble battered bas-reliefs, with the chain of tragic

Arch of Constantine

View of the Forum, by William Parrott

Arch of Constantine

statues – fettered, drooping barbarians – round its summit, I assume you to have profoundly admired, toward the piazzetta of the church of San Giovanni e Paolo, on the slope of Cælian. No spot in Rome can show a cluster of more charming accidents. The ancient brick apse of the church peeps down into the trees of the little wooded walk before the neighbouring church of San Gregorio, intensely venerable beneath its excessive modernisation; and a series of heavy brick buttresses, flying across to an opposite wall, overarches the short, steep paved passage which leads into the small square. This is flanked on one side by the long mediæval portico of the church of the two saints, sustained by eight time-blackened columns of granite and marble. On another rise the great scarce-windowed walls of a Passionist convent, and on the third the portals of a grand villa, whose tall porter, with his cockade and silver-topped staff, standing sublime behind his grating, seems a kind of mundane St. Peter, I suppose, to the beggars who sit at the church door or lie in the sun along the farther slope which leads to the gate of the convent. The place always seems to me the perfection of an out-of-the-way corner – a place you would think twice before telling people about, lest you should find them there the next time you were to go. It is such a group of objects, singly and in their happy combination, as one must come to Rome to find at one's house door; but what makes it peculiarly a picture is the beautiful dark red campanile of the church, which stands embedded in the mass of the convent. It begins, as so many things in Rome begin, with a stout foundation of antique travertine, and rises high, in delicately quaint mediæval brickwork – little tiers and apertures sustained on miniature columns and adorned with small cracked slabs of green and yellow marble, inserted almost at random. When there are three or four brown-breasted contadini sleeping in the sun before the convent doors, and a departing monk leading his shadow down over them, I think you will not find anything in Rome more *sketchable*.

If you stop, however, to observe everything worthy of your water-colours you will never reach St. John Lateran. My business was much less with the interior of that vast and empty, that cold clean temple, which I have never found peculiarly interesting, than with certain charming features of its surrounding precinct – the crooked old court beside it, which admits you to the Baptistery and to a delightful rear-view of the queer architectural odds and ends that may in Rome compose a florid ecclesiastical façade. There are more of these, a stranger jumble of chance detail, of lurking recesses and wanton projections and inexplicable windows, than I have memory or phrase for; but the gem of the collection is the oddly perched peaked turret, with its yellow travertine welded upon the rusty brickwork, which was not meant to be suspected, and the brickwork retreating beneath and leaving it in the odd position of a tower *under* which you may see the sky. As to the great front of the church overlooking the Porta San Giovanni, you are not admitted behind the scenes; the term is quite in keeping, for the architecture has a vastly theatrical air. It is extremely imposing – that of St. Peter's alone is more so; and when from far off on the Campagna you see the colossal images of the mitred saints along the top standing distinct against the sky, you forget their coarse construction and their inflated draperies. The view from the great space which stretches from the church steps to the city wall is the very prince of views. Just beside you, beyond the great alcove of mosaic, is the Scala Santa, the marble staircase which (says the legend) Christ descended under the weight of Pilate's judgment, and which all Christians must forever ascend on their knees; before you is the city gate which opens upon the Via Appia Nuova, the long gaunt file of arches of the Claudian aqueduct, their jagged ridge stretching away like the vertebral column of some monstrous mouldering skeleton, and upon the blooming brown and purple flats and dells of the Campagna and the glowing blue of the Alban Mountains, spotted with their white, high-nestling towns; while to your left is the great grassy space, lined with dwarfish mulberry-trees, which stretches across to the damp little sister-basilica of Santa Croce in Gerusalemme. During a former visit to Rome I lost my heart to this idle tract, and wasted much time in sitting on the steps of the church and watching certain white-cowled friars who were sure to be passing there for the delight of my eyes. There are fewer friars now, and there are a great many of the king's recruits, who inhabit the ex-conventual barracks adjoining Santa Croce and are led forward to practise their goose-step on the sunny turf. Here too the poor old cardinals who are no longer to be seen on the Pincio descend from their mourning-coaches and relax their venerable knees. These members alone still testify to the traditional splendour of the princes of the Church; for as they advance the lifted black petticoat reveals a flash of scarlet stockings and makes you groan at the victory of civilisation over colour.

If St. John Lateran disappoints you internally, you have an easy compensation in pacing the long lane which connects it with Santa Maria Maggiore and entering the singularly perfect nave of that most delightful of churches. The first day of my stay in Rome under the old dispensation I spent in wandering at random through the city, with accident for my *valet-de-place*. It served me to perfection and introduced me to the best things; among others to an immediate happy relation with Santa Maria Maggiore. First impressions, memorable impressions, are generally irrecoverable; they often leave one the wiser, but they rarely return in the same form. I remember, of my coming uninformed and unprepared into the place of worship and of curiosity that I have named, only that I sat for half an hour on the edge of the base of one of the marble columns of the beautiful nave and enjoyed a perfect revel of – what shall I call it? – taste, intelligence, fancy, perceptive emotion? The place proved so endlessly suggestive that perception became a throbbing confusion of images, and I departed with a sense of knowing a good deal that is not set down in Murray. I have seated myself more than once again at the base of the same column; but you live your life only once, the parts as well as the whole. The obvious charm of the church is the elegant grandeur of the nave – its perfect shapeliness and its rich simplicity, its long double row of white marble columns and its high flat roof, embossed with intricate gildings and mouldings. It opens into a choir of an extraordinary splendour of effect, which I recommend you to look out for of a fine afternoon. At such a time the glowing western light, entering the high windows of the tribune, kindles the scattered masses of colour into sombre brightness, scintillates on the great solemn mosaic of the vault, touches the porphyry columns of the superb baldachino with ruby lights, and buries its shining shafts in the deep-toned shadows that hang about frescoes and sculptures and mouldings. The deeper charm even than in such things, however, is the social or historic note or tone or atmosphere of the church – I fumble, you see, for my right expression; the sense it gives you, in common with most of the Roman churches, and more than any of them, of having been prayed in for several centuries by an endlessly curious and complex society. It takes no great attention to let it come to you that the authority of Italian Catholicism has lapsed not a little in these days; not less also perhaps than to feel that, as they stand, these deserted temples were the fruit of a society leavened through and through by ecclesiastical manners, and that they formed for ages the constant background of the human drama. They are, as one may say, the *churchiest* churches in Europe – the fullest of gathered memories, of the experience of their office. There's not a figure one has read of in old-world annals that isn't to be imagined on proper occasion kneeling before the lamp-decked Confession beneath the altar of Santa Maria Maggiore. One sees after all, however, even among the most palpable realities, very much what the play of one's imagination projects there; and I present my remarks simply as a reminder that one's constant excursions into these places are not the least interesting episodes of one's walks in Rome.

I had meant to give a simple illustration of the church-habit, so to speak, but I have given it at such a length as leaves scant space to touch on the innumerable topics brushed by the pen that begins to take Roman notes. It is by the aimless *flânerie* which leaves you free to follow capriciously every hint of entertainment that you get to know Rome. The greater part of the life about you

S. Maria Maggiore

goes on in the streets; and for an observer fresh from a country in which town scenery is at the least montonous incident and character and picture seem to abound. I become conscious with compunction, let me hasten to add, that I have launched myself thus on the subject of Roman churches and Roman walks without so much as a preliminary allusion to St. Peter's. One is apt to proceed thither on rainy days with intentions of exercise – to put the case only at that – and to carry these out body and mind. Taken as a walk not less than as a church, St. Peter's of course reigns alone. Even for the profane "constitutional" it serves where the Boulevards, where Piccadilly and Broadway, fall short, and if it didn't offer to our use the grandest area in the world it would still offer the most diverting. Few great works of art last longer to the curiosity, to the perpetually transcended attention. You think you have taken the whole thing in, but it expands, it rises sublime again, and leaves your measure itself poor. You never let the ponderous leather

View of Rome from the Convent of San Onofrio, by David Roberts

down behind you – your weak lift of a scant edge of whose padded vastness resembles the liberty taken in folding back the parchment corner of some mighty folio page – without feeling all former visits to have been but missed attempts at apprehension and the actual to achieve your first real possession. The conventional question is ever as to whether one hasn't been "disappointed in the size", but a few honest folk here and there, I hope, will never cease to say no. The place struck me from the first as the hugest thing conceivable – a real exaltation of one's idea of space; so that one's entrance, even from the great empty square which either glares beneath the deep blue sky or makes of the cool far-cast shadow of the immense front something that resembles a big slate-coloured country on a map, seems not so much a going in somewhere as a going out. The mere man of pleasure in quest of new sensations might well not know where to better his encounter there of the sublime shock that brings him, within the threshold, to an immediate gasping pause. There are days when the vast nave looks mysteriously vaster than on others and the gorgeous baldachino a longer journey beyond the far-spreading tessellated plain of the pavement, and when the light has yet a quality which lets things loom their largest, while the scattered figures – I mean the human, for there are plenty of others – mark happily the scale of items and parts. Then you have only to stroll and stroll and gaze and gaze; to watch the glorious altar-canopy lift its bronze architecture, its colossal embroidered contortions, like a temple within a temple, and feel yourself, at the bottom of the abysmal shaft of the dome, dwindle to a crawling dot.

Much of the constituted beauty resides in the fact that it is all general beauty, that you are appealed to by no specific details, or that these at least, practically never importunate, are as taken for granted as the lieutenants and captains are taken for granted in a great standing army – among whom indeed individual aspects may figure here the rather shifting range of decorative dignity in which details, when observed, often prove poor

St. Peter's from the back of the colonnade

101

(though never not massive and substantially precious) and sometimes prove ridiculous. The sculptures, with the sole exception of Michael Angelo's ineffable "Pietà", which lurks obscurely in a side-chapel – this indeed to my sense the rarest artistic *combination* of the greatest things the hand of man has produced – are either bad or indifferent; and the universal incrustation of marble, though sumptuous enough, has a less brilliant effect than much later work of the same sort, that for instance of St. Paul's without the Walls. The supreme beauty is the splendidly sustained simplicity of the whole. The thing represents a prodigious imagination extraordinarily strained, yet strained, at its happiest pitch, without breaking. Its happiest pitch I say, because this is the only creation of its strenuous author in presence of which you are in presence of serenity. You may invoke the idea of ease at St. Peter's without a sense of sacrilege – which you can hardly do, if you are at all spiritually nervous, in Westminster Abbey or Notre Dame. The vast enclosed clearness has much to do with the idea. There are no shadows to speak of, no marked effects of shade; only effects of light innumerable – points at which this element seems to mass itself in airy density and scatter itself in enchanting gradations and cadences. It performs the office of gloom or of mystery in Gothic churches; hangs like a rolling mist along the gilded vault of the nave, melts into bright interfusion the mosaic scintillations of the dome, clings and clusters and lingers, animates the whole huge and otherwise empty shell. A good Catholic, I suppose, is the same Catholic anywhere, before the grandest as well as the humblest altars; but to a visitor not formally enrolled St. Peter's speaks less of aspiration than of full and convenient assurance. The soul infinitely expands there, if one will, but all on its quite human level. It marvels at the reach of our dream and the immensity of our resources. To be so impressed and put in our place, we say, is to be sufficiently "saved"; we can't be more than that in heaven itself; and what specifically celestial beauty such a show or such a substitute may lack it makes up for in certainty and tangibility. And yet if one's hours on the scene are not actually

Piazza del Popolo

spent in praying, the spirit seeks it again as for the finer comfort, for the blessing, exactly, of its example, its protection and its exclusion. When you are weary of the swarming democracy of your fellow-tourists, of the unremunerative aspects of human nature on Corso and Pincio, of the oppressively frequent combination of coronets on carriage panels and stupid faces in carriages, of addled brains and lacquered boots, of ruin and dirt and decay, of priests and beggars and takers of advantage, of the myriad tokens of a halting civilisation, the image of the great temple depresses the balance of your doubts, seems to rise above the highest tide of vulgarity and make you still believe in the heroic will and the heroic act. It's a relief, in other words, to feel that there's nothing but a cab-fare between your pessimism and one of the greatest of human achievements.

This might serve as a Lenten peroration to these remarks of mine which have strayed so woefully from their jovial text, save that I ought fairly to confess that my last impression of the Carnival was altogether Carnivalesque. The merry-making of Shrove Tuesday had life and felicity; the dead letter of tradition broke out into nature and grace. I pocketed my scepticism and spent a long afternoon on the Corso. Almost every one was a masker, but you had no need to conform; the pelting rain of confetti effectually disguised you. I can't say I found it all very exhilarating; but here and there I noticed a brighter episode – a capering clown inflamed with contagious jollity, some finer humourist forming a circle every thirty yards to crow at his indefatigable sallies. One clever performer so especially pleased me that I should have been glad to catch a glimpse of the natural man. You imagined for him that he was taking a prodigious intellectual holiday and that his gaiety was in inverse ratio to his daily mood. Dressed as a needy scholar, in an ancient evening-coat and with a rusty black hat and gloves fantastically patched, he carried a little volume carefully under his arm. His humours were in excellent taste, his whole manner the perfection of genteel comedy. The crowd seemed to relish him vastly, and he at once commanded a gleefully attentive audience. Many of his sallies I lost; those I caught were excellent. His trick was often to begin by taking some one urbanely and caressingly by the chin and complimenting him on the *intelligenza della sua fisionomia*. I kept near him as long as I could; for he struck me as a real ironic artist, cherishing a disinterested, and yet at the same time a motived and a moral, passion for the grotesque. I should have liked, however – if indeed I shouldn't have feared – to see him the next morning, or when he unmasked that night over his hard-earned supper in a smoky *trattoria*. As the evening went on the cloud

S. Francesco Romana

thickened and became a motley press of shouting, pushing, scrambling, everything but squabbling, revellers. The rain of missiles ceased at dusk, but the universal deposit of chalk and flour was trampled into a cloud made lurid by flaring pyramids of the gas-lamps that replaced for the occasion the stingy Roman luminaries. Early in the evening came off the classic exhibition of the *moccoletti*, which I but half saw, like a languid reporter resigned beforehand to be cashiered for want of enterprise. From the mouth of a side-street, over a thousand heads, I caught a huge slow-moving illuminated car, from which blue-lights and rockets and Roman candles were in course of discharge, meeting all in a dim fuliginous glare far above the house-tops. It was like a glimpse of some public orgy in ancient Babylon. In the small hours of the morning, walking homeward from a private entertainment, I found Ash-Wednesday still kept at bay. The Corso, flaring with light, smelt like a circus. Every one was taking friendly liberties with every one else and using up the dregs of his festive energy in convulsive hootings and gymnastics. Here and there certain indefatigable spirits, clad all in red after the manner of devils and leaping furiously about with torches, were supposed to affright you. But they shared the universal geniality and bequeathed me no midnight fears as a pretext for keeping Lent, the *carnevale dei preti*, as I read in that profanely radical sheet the *Capitale*. Of this too I have been having glimpses. Going lately into Santa Francesca Romana, the picturesque church near the Temple of Peace, I found a feast for the eyes – a dim crimson-toned light through curtained windows, a great festoon of tapers round the altar, a bulging girdle of lamps before the sunken shrine beneath, and a dozen white-robed Dominicans scattered in the happiest composition on the pavement. It was better than the *moccoletti*.

1873.

CHAPTER V
ROMAN RIDES

Entrance to the Vatican

 SHALL ALWAYS REMEMBER the first I took: out of the Porta del Popolo, to where the Ponte Molle, whose single arch sustains a weight of historic tradition, compels the sallow Tiber to flow between its four great-mannered ecclesiastical statues, over the crest of the hill and along the old posting-road to Florence. It was mild midwinter, the season peculiarly of colour on the Roman Campagna; and the light was full of that mellow purple glow, that tempered intensity, which haunts the after-visions of those who have known Rome like the memory of some supremely irresponsible pleasure. An hour away I pulled up and at the edge of a meadow gazed away for some time into remoter distances. Then and there, it seemed to me, I measured the deep delight of knowing the Campagna. But I saw more things in it than I can easily tell. The country rolled away around me into slopes and dells of long-drawn grace, chequered with purple and blue and blooming brown. The lights and shadows were at play on the Sabine Mountains – an alternation of tones so exquisite as to be conveyed only by some fantastic comparison to sapphire and amber. In the foreground a contadino in his cloak and peaked hat jogged solitary on his ass; and here and there in the distance, among blue undulations, some white village, some grey tower, helped deliciously to make the picture the typical "Italian landscape" of old-fashioned art. It was so bright and yet so sad, so still and yet so charged, to the supersensuous ear, with the murmur of an extinguished life, that you could only say it was intensely and adorably strange, could only impute to the whole overarched scene an unsurpassed secret for bringing tears of appreciation to no matter how ignorant – archeologically ignorant – eyes. To ride once, in these conditions, is of course to ride again and to allot to the Campagna a generous share of the time one spends in Rome.

It is a pleasure that doubles one's horizon, and one can scarcely say whether it enlarges or limits one's impression of the city proper. It certainly makes St. Peter's seem a trifle smaller and blunts the edge of one's curiosity in the Forum. It must be the effect of the experience, at all extended, that when you think of Rome afterwards you will think still respectfully and regretfully enough of the Vatican and the Pincio, the streets and the picture-making street life; but will even more wonder, with an irrepressible contraction of the heart, when again you shall feel yourself bounding over the flower-smothered turf, or pass from one framed picture to another beside the open arches of the crumbling aqueducts. You look back at the City so often from some grassy hill-top – hugely compact within its walls, with St. Peter's overtopping all things and yet seeming small, and the vast girdle of marsh and meadow receding on all sides to the mountains and the sea – that you come to remember it at last as hardly more than a respectable parenthesis in a great sweep of generalisation. Within the walls, on the other hand, you think of your intended ride as the most romantic of all your possibilities; of the Campagna generally as an illimitable experience. One's rides certainly give Rome an inordinate scope for the reflective – by which I suppose I mean after all the æsthetic and the "esoteric" – life. To dwell in a city which, much as you grumble at it, is after all very fairly a modern city; with crowds and shops and theatres and cafés and balls and receptions and dinner-parties and all the modern confusion of social pleasures and pains; to have at your door the good and evil of it all; and yet to be able in half an hour to gallop away and leave it a hundred miles, a hundred years, behind, and to look at the tufted broom blowing on a lonely tower-top in the still blue air, and the pale pink asphodels trembling none the less for the stillness, and the shaggy-legged shepherds leaning on their sticks in motionless brotherhood with the heaps of ruin, and the scrambling goats and staggering little kids treading out wild desert smells from the top of hollow-sounding mounds; and then to come back through one of the great gates and a couple of hours later find yourself in the "world", dressed, introduced, entertained, inquiring, talking about "Middlemarch" to a young English lady or listening to Neapolitan songs from a gentleman in a very low-cut shirt – all this is to lead in a manner a double life and to gather from the hurrying hours more impressions than a mind of modest capacity quite knows how to dispose of.

I touched lately upon this theme with a friend who, I fancied, would understand me, and who immediately assured me that he had just spent a day that this mingled diversity of sensation made to the days one spends elsewhere what an uncommonly good novel may be to the daily paper. "There was an air of idleness about it, if you will," he said, "and it was certainly pleasant enough to have been wrong Perhaps, being after all unused to long stretches of dissipation, this was why I had a half-feeling that I was reading an odd chapter in the history of a person very much more of a *héros de roman* than myself." Then he proceeded to relate how he had taken a long ride with a lady whom he extremely admired. "We turned off from the Tor di Quinto Road to that castellated farm-house you know of – once a Ghibelline fortress – whither Claude Lorraine used to come to paint pictures of which the surrounding landscape is still so artistically, so compositionally,

Roman Campagna

107

suggestive. We went into the inner court, a cloister almost, with the carven capitals of its loggia columns, and looked at a handsome child swinging shyly against the half-opened door of a room whose impenetrable shadow, behind her, made her, as it were, a sketch in bituminous water-colours. We talked with the farmer, a handsome, pale, fever-tainted fellow with a well-to-do air that didn't in the least deter his affability from a turn compatible with the acceptance of small coin; and then we galloped away and away over the meadows which stretch with hardly a break to Veii. The day was strangely delicious, with a cool grey sky and just a touch of moisture in the air stirred by our rapid motion. The Campagna, in the colourless even light, was more solemn and romantic than ever; and a ragged shepherd, driving a meagre straggling flock, whom we stopped to ask our way of, was a perfect type of pastoral, weather-beaten misery. He was precisely the shepherd for the foreground of a scratchy etching. There were faint odours of spring in the air, and the grass here and there was streaked with great patches of daisies; but it was spring with a foreknowledge of autumn, a day to be enjoyed with a substrain of sadness, the foreboding of regret, a day somehow to make one feel as if one had seen and felt a great deal – quite, as I say, like a *héros de roman*. Touching such characters, it was the illustrious Pelham, I think, who, on being asked if he rode, replied that he left those violent exercises to the ladies. But under such a sky, in such an air, over acres of daisied turf, a long, long gallop is certainly a supersubtle joy. The elastic bound of your horse is the poetry of motion; and if you are so happy as to add to it not the prose of companionship riding comes almost to affect you as a spiritual exercise. My gallop, at any rate," said my friend, "threw me into a mood which gave an extraordinary zest to the rest of the day." He was to go to a dinner party at a villa on the edge of Rome, and Madame X— —, who was also going, called for him in her carriage. "It was a long drive," he went on, "through the Forum, past the Colosseum. She told me a long story about a most interesting person. Toward the end my eyes caught through the carriage window a slab of rugged sculptures. We were passing under the Arch of Constantine. In the hall pavement of the villa is a rare antique mosaic —one of the largest and most perfect; the ladies on their way to the drawing-room trail over it the flounces of Worth. We drove home late, and there's my day."

On your exit from most of the gates of Rome you have generally half-an-hour's progress through winding

Tomb in the Campagna

The Forum viewed from the Farnese Gardens, by J. B. C. Corot

lanes, many of which are hardly less charming than the open meadows. On foot the walls and high hedges would vex you and spoil your walk; but in the saddle you generally overtop them, to an endless peopling of the minor vision. Yet a Roman wall in the springtime is for that matter almost as interesting as anything it conceals. Crumbling grain by grain, coloured and mottled to a hundred tones by sun and storm, with its rugged structure of brick extruding through its coarse complexion of peeling stucco, its creeping lacework of wandering ivy starred with miniature violets, and its wild fringe of stouter flowers against the sky – it is as little as possible a blank partition; it is practically a luxury of landscape. At the moment at which I write, in mid-April, all the ledges and cornices are wreathed with flaming poppies, nodding there as if they knew so well what faded greys and yellows are an offset to their scarlet. But the best point in a dilapidated enclosing surface of vineyard or villa is of course the gateway, lifting its great arch of cheap rococo scroll-work, its balls and shields and mossy dish-covers – as they always perversely figure to me – and flanked with its dusky cypresses. I never pass one without taking out my mental sketch-book and jotting it down as a vignette in the insubstantial record of my ride. They are as sad and dreary as if they led to the moated grange where Mariana waited in desperation for something to happen; and it's easy to take the usual inscription over the porch as a recommendation to those who enter to renounce all hope of anything but a glass of more or less agreeably acrid *vino romano*. For what you chiefly see over the walls and at the end of the straight short avenue of rusty cypresses are the appurtenances of a *vigna* – a couple of acres of little upright sticks blackening in the sun, and a vast sallow-faced, scantily windowed mansion, whose expression denotes little of the life of the mind beyond what goes to the driving of a hard bargain over the tasted

Temple of Venus

hogsheads. If Mariana is there she certainly has no pile of old magazines to beguile her leisure. The life of the mind, if the term be in any application here not ridiculous, appears to any asker of curious questions, as he wanders about Rome, the very thinnest deposit of the past. Within the rococo gateway, which itself has a vaguely æsthetic self-consciousness, at the end of the cypress walk, you will probably see a mythological group in rusty marble – a Cupid and Psyche, a Venus and Paris, an Apollo and Daphne – the relic of an age when a Roman proprietor thought it fine to patronise the arts. But I imagine you are safe in supposing it to constitute the only allusion savouring of culture that has been made on the premises for three or four generations.

There is a franker cheerfulness – though certainly a proper amount of that forlornness which lurks about every object to which the Campagna forms a background – in the primitive little taverns where, on the homeward stretch, in the waning light, you are often glad to rein up and demand a bottle of their best. Their best and their worst are indeed the same, though with a shifting price, and plain *vino bianco* or *vino rosso* (rarely both) is the sole article of refreshment in which they deal. There is a ragged bush over the door, and within, under a dusky vault, on crooked cobble-stones, sit half-a-dozen contadini in their indigo jackets and goatskin breeches and with their elbows on the table. There is generally a rabble of infantile beggars at the door, pretty enough in their dusty rags, with their fine eyes and intense Italian smile, to make you forget your private vow of doing your individual best to make these people, whom you like so much, unlearn their old vices. Was Porta Pia bombarded three years ago that Peppino should still grow up to whine for a copper? But the Italian shells had no direct message for Peppino's stomach – and you are going to a dinner party at a villa. So Peppino "points" an instant for the copper in the dust and grows up a Roman beggar. The whole little place represents the most primitive form of hostelry; but along any of the roads leading out of the city you may find establishments of a higher type, with Garibaldi, superbly mounted and foreshortened, painted on the wall, or a lady in a low-necked dress opening a fictive lattice with irresistible hospitality, and a yard with the classic vine-wreathed arbour casting thin shadows upon benches and tables draped and cushioned with the white dust from which the highways from the gates borrow most of their local colour. None the less, I say, you avoid the highroads, and, if you are a person of taste, don't grumble at the occasional need of following the walls of the city. City walls, to a properly constituted American, can never be an object of indifference; and it is emphatically "no end of a sensation" to pace in the shadow of this massive cincture of Rome. I have found myself, as I skirted its base, talking of trivial things, but never without a sudden reflection on the deplorable impermanence of first impressions. A twelve-month ago the raw plank fences of a Boston suburb, inscribed with the virtues of healing drugs, bristled along my horizon: now I glance with idle eyes at a compacted antiquity in which a more learned sense may read portentous dates and signs – Servius, Aurelius, Honorius. But even to idle eyes the prodigious, the continuous thing bristles with eloquent passages. In some places, where the huge brickwork is black with time and certain strange square towers look down at you with still blue eyes, the Roman sky peering through lidless loopholes, and there is nothing but

*Albano, Tomb of Pompeius Magnus
on the Via Appia*

white dust in the road and solitude in the air, I might take myself for a wandering Tartar touching on the confines of the Celestial Empire. The wall of China must have very much such a gaunt robustness. The colour of the Roman ramparts is everywhere fine, and their rugged patchwork has been subdued by time and weather into a mellow harmony that the brush only asks to catch up. On the northern side of the city, behind the Vatican, St. Peter's and the Trastevere, I have seen them glowing in the late afternoon with the tones of ancient bronze and rusty gold. Here at various points they are embossed with the Papal insignia, the tiara with its flying bands and crossed keys; to the high style of which the grace that attaches to almost any lost cause – even if not quite the "tender" grace of a day that is dead – considerably adds a style. With the dome of St. Peter's resting on their cornice and the hugely clustered architecture of the Vatican rising from them as from a terrace, they seem indeed the valid bulwark of an ecclesiastical city. Vain bulwark, alas! sighs the sentimental tourist, fresh from the meagre entertainment of this latter Holy Week. But he may find monumental consolation in this neighbourhood at a source where, as I pass, I never fail to apply for it. At half-an-hour's walk beyond Porta San Pancrazio, beneath the wall of the Villa Doria, is a delightfully pompous ecclesiastical gateway of the seventeenth century, erected by Paul V, to commemorate his restoration of the aqueducts through which the stream bearing his name flows towards the fine florid portico protecting its clear-sheeted outgush on the crest of the Janiculan. It arches across the road in the most ornamental manner of the period, and one can hardly pause before it without seeming to assist at a ten minutes' revival of old Italy – without feeling as if one were in a cocked hat and sword and were coming up to Rome, in another mood than Luther's, with a letter of recommendation to the mistress of a cardinal.

The Campagna differs greatly on the two sides of the Tiber; and it is hard to say which, for the rider, has the greater charm. The half-dozen rides you may take from Porta San Giovanni possess the perfection of traditional Roman interest and lead you through a far-strewn wilderness of ruins – a scattered maze of tombs and towers and nameless fragments of antique masonry. The landscape here has two great features; close before you on one side is the long, gentle swell of the Alban Hills, deeply, fantastically blue in most weathers, and marbled with the vague white masses of their scattered towns and villas. It would be difficult to draw the hard figure to a softer curve than that with which the heights sweep from Albano to the plain; this a perfect example of the classic beauty of line in the Italian landscape – that beauty which, when it fills the background of a picture, makes us look in the foreground for a broken column couched upon flowers and a shepherd piping to dancing nymphs. At your side, constantly, you have the broken line of the Claudian Aqueduct, carrying its broad arches far away into the plain. The meadows along which it lies are not the smoothest in the world for a gallop, but there is no pleasure greater than to wander near it. It stands knee-deep in the flower-strewn grass, and its rugged piers are hung with ivy as the columns of a church are draped for a festa. Every archway is a picture, massively framed, of the distance beyond – of the snow-tipped Sabines and lonely Soracte. As the spring advances the whole Campagna smiles and waves with flowers; but I think they are nowhere more rank and lovely than in the shifting shadow of the aqueducts, where they muffle the feet of the columns and smother the half-dozen brooks which wander in and out like silver meshes between the legs of a file of giants. They make a niche for themselves too in every crevice and tremble on the vault of the empty conduits. The ivy hereabouts in the springtime is peculiarly brilliant and delicate; and though it cloaks and muffles these Roman fragments far less closely than the castles and abbeys of England it hangs with the light elegance of all Italian vegetation. It is partly doubtless because their mighty outlines are still unsoftened that the aqueducts are so impressive. They seem the very source of the solitude in which they stand; they look like architectural spectres and loom through the light mists of their grassy desert, as you recede along the line, with the same insubstantial vastness as if they rose out of Egyptian sands. It is a great neighbourhood of ruins, many of which, it must be confessed, you have applauded in many an album. But station a peasant with sheepskin coat and bandaged legs in the shadow of a tomb or tower best known to drawing-room art, and scatter a dozen goats on the mound above him, and the picture has a charm which has not yet been sketched away.

The other quarter of the Campagna has wider fields and smoother turf and perhaps a greater number of delightful rides; the earth is sounder, and there are fewer pitfalls and ditches. The land for the most part lies higher and catches more wind, and the grass is here and there for great stretches as smooth and level as a carpet. You have no Alban Mountains before you, but you have in the distance the waving ridge of the nearer Apennines, and west of them, along the course of the

Tiber, the long seaward level of deep-coloured fields, deepening as they recede to the blue and purple of the sea itself. Beyond them, of a very clear day, you may see the glitter of the Mediterranean. These are the occasions perhaps to remember most fondly, for they lead you to enchanting nooks, and the landscape has details of the highest refinement. Indeed when my sense reverts to the lingering impressions of so blest a time, it seems a fool's errand to have attempted to express them, and a waste of words to do more than recommend the reader to go citywards at twilight of the end of March, making for Porta Cavalleggieri, and note what he sees. At this hour the Campagna is to the last point its melancholy self, and I remember roadside "effects" of a strange and intense suggestiveness. Certain mean, mouldering villas behind grass-grown courts have an indefinably sinister look; there was one in especial of which it was impossible not to argue that a despairing creature must have once committed suicide there, behind bolted door and barred window, and that no one has since had the pluck to go in and see why he never came out. Every wayside mark of manners, of history, every stamp of the past in the country about Rome, touches my sense to a thrill, and I may thus exaggerate the appeal of very common things. This is the more likely because the appeal seems ever to rise out of heaven knows what depths of ancient trouble. To delight in the aspects of *sentient* ruin might appear a heartless pastime, and the pleasure, I confess, shows the note of perversity. The sombre and the hard are as common an influence from southern things as the soft and the bright, I think; sadness rarely fails to assault a northern observer when he misses what he takes for comfort. Beauty is no compensation for the loss, only making it more poignant. Enough beauty of climate hangs over these Roman cottages and farm-houses – beauty of light, of atmosphere and of vegetation; but their charm for the maker-out of the stories in things is the way the golden air shows off their desolation. Man lives more with Nature in Italy than in New or than in Old England; she does more work for him and gives him more holidays than in our short-summered climes, and his home is therefore much more bare of devices for helping him to do without her, forget her and forgive her. These reflections are perhaps the source of the character you find in a moss-coated stone stairway climbing outside of a wall; in a queer inner court, befouled with rubbish and drearily bare of convenience; in an ancient quaintly carven well, worked with infinite labour from an overhanging window; in an arbour of time-twisted vines under which you may sit with your feet in the dirt and remember as a dim fable that there are races for which the type of domestic allurement is the parlour hearth-rug. For reasons apparent or otherwise these things amuse me beyond expression, and I am never weary of staring into gateways, of lingering by dreary, shabby, half-barbaric farm-yards, of feasting a foolish gaze on sun-cracked plaster and unctuous indoor shadows.

I mustn't forget, however, that it's not for wayside effects that one rides away behind St. Peter's, but for the strong sense of wandering over boundless space, of seeing great classic lines of landscape, of watching them dispose themselves into pictures so full of "style" that you can think of no painter who deserves to have you admit that they suggest him – hardly knowing whether it is better pleasure to gallop far and drink deep of air and grassy distance and the whole delicious opportunity, or to walk and pause and linger, and try and grasp some ineffaceable memory of sky and colour and outline. Your pace can hardly help falling into a contemplative measure at the time, everywhere so wonderful, but in Rome so persuasively divine, when the winter begins palpably to soften and quicken. Far out on the Campagna, early in February, you feel the first vague earthly emanations, which in a few weeks come wandering into the heart of the city and throbbing through the close, dark streets. Springtime in Rome is an immensely poetic affair; but you must stand often far out in the ancient waste, between grass and sky, to measure its deep, full, steadily accelerated rhythm. The winter has an incontestable beauty, and is pre-eminently the time of colour – the time when it is no affectation, but homely verity, to talk about the "purple" tone of the atmosphere. As February comes and goes your purple is streaked with green and the rich, dark bloom of the distance begins to lose its intensity. But your loss is made up by other gains; none more precious than that inestimable gain to the ear – the disembodied voice of the lark. It comes with the early flowers, the white narcissus and the cyclamen, the half-buried violets and the pale anemones, and makes the whole atmosphere ring like a vault of tinkling glass. You never see the source of the sound, and are utterly unable to localise his note, which seems to come from everywhere at once, to be some hundred-throated voice of the air. Sometimes you fancy you just catch him,

Carriages

a mere vague spot against the blue, an intenser throb in the universal pulsation of light. As the weeks go on the flowers multiply and the deep blues and purples of the hills, turning to azure and violet, creep higher toward the narrowing snow-line of the Sabines. The temperature rises, the first hour of your ride you feel the heat, but you beguile it with brushing the hawthorn-blossoms as you pass along the hedges, and catching at the wild rose and honeysuckle; and when you get into the meadows there is stir enough in the air to lighten the dead weight of the sun. The Roman air, however, is not a tonic medicine, and it seldom suffers exercise to be all exhilarating. It has always seemed to me indeed part of the charm of the latter that your keenest consciousness is haunted with a vague languor. Occasionally when the sirocco blows that sensation becomes strange and exquisite. Then, under the grey sky, before the dim distances which the south-wind mostly brings with it, you seem to ride forth into a world from which all hope has departed and in which, in spite of the flowers that make your horse's footfalls soundless, nothing is left save some queer probability that your imagination is unable to measure, but from which it hardly shrinks. This quality in the Roman element may now and then "relax" you almost to ecstasy; but a season of sirocco would be an overdose of morbid pleasure. You may at any rate best feel the peculiar beauty of the Campagna on those mild days of winter when the mere quality and temper of the sunshine suffice to move the landscape to joy, and you pause on the brown grass in the sunny stillness and, by listening long enough, almost fancy you hear the shrill of the midsummer cricket. It is detail and ornament that vary from month to month, from week to week even, and make your returns to the same places a constant feast of unexpectedness; but the great essential features of the prospect preserve throughout the year the same impressive serenity. Soracte, be it January or May, rises from its blue horizon like an island from the sea and with an elegance of contour which no mood of the year can deepen or diminish. You know it well; you have seen it often in the mellow backgrounds of Claude; and it has such an irresistibly classic, academic air that while you look at it you begin to take your saddle for a faded old arm-chair in a palace gallery. A month's rides in different directions will show you a dozen prime Claudes. After I had seen them all I went piously to the Doria gallery to refresh my memory of its two famous specimens and to enjoy to the utmost their delightful air of reference to something that had become a part of my personal experience. Delightful it certainly is to feel the common element in one's own sensibility and those of a genius whom that element has helped to do great things. Claude must have haunted the very places

Poplars near Rome, by P. H. de Valenciennes

of one's personal preference and adjusted their divine undulations to his splendid scheme of romance, his view of the poetry of life. He was familiar with aspects in which there wasn't a single uncompromising line. I saw a few days ago a small finished sketch from his hand, in the possession of an American artist, which was almost startling in its clear reflection of forms unaltered by the two centuries that have dimmed and cracked the paint and canvas.

This unbroken continuity of the impressions I have tried to indicate is an excellent example of the intellectual background of all enjoyment in Rome. It effectually prevents pleasure from becoming vulgar, for your sensation rarely begins and ends with itself; it reverberates – it recalls, commemorates, resuscitates something else. At least half the merit of everything you enjoy must be that it suits you absolutely; but the larger half here is generally that it has suited some one else and that you can never flatter yourself you have discovered it. It has been addressed to some use a million miles out of your range, and has had great adventures before ever condescending to please you. It was in admission of this truth that my discriminating friend who showed me the Claudes found it impossible to designate a certain delightful region which you enter at the end of an hour's riding from Porta Cavalleggieri as anything but Arcadia. The exquisite correspondence of the term in this case altogether revived its faded bloom; here veritably the oaten pipe must have stirred the windless air and the satyrs have laughed among the brookside reeds. Three or four long grassy dells stretch away in a chain between low hills over which delicate trees are so discreetly scattered that each one is a resting place for a shepherd. The elements of the scene are simple enough, but the composition has extraordinary refinement. By one of those happy chances which keep observation in Italy always in her best humour a shepherd had thrown himself down under one of the trees in the very attitude of Melibœus. He had been washing his feet, I suppose, in the neighbouring brook, and had found it pleasant afterwards to roll his short breeches well up on his thighs. Lying thus in the shade, on his elbow, with his naked legs stretched out on the turf and his soft peaked hat over his long hair crushed back like the veritable bonnet of Arcady, he was exactly the figure of the background of this happy valley. The poor fellow, lying there in rustic weariness and ignorance, little fancied that he was a symbol of old-world meanings to new-world eyes.

Such eyes may find as great a store of picturesque meanings in the cork-woods of Monte Mario, tenderly loved of all equestrians. These are less severely pastoral than our Arcadia, and you might more properly lodge there a damosel of Ariosto

Near Arricia

than a nymph of Theocritus. Among them is strewn a lovely wilderness of flowers and shrubs, and the whole place has such a charming woodland air, that, casting about me the other day for a compliment, I declared that it reminded me of New Hampshire. My compliment had a double edge, and I had no sooner uttered it than I smiled – or sighed – to perceive in all the undiscriminated botany about me the wealth of detail, the idle elegance and grace of Italy alone, the natural stamp of the land which has the singular privilege of making one love her unsanctified beauty all but as well as those features of one's own country toward which nature's small allowance doubles that of one's own affection. For this effect of casting a spell no rides have more value than those you take in Villa Doria or Villa Borghese; or don't take, possibly, if you prefer to reserve these particular regions – the latter in especial – for your walking hours. People do ride, however, in both villas, which deserve honourable mention in this regard. Villa Doria, with its noble site, its splendid views, its great groups of stone-pines, so clustered and yet so individual, its lawns and flowers and fountains, its altogether princely disposition, is a place where one may pace, well mounted, of a brilliant day, with an agreeable sense of its being rather a more elegant pastime to balance in one's stirrups than to trudge on even the smoothest gravel. But at Villa Borghese the walkers have the best of it; for they are free of those adorable outlying corners and bosky byways which the rumble of barouches never reaches. In March the place becomes a perfect epitome of the spring. You cease to care much for the melancholy greenness of the disfeatured statues which has been your chief winter's intimation of verdure; and before you are quite conscious of the tender streaks and patches in the great quaint grassy arena round which the Propaganda students, in their long skirts, wander slowly, like dusky seraphs revolving the gossip of Paradise, you spy the brave little violets uncapping their azure brows beneath the high-stemmed pines. One's walks here would take us too far, and one's pauses detain us too long, when in the quiet parts under the wall one comes across a group of charming small school-boys in full-dress suits and white cravats, shouting over their play in clear Italian, while a grave young priest, beneath a tree, watches them over the top of his book. It sounds like nothing, but the force behind it and the frame round it, the setting, the air, the chord struck, make it a hundred wonderful things.

1873.

Piazza Barberini, by Gustav Palm

CHAPTER VI

FROM A ROMAN NOTEBOOK

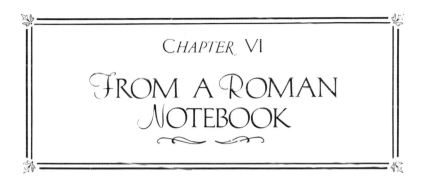

Subiaco

DECEMBER 28TH, 1872. – In Rome again for the last three days – that second visit which, when the first isn't followed by a fatal illness in Florence, the story goes that one is doomed to pay. I didn't drink of the Fountain of Trevi on the eve of departure the other time; but I feel as if I had drunk of the Tiber itself. Nevertheless as I drove from the station in the evening I wondered what I should think of it at this first glimpse hadn't I already known it. All manner of evil perhaps. Paris, as I passed along the Boulevards three evenings before to take the train, was swarming and glittering as befits a great capital. Here, in the black, narrow, crooked, empty streets, I saw nothing I would fain regard as eternal. But there were new gas-lamps round the spouting Triton in Piazza Barberini and a newspaper stall on the corner of the Condotti and the Corso – salient signs of the emancipated state. An hour later I walked up to Via Gregoriana by Piazza di Spagna. It was all silent and deserted, and the great flight of steps looked surprisingly small. Everything seemed meagre, dusky, provincial. Could Rome after all really *be* a world-city? That queer old rococo garden gateway at the top of the Gregoriana stirred a dormant memory; it awoke into a consciousness of the delicious mildness of the air, and very soon, in a little crimson drawing-room, I was reconciled and re-initiated. . . . Everything is dear (in the way of lodgings) but it hardly matters, as everything is taken and some one else paying for it. I must make up my mind to a bare perch. But it seems poorly perverse here to aspire to an "interior" or to be conscious of the economic side of life. The æsthetic is so intense that you feel you should live on the taste of it, should extract the nutritive essence of the atmosphere. For positively it's *such* an atmosphere! The weather is perfect, the sky as blue as the most exploded tradition fames it, the whole air glowing and throbbing with lovely colour. . . . The glitter of Paris is now all gaslight. And oh the monotonous miles of rain-washed asphalt!

Piazza di Spagna

DECEMBER 30TH. – I have had nothing to do with the "ceremonies". In fact I believe there have hardly been any – no midnight mass at the Sistine chapel, no silver trumpets at St. Peter's. Everything is remorselessly clipped and curtailed – the Vatican in deepest mourning. But I saw it in its superbest scarlet in '69 . . . I went yesterday with L. to the Colonna gardens – an adventure that would have reconverted me to Rome if the thing weren't already done. It's a rare old place – rising in mouldy bosky terraces and mossy stairways and winding walks from the back of the palace to the top of the Quirinal. It's the grand style of gardening, and resembles the present natural manner as a chapter of Johnsonian rhetoric resembles a piece of clever contemporary journalism. But it's a better style in horticulture than in literature; I prefer one of the long-drawn blue-green Colonna vistas, with a maimed and mossy-coated garden goddess at the end, to the finest possible quotation from a last-century classic. Perhaps the best thing there is the old orangery with its trees in fantastic terra-cotta tubs. The late afternoon light was gilding the monstrous jars and suspending golden chequers among the golden-fruited leaves. Or perhaps the best thing is the broad terrace with its mossy balustrade and its benches; also its view of the great naked Torre di Nerone (I think) which might look stupid if the rosy brickwork didn't take such a colour in the blue air. Delightful, at any rate, to stroll and talk there in the afternoon sunshine.

JANUARY 2ND, 1873. – Two or three drives with A. – one to St. Paul's without the Walls and back by a couple of old churches on the Aventine. I was freshly struck with the rare distinction of the little Protestant cemetery at the Gate, lying in the shadow of the black sepulchral Pyramid and the thick-growing black cypresses. Bathed in the clear Roman light the place is heart-breaking for what it asks you – in such a world as *this* – to renounce. If it should "make one in love with death to lie there", that's only if death should be conscious. As the case stands the weight of a tremendous past presses upon the flowery sod, and the sleeper's mortality feels the contact of all the mortality with which the brilliant air is tainted. . . . The restored Basilica is incredibly splendid. It seems a last pompous effort of formal Catholicism, and there are few more striking emblems of later Rome – the Rome foredoomed to see Victor Emmanuel in the Quirinal, the Rome of abortive councils and unheeded anathemas. It rises there, gorgeous and useless, on its miasmatic site, with an air of conscious bravado – a florid advertisement of the superabundance of faith. Within it's magnificent, and its magnificence has no shabby spots – a rare thing in Rome. Marble and mosaic, alabaster and malachite, lapis and porphyry, incrust it from pavement to cornice and flash back their polished lights at each other with such a splendour of effect that you seem to stand at the heart of some immense prismatic crystal. One has to come to Italy to know marbles and love them. I remember the fascination of the first great show of them I met in Venice – at the Scalzi and Gesuiti. Colour has no other form so cool and unfading a purity and lustre. Softness of tone and hardness of substance – isn't that the sum of the artist's desire? G., with his beautiful caressing, open-lipped Roman utterance, so easy to understand and, to my ear, so finely suggestive of genuine Latin, not our horrible Anglo-Saxon and Protestant kind, urged upon us the charms of a return by the Aventine and the sight of a couple of old churches. The best is Santa Sabina, a very fine old structure of the fifth century, mouldering in its dusky solitude and consuming its own antiquity. What a massive heritage Christianity and Catholicism are leaving here! What a substantial fact, in all its decay, this memorial Christian temple outliving its uses among the sunny gardens and vineyards! It has a noble nave, filled with a stale smell which (like that of the onion) brought tears to my eyes, and bordered with twenty-four fluted marble columns of Pagan origin. The crudely primitive little mosaics along the entablature are extremely curious. A Dominican monk, still young, who showed us the church, seemed a creature generated from its musty shadows and odours. His physiognomy was wonderfully *de l'emploi*, and his voice, most agreeable, had the strangest jaded humility. His lugubrious salute and sanctimonious impersonal appropriation of my departing franc would have been a master-touch on the stage. While we were still in the church a bell rang that he had to go and answer, and as he came back and approached us along the nave he made with his white gown and hood and his cadaverous face, against the dark church background, one of those pictures which, thank the Muses, have not yet been reformed out of Italy. It was the exact illustration, for insertion in a text, of heaven knows how many old romantic and conventional literary Italianisms – plays, poems, mysteries of Udolpho. We got back into the carriage and talked of profane things and went home to dinner – drifting recklessly, it seemed to me, from æsthetic luxury to social.

On the 31st we went to the musical vesper-service at the Gesù – hitherto done so splendidly before the Pope and the cardinals. The manner of it was eloquent of change – no Pope, no cardinals, and indifferent music; but a great *mise-en-scène* nevertheless. The church is gorgeous; late Renaissance, of great proportions, and full, like so many others, but in a pre-eminent degree, of seventeenth and eighteenth century Romanism. It doesn't impress the imagination, but richly feeds the curiosity, by which I mean one's sense of the curious; suggests no legends, but innumerable anecdotes à la Stendhal. There is a vast dome, filled with a florid concave fresco of tumbling foreshortened angels, and all over the ceilings and cornices a wonderful outlay of dusky gildings and mouldings. There are various Bernini saints and seraphs in stucco-sculpture, astride of the tablets and door-tops, backing against their rusty machinery of coppery *nimbi* and egg-shaped cloudlets. Marble, damask and tapers in gorgeous profusion. The high altar a great screen of twinkling chandeliers. The choir perched in a little loft high up in the right transept, like a balcony in a side-scene at the opera, and indulging in surprising roulades and flourishes. . . . Near me sat a handsome, opulent-looking nun – possibly an abbess or prioress of noble lineage. Can a holy woman of such a complexion listen to a fine operatic barytone in a sumptuous temple and receive none but ascetic impressions? What a crossfire of influences does Catholicism provide!

JANUARY 4TH. – A drive with A. out of Porta San Giovanni and along Via Appia Nuova. More and more beautiful as you get well away from the walls and the great view opens out before you – the rolling green-brown dells and flats of the Campagna, the long, disjointed arcade of the aqueducts, the deep-shadowed blue of the Alban hills, touched into pale lights by their scattered towns. We stopped at the ruined basilica of San Stefano, an affair of the fifth century, rather meaningless without a learned companion. But the perfect little sepulchral chambers of the Pancratii, disinterred beneath the church, tell their own tale – in their hardly dimmed frescoes, their beautiful sculptured coffin and great sepulchral slab. Better still the tomb of the Valerii adjoining it – a single chamber with an arched roof, covered with stucco mouldings perfectly intact, exquisite figures and arabesques as sharp and delicate as if the plasterer's scaffold had just been taken from under them.

Near the gate of S. Lorenzo

Strange enough to think of these things – so many of them as there are – surviving their immemorial eclipse in this perfect shape and coming up like long-lost divers from the sea of time.

JANUARY 16TH. – A delightful walk last Sunday with F. to Monte Mario. We drove to Porta Angelica, the little gate hidden behind the right wing of Bernini's colonnade, and strolled thence up the winding road to the Villa Mellini, where one of the greasy peasants huddled under the wall in the sun admits you for half a franc into the finest old ilex-walk in Italy. It is all vaulted grey-green shade with blue Campagna stretches in the interstices. The day was perfect; the still sunshine, as we sat at the twisted base of the old trees, seemed to have the drowsy hum of midsummer – with that charm of Italian vegetation that comes to us as its confession of having scenically served, to weariness at last, for some pastoral these many centuries a classic. In a certain cheapness and thinness of substance – as compared with the English stoutness, never left athirst – it reminds me of our own, and it is relatively dry enough and pale enough to explain the contempt of many unimaginative Britons. But it has an idle abundance and wantonness, a romantic shabbiness and dishevelment. At the Villa Mellini is the famous lonely pine which "tells" so in the landscape from other points, bought off from the axe by (I believe) Sir George Beaumont, commemorated in a like connection in Wordsworth's great sonnet. He at least was not an unimaginative Briton. As you stand under it, its far-away shallow dome, supported on a single column almost white enough to be marble, seems to dwell in the dizziest depths of the blue. Its pale grey-blue boughs and its silvery stem make a wonderful harmony with the ambient air. The Villa Mellini is full of the elder Italy of one's imagination – the Italy of Boccaccio and Ariosto. There are twenty places where the Florentine story-tellers might have sat round on the grass. Outside the villa walls, beneath the overcrowding orange-boughs, straggled old Italy as well – but not in Boccaccio's velvet: a row of ragged and livid contadini, some simply stupid in their squalor, but some downright brigands of romance, or of reality, with matted locks and terribly sullen eyes.

A couple of days later I walked for old acquaintance sake over to San Onofrio on the Janiculan. The approach is one of the dirtiest adventures in Rome, and though the view is fine from the little terrace, the church and convent are of a meagre and musty pattern. Yet here – almost like pearls in a dunghill – are hidden mementos of two of the most exquisite of Italian minds. Torquato Tasso spent the last months of his life here, and you may visit his room and various warped and faded relics. The most interesting is a cast of his face taken after death – looking, like all such casts, almost more than mortally gallant and distinguished. But who should look all ideally so if not he? In a little shabby, chilly corridor adjoining is a fresco of Leonardo, a Virgin and Child with the *donatorio*. It is very small, simple and faded, but it has all the artist's magic, that mocking, illusive refinement and hint of a vague *arrière-pensée* which mark every stroke of Leonardo's brush. Is it the perfection of irony or the perfection of tenderness? What does he mean, what does he affirm, what does he deny? Magic wouldn't be magic, nor the author of such things stand so absolutely alone, if we were ready with an explanation. As I glanced from the picture to the poor stupid little red-faced brother at my side I wondered if the thing mightn't pass for an elegant epigram on monasticism. Certainly, at any rate, there is more intellect in it than under all the monkish tonsures it has seen coming and going these three hundred years.

JANUARY 21ST. – The last three or four days I have regularly spent a couple of hours from noon baking myself in the sun of the Pincio to get rid of a cold. The weather perfect and the crowd (especially to-day) amazing. Such a staring, lounging, dandified, amiable crowd! Who does the vulgar stay-at-home work of Rome? All the grandees and half the foreigners are there in their carriages, the *bourgeoisie* on foot staring at them and the beggars lining all the approaches. The great difference between public places in America and Europe is in the number of unoccupied people of every age and condition sitting about early and late on benches and gazing at you, from your hat to your boots, as you pass. Europe is certainly the continent of the practised stare. The ladies on the Pincio have to run the gauntlet; but they seem to do so complacently enough. The European woman is brought up to the sense of having a definite part in the way of manners or manner to play in public. To lie back in a barouche alone, balancing a parasol and seeming to ignore the extremely immediate gaze of two serried ranks of male creatures on each side of her path, save here and there to recognise one of them with an imperceptible nod, is one of her daily duties. The number of young men here who, like the cœnobites of old, lead the purely contemplative life is enormous. They muster in especial force on the Pincio, but the Corso all day is thronged with them. They are well-dressed, good-humoured, good-looking, polite; but they seem never to do a harder stroke of work than to stroll from the Piazza Colonna to the Hôtel de Rome or *vice versâ*. Some of them don't even stroll, but stand leaning by the hour against the doorways, sucking the knobs of their canes, feeling their back hair and settling their shirt-cuffs. At my café in the morning several stroll in already (at nine o'clock) in light, in "evening" gloves. But they order nothing, turn on their heels, glance at the mirrors and stroll out again. When it rains they herd under the *portes-cochères* and in the smaller cafés. . . . Yesterday Prince Humbert's little *primogenito* was on the Pincio in an open landau with his governess. He's a sturdy blond little man and the image of the King. They had stopped to listen to the music, and the crowd was planted about the carriage-wheels, staring and criticising under the child's snub little nose. It appeared bold cynical curiosity, without the slightest manifestation of "loyalty", and it gave me a singular sense of the vulgarisation of Rome under the new régime. When the Pope drove abroad it was a solemn spectacle; even if you neither kneeled nor uncovered you were irresistibly impressed. But the Pope never stopped to listen to opera tunes, and he had no little popelings, under the charge of superior nurse-maids, whom you might take liberties with. The family at Quirinal make something of a merit, I believe, of their modest and inexpensive way of life. The merit is great; yet, representationally, what a change for the worse from an order which proclaimed stateliness a part of its essence! The divinity that doth hedge a king must be pretty well on the wane. But how many more fine old traditions will the extremely sentimental traveller miss in the Italians over whom that little jostled prince in the landau will have come into his kinghood? . . . The Pincio continues to beguile; it's a great resource. I am forever being reminded of the "æsthetic luxury", as I called it above, of living in Rome. To be able to choose of an afternoon for a lounge (respectfully speaking) between St. Peter's and the high precinct you approach by the gate just beyond Villa Medici – counting nothing else – is a proof that if in Rome you may suffer from ennui, at least your ennui has a throbbing soul in it. It is something to say for the Pincio that you don't always choose St. Peter's. Sometimes I lose patience with its parade of eternal idleness, but at others this very idleness is balm to one's conscience. Life on just these terms seems so easy, so monotonously sweet, that you feel it would be unwise, would be really unsafe, to change. The Roman air is charged with elixir, the Roman cup seasoned with some insidious

Market Girls, Piazza Madama

A View of the Tiber with the Church of S. Andrea, Rome, by William Linton

drop, of which the action is fatally yet none the less agreeably, "lowering".

JANUARY 26TH. – With S. to the Villa Medici – perhaps on the whole the most enchanting place in Rome. The part of the garden called the Boschetto has an incredible, impossible charm; an upper terrace, behind locked gates, covered with a little dusky forest of evergreen oaks. Such a dim light as of a fabled, haunted place, such a soft suffusion of tender grey-green tones, such a company of gnarled and twisted little miniature trunks – dwarfs playing with each other at being giants – and such a shower of golden sparkles drifting in from the vivid west! At the end of the wood is a steep, circular mound, up which the short trees scramble amain, with a long mossy staircase climbing up to a belvedere. This staircase, rising suddenly out of the leafy dusk to you don't see where, is delightfully fantastic. You expect to see an old woman in a crimson petticoat and with a distaff come hobbling down and turn into a fairy and offer you three wishes. I should name for my own first wish that one didn't have to be a Frenchman to come and live and dream and work at the Académie de France. Can there be for a while a happier destiny than that of a young artist conscious of talent and of no errand but to educate, polish and perfect it, transplanted to these sacred shades? One has fancied Plato's Academy – his gleaming colonnades, his blooming gardens and Athenian sky; but was it as good as this one, where Monsieur Hébert does the Platonic? The blessing in Rome is not that this or that or the other isolated object is so very unsurpassable; but that the general air so contributes to interest, to impressions that are not as any other impressions anywhere in the world. And from this general air the Villa Medici has distilled an essence of its own – walled it in and made it delightfully private. The great façade on the gardens is like an enormous rococo clock-face all incrusted with images and arabesques and tablets. What mornings and afternoons one might spend there, brush in hand, unpreoccupied, untormented, pensioned, satisfied – either persuading one's self that one would be "doing something" in consequence or not caring if one shouldn't be.

AT A LATER DATE – MIDDLE OF MARCH. – A ride with S. W. out of the Porta Pia to the meadows beyond the Ponte Nomentana – close to the site of

French Academy

130

Phaon's villa where Nero in hiding had himself stabbed. It all spoke as things here only speak, touching more chords than one can *now* really know or say. For these are predestined memories and the stuff that regrets are made of; the mild divine efflorescence of spring, the wonderful landscape, the talk suspended for another gallop. . . . Returning, we dismounted at the gate of the Villa Medici and walked through the twilight of the vaguely perfumed, bird-haunted alleys to H.'s studio, hidden in the wood like a cottage in a fairy tale. I spent there a charming half-hour in the fading light, looking at the pictures while my companion discoursed of her errand. The studio is small and more like a little salon; the painting refined, imaginative, somewhat morbid, full of consummate French ability. A portrait, idealised and etherealised, but a likeness of Mme. de — — (from last year's Salon) in white satin, quantities of lace, a coronet, diamonds and pearls; a striking combination of brilliant silvery tones. A "Femme Sauvage", a naked dusky girl in a wood, with a wonderfully clever pair of shy, passionate eyes. The author is different enough from any of the numerous American artists. They may be producers, but he's a product as well – a product of influences of a sort of which we have as yet no general command. One of them is his charmed lapse of life in that unprofessional-looking little studio, with his enchanted wood on one side and the plunging wall of Rome on the other.

JANUARY 30TH. – A drive the other day with a friend to Villa Madama, on the side of Monte Mario; a place like a page out of one of Browning's richest evocations of this clime and civilisation. Wondrous in its haunting melancholy, it might have inspired half "The Ring and the Book" at a stroke. What a grim commentary on history such a scene – what an irony of the past! The road up to it through the outer enclosure is almost impassable with mud and stones. At the end, on a terrace, rises the once elegant Casino, with hardly a whole pane of glass in its façade, reduced to its sallow stucco and degraded ornaments. The front away from Rome has in the basement a great loggia, now walled in from the weather, preceded by a grassy belittered platform with an immense sweeping view of the Campagna; the sad-looking, more than sad-looking, evil-looking, Tiber beneath (the colour of gold, the sentimentalists say, the colour of mustard, the realists); a great vague stretch beyond, of various complexions and uses; and on the horizon the ever-iridescent mountains. The place has become the shabbiest farm-house, with muddy water in the old *pièces d'eau* and dunghills on the old parterres. The "feature" is the contents of the loggia: a vaulted roof and walls decorated by

Giulio Romano; exquisite stucco-work and still brilliant frescoes; arabesques and figurini, nymphs and fauns, animals and flowers – gracefully lavish designs of every sort. Much of the colour – especially the blues – still almost vivid, and all the work wonderfully ingenious, elegant and charming. Apartments so decorated can have been meant only for the recreation of people greater than any we know, people for whom life was impudent ease and success. Margaret Farnese was the lady of the house, but where she trailed her cloth of gold the chickens now scamper between your legs over rotten straw. It is all inexpressibly dreary. A stupid peasant scratching his head, a couple of critical Americans picking their steps, the walls tattered and befouled breast-high, dampness and decay striking in on your heart, and the scene overbowed by these heavenly frescoes, mouldering there in their airy artistry! It's poignant; it provokes tears; it tells so of the waste of effort. Something human seems to pant beneath the grey pall of time and to implore you to rescue it, to pity it, to stand by it somehow. But you leave it to its lingering death without compunction, almost with pleasure; for the place seems vaguely crime-haunted – paying at least the penalty of some hard immorality. The end of a Renaissance pleasure-house. Endless for the didactic observer the moral, abysmal for the story-seeker the tale.

FEBRUARY 12TH. – Yesterday to the Villa Albani. Over-formal and (as my companion says) too much like a tea-garden; but with beautiful stairs and splendid geometrical lines of immense box-hedge, intersected with high pedestals supporting little antique busts. The light to-day magnificent; the Alban hills of an intenser broken purple than I had yet seen them – their white towns blooming upon it like vague projected lights. It was like a piece of very modern painting, and a good example of how Nature has at times a sort of mannerism which ought to make us careful how we condemn out of hand the more refined and affected artists. The collection of marbles in the Casino (Winckelmann's) admirable and to be seen again. The famous Antinous crowned with lotus a strangely beautiful and impressive thing. The "Greek manner", on the showing of something now and again encountered here, moves one to feel that even for purely romantic and imaginative effects it surpasses any since invented. If there be not imagination, even in our comparatively modern sense of the word, in the baleful beauty of that perfect young profile there is none in "Hamlet" or in "Lycidas". There is five hundred times as much as in "The Transfiguration". With this at any rate to point to it's not for sculpture not professedly to produce any emotion producible by

Poniatowsky, Rome, by Thorald Brendstrup

painting. There are numbers of small and delicate fragments of bas-reliefs of exquisite grace, and a huge piece (two combatants – one, on horseback, beating down another – murder made eternal and beautiful) attributed to the Parthenon and certainly as grandly impressive as anything in the Elgin marbles. S. W. suggested again the Roman villas as a "subject". Excellent if one could find a feast of facts à la Stendhal. A lot of vague ecstatic descriptions and anecdotes wouldn't at all pay. There have been too many already. Enough facts are recorded, I suppose; one should discover them and soak them for a twelvemonth. And yet a Roman villa, in spite of statues, ideas and atmosphere, affects me as of a scanter human and social *portée*, a shorter, thinner reverberation, than an old English country-house, round which experience seems piled so thick. But this perhaps is either hair-splitting or "racial" prejudice.

MARCH 9TH. – The Vatican is still deadly cold; a couple of hours there yesterday with R. W. E. Yet he, illustrious and enviable man, fresh from the East, had no overcoat and wanted none. Perfect bliss, I think, would be to live in Rome without thinking of overcoats. The Vatican seems very familiar, but strangely smaller than of old. I never lost the sense before of confusing vastness. *Sancta simplicitas!* All my old friends however stand there in undimmed radiance, keeping most of them their old pledges. I am perhaps more struck now with the enormous amount of padding – the number of third-rate, fourth-rate things that weary the eye desirous to approach freshly the twenty and thirty best. In spite of the padding there are dozens of treasures that one passes regretfully; but the impression of the whole place is the great thing – the feeling that through these solemn vistas flows the source of an incalculable part of our present conception of Beauty.

APRIL 10TH. – Last night, in the rain, to the Teatro Valle to see a comedy of Goldoni in Venetian dialect –

Interior of St. Peter's

"I Quattro Rustighi". I could but half follow it; enough, however, to be sure that, for all its humanity of irony, it wasn't so good as Molière. The acting was capital – broad, free and natural; the play of talk easier even than life itself; but, like all the Italian acting I have seen, it was wanting in *finesse*, that shade of the shade by which, and by which alone, one really knows art. I contrasted the affair with the evening in December last that I walked over (also in the rain) to the Odéon and saw the "Plaideurs" and the "Malade Imaginaire". There, too, was hardly more than a handful of spectators; but what rich, ripe, fully representational and above all intellectual comedy, and what polished, educated playing! These Venetians in particular, however, have a marvellous *entrain* of their own; they seem even less than the French to recite. In some of the women – ugly, with red hands and shabby dresses – an extraordinary gift of natural utterance, of seeming to invent joyously as they go.

LATER. – Last evening in H.'s box at the Apollo to hear Ernesto Rossi in "Othello". He shares supremacy with Salvini in Italian tragedy. Beautiful great theatre with boxes you can walk about in; brilliant audience. The Princess Margaret was there – I have never been to the theatre that she was not – and a number of other princesses in neighbouring boxes. G. G. came in and instructed us that they were the M., the L., the P., &c. Rossi is both very bad and very fine; bad where anything like taste and discretion is required, but "all there", and more than there, in violent passion. The last act reduced too much, however, to mere exhibitional sensibility. The interesting thing to me was to observe the Italian conception of the part – to see how crude it was, how little it expressed the hero's moral side, his depth, his dignity – anything more than his being a creature terrible in mere tantrums. The great point was his seizing Iago's head and whacking it half-a-dozen times on the floor, and then flinging him twenty yards away. It was wonderfully done, but in the doing of it and in the evident relish for it in the house there was I scarce knew what force of easy and thereby rather cheap expression.

APRIL 27TH. – A morning with L. B. at Villa Ludovisi, which we agreed that we shouldn't soon forget. The villa now belongs to the King, who has lodged his morganatic wife there. There is nothing so blissfully *right* in Rome, nothing more consummately consecrated to style. The grounds and gardens are immense, and the great rusty-red city wall stretches away behind them and makes the burden of the seven hills seem vast without making *them* seem small. There is everything – dusky avenues trimmed by the clippings of centuries, groves and dells and glades and glowing pastures and reedy fountains and great flowering meadows studded with enormous slanting pines. The day was delicious, and the trees all one melody, the whole place a revelation of what Italy and hereditary pomp can do together. Nothing could be more in the grand manner than this garden view of the city ramparts, lifting their fantastic battlements above the trees and flowers. They are all tapestried with vines and made to serve as sunny fruit-walls – grim old defence as they once were; now giving nothing but a splendid buttressed privacy. The sculptures in the little Casino are few, but there are two great ones – the beautiful sitting Mars and the head of the great Juno, the latter thrust into a corner behind a shutter. These things it's almost impossible to praise; we can only mark them well and keep them clear, as we insist on silence to hear great music. . . . If I don't praise Guercino's Aurora in the greater Casino, it's for another reason; this is certainly a very muddy masterpiece. It figures on the ceiling of a small low hall; the painting is coarse and the ceiling too near. Besides, it's unfair to pass straight from the Greek mythology to the Bolognese. We were left to roam at will through the house; the custode shut us in and went to walk in the park. The apartments were all open, and I had an opportunity to reconstruct, from its *milieu* at least, the character of a morganatic queen. I saw nothing to indicate that it was not amiable; but I should have thought more highly of the lady's discrimination if she had had the Juno removed from behind her shutter. In such a house, girdled about with such a park, methinks I could be amiable – and perhaps discriminating too. The Ludovisi Casino is small, but the perfection of the life of ease might surely be led there. There are English houses enough in wondrous parks, but they expose you to too many small needs and observances – to say nothing of a red-faced butler dropping his *h*'s. You are oppressed with the detail of accommodation. Here the billiard-table is old-fashioned, perhaps a trifle crooked; but you have Guercino above your head, and Guercino, after all, is almost as good as Guido. The rooms, I noticed, all pleased by their shape, by a lovely proportion, by a mass of delicate ornamentation on the high concave ceilings. One might live over again in them some deliciously benighted life of a forgotten type – with graceful old *sale*, and immensely thick walls, and a winding stone staircase, and a view from the loggia at the top; a view of twisted parasol-pines balanced, high above a wooden horizon, against a sky of faded sapphire.

MAY 17TH. – It was wonderful yesterday at St. John Lateran. The spring now has turned to perfect summer; there are cascades of verdure over all the walls; the early flowers are a fading memory, and the new grass knee-deep in the Villa Borghese. The winter aspect of the region about the Lateran is one of the best things in Rome; the sunshine is nowhere so golden and the lean shadows nowhere so purple as on the long grassy walk to Santa Croce. But yesterday I seemed to see nothing but green and blue. The expanse before Santa Croce was vivid green; the Campagna rolled away in great green billows, which seemed to break high about the gaunt aqueducts; and the Alban Hills, which in January and February keep shifting and melting along the whole scale of azure, were almost monotonously fresh, and had lost some of their finer modelling. But the sky was ultramarine and everything radiant with light and warmth – warmth which a soft steady breeze kept from excess. I strolled some time about the church, which has a grand air enough, though I don't seize the point of view of Miss — —, who told me the other day how vastly finer she thought it than St. Peter's. But on Miss — —'s lips this seemed a very pretty paradox. The choir and transepts have a sombre splendour, and I like the old vaulted passage with its slabs and monuments behind the choir. The charm of charms at St. John Lateran is the admirable twelfth-century cloister, which was never more charming than yesterday. The shrubs and flowers about the ancient well were blooming away in the intense light, and the twisted pillars and chiselled capitals of the perfect little colonnade seemed to enclose them like the sculptured rim of a precious vase. Standing out among the flowers you may look up and see a section of the summit of the great façade of the church. The robed and mitred apostles, bleached and rain-washed by the ages, rose into the blue air like huge snow figures. I spent at the incorporated museum a subsequent hour of fond vague attention, having it quite to myself. It is rather scantily stocked, but the great cool halls open out impressively one after the other, and the wide spaces between the statues seem to suggest at first that each is a masterpiece. I was in the loving mood of one's last days in Rome, and when I had nothing else to admire I admired the magnificent thickness of the embrasures of the doors and windows. If there were no objects of interest at all in the Lateran the palace would be worth walking through every now and then, to keep up one's idea of solid architecture. I went over to the Scala Santa, where was no one but a very shabby priest sitting like a ticket-taker at the door. But he let me pass, and I ascended

Cloisters of St. John Lateran

one of the profane lateral stairways and treated myself to a glimpse of the Sanctum Sanctorum. Its threshold is crossed but once or twice a year, I believe, by three or four of the most exalted divines, but you may look into it freely enough through a couple of gilded lattices. It is very sombre and splendid, and conveys the impression of a very holy place. And yet somehow it suggested irreverent thoughts; it had to my fancy – perhaps on account of the lattice – an Oriental, a Mahometan note. I expected every moment to see a sultana appear in a silver veil and silken trousers and sit down on the crimson carpet.

Farewell, packing, the sharp pang of going. One would like to be able after five months in Rome to sum up, for tribute and homage, one's experience, one's gains, the whole adventure of one's sensibility. But one has really vibrated too much – the addition of so many items isn't easy. What is simply clear is the sense of an acquired passion for the place and of an incalculable number of gathered impressions. Many of these have been intense and momentous, but one has trodden on the other – there are always the big fish that swallow up the little – and one can hardly say what has become of them. They store themselves noiselessly away, I suppose, in the dim but safe places of memory and "taste", and we live in a quiet faith that they will emerge into vivid relief if life or art should demand them. As for the passion we needn't perhaps trouble ourselves about that. Fifty swallowed palmfuls of the Fountain of Trevi couldn't make us more ardently sure that we shall at any cost come back.

1873.

CHAPTER VII
A CHAIN OF CITIES

Perugia

 NE DAY IN MIDWINTER, some years since, during a journey from Rome to Florence perforce too rapid to allow much wayside sacrifice to curiosity, I waited for the train at Narni. There was time to stroll far enough from the station to have a look at the famous old bridge of Augustus, broken short off in mid-Tiber. While I stood admiring the measure of impression was made to overflow by the gratuitous grace of a white-cowled monk who came trudging up the road that wound to the gate of the town. Narni stood, in its own presented felicity, on a hill a good space away, boxed in behind its perfect grey wall, and the monk, to oblige me, crept slowly

Street at Narni

ASSISI

along and disappeared within the aperture. Everything was distinct in the clear air, and the view exactly as like the bit of background by an Umbrian master as it ideally should have been. The winter is bare and brown enough in southern Italy and the earth reduced to more of a mere anatomy than among ourselves, for whom the very *crânerie* of its exposed state, naked and unashamed, gives it much of the robust serenity, not of a fleshless skeleton, but of a fine nude statue. In these regions, at any rate, the tone of the air, for the eye, during the brief desolation, has often an extraordinary charm: nature still smiles as with the deputed and provisional charity of colour and light, the duty of not ceasing to cheer man's heart. Her whole behaviour, at the time, cast such a spell on the broken bridge, the little walled town and the trudging friar, that I turned away with the impatient vow and the fond vision of how I would take the journey again and pause to my heart's content at Narni, at Spoleto, at Assisi, at Perugia, at Cortona, at Arezzo. But we have generally to clip our vows a little when we come to fulfil them; and so it befell that when my blest springtime arrived I had to begin as resignedly as possible, yet with comparative meagreness, at Assisi.

I suppose enjoyment would have a simple zest which it often lacks if we always did things at the moment we want to, for it's mostly when we can't that we're thoroughly sure we *would*, and we can answer too little for moods in the future conditional. Winter at least seemed to me to have put something into these seats of antiquity that the May sun had more or less melted away – a desirable strength of tone, a depth upon depth of queerness and quaintness. Assisi had been in the January twilight, after my mere snatch at Narni, a vignette out of some brown old missal. But you'll have to be a fearless explorer now to find of a fine spring day any such cluster of curious objects as doesn't seem made to match before anything else Mr. Baedeker's polyglot estimate of its chief recommendations. This great man was at Assisi in force, and a brand-new inn for his accommodation has just been opened cheek by jowl with the church of St. Francis. I don't know that even the dire discomfort of this harbourage makes it seem less impertinent; but I confess I sought its protection, and the great view seemed hardly less beautiful from my window than from the gallery of the convent. This view embraces the whole wide reach of Umbria, which becomes as twilight deepens a purple counterfeit of the misty sea. The visitor's first errand is with the church; and it's fair furthermore to admit that when he has crossed that threshold the position and quality of his hotel cease for the time to be matters of moment. This twofold temple of St. Francis is one of the very sacred places of Italy, and it would be hard

140

to breathe anywhere an air more heavy with holiness. Such seems especially the case if you happen thus to have come from Rome, where everything ecclesiastical is, in aspect, so very much of this world – so florid, so elegant, so full of accommodations and excrescences. The mere site here makes for authority, and they were brave builders who laid the foundation-stones. The thing rises straight from a steep mountain-side and plunges forward on its great substructure of arches even as a crowned headland may frown over the main. Before it stretches a long, a grassy piazza, at the end of which you look up a small grey street, to see it first climb a little way the rest of the hill and then pause and leave a broad green slope, crested, high in the air, with a ruined castle. When I say before it I mean before the upper church; for by way of doing something supremely handsome and impressive the sturdy architects of the thirteenth century piled temple upon temple and bequeathed a double version of their idea. One may imagine them to have intended perhaps an architectural image of the relation between heart and head. Entering the lower church at the bottom of the great flight of steps which leads from the upper door, you seem to push at least into the very heart of Catholicism.

For the first minutes after leaving the clearer gloom you catch nothing but a vista of low black columns closed by the great fantastic cage surrounding the altar, which is thus placed, by your impression, in a sort of gorgeous cavern. Gradually you distinguish details, become accustomed to the penetrating chill, and even manage to make out a few frescoes; but the general effect remains splendidly sombre and subterranean. The vaulted roof is very low and the pillars dwarfish, though immense in girth, as befits pillars supporting substantially a cathedral. The tone of the place is a triumph of mystery, the richest harmony of lurking shadows and dusky corners, all relieved by scattered images and scintillations. There was little light but what came through the windows of the choir over which the red curtains had been dropped and were beginning to glow with the downward sun. The choir was guarded by a screen behind which a dozen venerable voices droned vespers; but over the top of the screen came the heavy radiance and played among the ornaments of the high fence round the shrine, casting the shadow of the whole elaborate mass forward into the obscured nave. The darkness of vaults and side-chapels is overwrought with vague frescoes, most of them by Giotto and his school, out of which confused richness the terribly distinct little faces characteristic of these artists stare at you with a solemn formalism. Some are faded and injured, and many so ill-lighted and ill-placed that you can only glance at them

Church of San Vascovato, Assisi

with decent conjecture; the great group, however – four paintings by Giotto on the ceiling above the altar – may be examined with some success. Like everything of that grim and beautiful master they deserve examination; but with the effect ever of carrying one's appreciation in and in, as it were, rather than of carrying it out and out, off and off, as happens for us with those artists who have been helped by the process of "evolution" to grow wings. This one, "going in" for emphasis at any price, stamps hard, as who should say, on the very spot of his idea – thanks to which fact he has a concentration that has never been surpassed. He was in other words, in proportion to his means, a genius supremely expressive; he makes the very shade of an intended meaning or a represented attitude so unmistakable that his figures affect us at moments as creatures all too suddenly, too alarmingly, too menacingly met. Meagre, primitive, undeveloped, he yet is immeasurably strong; he even suggests that if he had lived the due span of years later Michael Angelo might have found a rival. Not that he is given, however, to complicated postures or superhuman flights. The something strange that troubles and haunts us in his work spring rather from a kind of fierce familiarity.

It is part of the wealth of the lower church that it contains an admirable primitive fresco by an artist of genius rarely encountered, Pietro Cavallini, pupil of Giotto. This represents the Crucifixion; the three crosses rising into a sky spotted with the winged heads of angels while a dense crowd presses below. You will nowhere see anything more direfully lugubrious, or more approaching for direct force, though not of course for amplitude of style, Tintoretto's great renderings of the scene in Venice. The abject anguish of the crucified and the straddling authority and brutality of the mounted guards in the foreground are contrasted in a fashion worthy of a great dramatist. But the most poignant touch is the tragic grimaces of the little angelic heads that fall like hailstones through the dark air. It is genuine realistic weeping, the act of irrepressible "crying", that the painter has depicted, and the effect is pitiful at the same time as grotesque. There are many more frescoes besides; all the chapels on one side are lined with them, but these are chiefly interesting in their general impressiveness – as they people the dim recesses with startling presences, with apparitions out of scale. Before leaving the place I lingered long near the door, for I was sure I shouldn't soon again enjoy such a feast of scenic composition. The opposite end glowed with subdued colour; the middle portion was vague and thick and brown, with two or three scattered worshippers looming through the obscurity; while, all the way down, the polished pavement, its uneven slabs glittering dimly in the obstructed light, was of the very essence of expensive picture. It is certainly desirable, if one takes the lower church of Saint Francis to represent the human heart, that one should find a few bright places there. But if the general effect is of brightness terrorised and smothered, is the symbol less valid? For the contracted, prejudiced, passionate heart let it stand.

One thing at all events we can say, that we should rejoice to boast as capacious, symmetrical and well-ordered a head as the upper sanctuary. Thanks to these merits, in spite of a brave array of Giottesque work which has the advantage of being easily seen, it lacks the great character of its counterpart. The frescoes, which are admirable, represent certain leading events in the life of Saint Francis, and suddenly remind you, by one of those anomalies that are half the secret of the consummate *mise-en-scène* of Catholicism, that the apostle of beggary, the saint whose only tenement in life was the ragged robe which barely covered him, is the hero of this massive structure. Church upon church, nothing less will adequately shroud his consecrated clay. The great reality of Giotto's designs adds to the helpless wonderment with which we feel the passionate pluck of the Hero, the sense of being separated from it by an impassable gulf, the reflection on all that has come and gone to make morality at that vertiginous pitch impossible. There are no such high places of humility left to climb to. An observant friend who has lived long in Italy lately declared to me, however, that she detested the name of this moralist, deeming him chief propagator of the Italian vice most trying to the would-be lover of the people, the want of personal self-respect. There is a solidarity in the use of soap, and every cringing beggar, idler, liar and pilferer flourished for her under the shadow of the great Franciscan indifference to it. She was possibly right; at Rome, at Naples, I might have admitted she was right; but at Assisi, face to face with Giotto's vivid chronicle, we admire too much in its main subject the exquisite play of that subject's genius – we don't remit to him, and this for very envy, a single throb of his consciousness. It took in, that human, that divine embrace, everything *but* soap.

I should find it hard to give an orderly account of my next adventures or impressions at Assisi, which couldn't well be anything more than mere romantic *flânerie*. One may easily plead as the final result of a meditation at the shrine of Saint Francis a great and even an amused charity. This state of mind led me slowly up and down for a couple of hours through the steep little streets, and at last stretched itself on the grass with me in the shadow of the great ruined castle that decorates so grandly the eminence above the town. I remember edging along the sunless side of the small mouldy houses and pausing very often to look at nothing in particular. It was all very hot, very hushed, very resignedly but very persistently old. A wheeled vehicle in such a place is an event, and the *forestiero's* interrogative tread in the blank sonorous lanes has the privilege of bringing the inhabitants to their doorways. Some of the better houses, however, achieve a sombre stillness that protests against the least curiosity as to what may happen in any such century as this. You wonder, as you pass, what lingering old-world social types vegetate there, but you won't find out; albeit that in one very silent little street I had a glimpse of an open door which I have not forgotten. A long-haired peddler who must have been a Jew, and who yet carried without prejudice a burden of mass-books and rosaries, was offering his wares to a stout old priest. The priest had opened the door rather stingily and appeared half-heartedly to dismiss him. But the peddler held up something I couldn't see; the priest wavered with a timorous concession to profane curiosity and then furtively pulled the agent of sophistication, or whatever it might be, into the house. I should have liked to enter with that worthy.

I saw later some gentlemen of Assisi who also seemed bored enough to have found entertainment in his tray. They were at the door of the café on the Piazza, and were so thankful to me for asking them the way to the cathedral that, answering all in chorus, they lighted up with smiles as sympathetic as if I had done them a favour. Of that type were my mild, my delicate adventures. The Piazza has a fine old portico of an ancient Temple of Minerva – six fluted columns and a pediment, of beautiful proportions, but sadly battered and decayed. Goethe, I believe, found it much more interesting than the mighty mediæval church, and Goethe, as a cicerone, doubtless could have persuaded one that it was so; but in the humble society of Murray we shall most of us find a richer sense in the later monument. I found quaint old meanings enough in the dark yellow façade of the small cathedral as I sat on a stone bench by the oblong green stretched before it. This is a pleasing piece of Italian Gothic and, like several of its companions at Assisi, has an elegant wheel window and a number of grotesque little carvings of creatures human and bestial. If with Goethe I were to balance anything against the attractions of the double church I should choose the ruined castle on the hill above the town. I had been having glimpses of it all the afternoon at the end of steep street-vistas, and promising myself half-an-hour beside its grey walls at sunset. The sun was very late setting, and my half-hour became a long lounge in the lee of an abutment which arrested the gentle uproar of the wind. The castle is a splendid piece of ruin, perched on the summit of the mountain to whose slope Assisi clings and dropping a pair of stony arms to enclose the little town in its embrace. The city wall, in other words, struggles up the steep green hill and meets the crumbling skeleton of the fortress. On the side off from the town the mountain plunges into a deep ravine, the opposite face of which is formed by the powerful undraped shoulder of Monte Subasio, a fierce reflector of the sun. Gorge and mountain are wild enough, but their frown expires in the teeming softness of the great vale of Umbria. To lie aloft there on the grass, with silver-grey ramparts at one's back and the warm rushing wind in one's ears, and watch the beautiful plain mellow into the tones of twilight, was as exquisite a form of repose as ever fell to a tired tourist's lot.

Perugia too has an ancient stronghold, which one must speak of in earnest as that unconscious humourist the classic American traveller is supposed invariably to speak of the Colosseum: it will be a very handsome building when it's finished. Even Perugia is going the way of all Italy – straightening out her streets, preparing her ruins, laying her venerable ghosts. The castle is being completely *remis à neuf* – a Massachusetts schoolhouse couldn't cultivate a "smarter" ideal. There are shops in the basement and fresh putty on all the windows; so that the only thing proper to a castle it has kept is its magnificent position and range, which you may enjoy from the broad platform where the Perugini assemble at eventide. Perugia is chiefly known to fame as the city of Raphael's master; but it has a still higher claim to renown and ought to figure in the gazetteer of fond memory as the little City of the infinite View. The small dusky, crooked place tries by a hundred prompt pretensions, immediate contortions, rich mantling flushes and other ingenuities, to waylay your attention and keep it at home; but your consciousness, alert and uneasy from the first moment, is all abroad even when your back is turned to the vast alternative or when fifty house-walls conceal it, and you are forever rushing up by-streets and peeping round corners in the hope of another glimpse or reach of it. As it stretches away before you in that eminent indifference to limits which is at the same time at every step an eminent homage to style, it is altogether too free and fair for compasses and terms. You can only say, and rest upon it, that you prefer it to any other visible fruit of position or claimed empire of the eye that you are anywhere likely to enjoy.

For it is such a wondrous mixture of blooming plain and gleaming river and wavily-multitudinous mountain vaguely dotted with pale grey cities, that, placed as you are, roughly speaking, in the centre of Italy, you all but span the divine peninsula from sea to sea. Up the long vista of the Tiber you look – almost to Rome; past Assisi, Spello, Foligno, Spoleto, all perched on their respective heights and shining through the violet haze. To the north, to the east, to the west, you see a hundred variations of the prospect, of which I have kept no record. Two notes only I have made: one – though who hasn't made it over and over again? – on the exquisite elegance of mountain forms in this endless play of the excrescence, it being exactly as if there were variation of sex in the upheaved mass, with the effect here mainly of contour and curve and complexion determined in the feminine sense. It further came home to me that the command of such an outlook on the world goes far, surely, to give authority and centrality and experience, those of the great seats of dominion, even to so scant a cluster of attesting objects as here. It must deepen the civic consciousness and take off the edge of ennui. It performs this kindly office, at any rate, for the traveller who may overstay his curiosity as to Perugino and the Etruscan relics. It continually solicits his wonder and praise – it reinforces the historic page. I spent a week in the place, and when it was gone I had had enough of Perugino, but hadn't had enough of the View.

I should perhaps do the reader a service by telling him just how a week at Perugia may be spent. His first care must be to ignore the very dream of haste, walking everywhere very slowly and very much at random, and to impute an esoteric sense to almost anything his eye may happen to encounter. Almost everything in fact lends itself to the historic, the romantic, the æsthetic fallacy – almost everything has an antique queerness and richness that ekes out the reduced state; that of a grim and battered old adventuress, the heroine of many shames and scandals, surviving to an extraordinary age and a considerable penury, but with ancient gifts of princes and other forms of the wages of sin to show, and the most beautiful garden of all the world to sit and doze and count her beads in and remember. He must hang a great deal about the huge Palazzo Pubblico, which indeed is very well worth any acquaintance you may scrape with it. It masses itself gloomily above the narrow street to an immense elevation, and leads up the eye along a cliff-like surface of rugged wall, mottled with old scars and new repairs, to the loggia dizzily perched on its cornice. He must repeat his visit to the Etruscan Gate, by whose immemorial composition he must indeed linger to resolve it back into the elements originally attending it. He must uncap to the irrecoverable, the inimitable style of the statue of Pope Julius III, before the cathedral, remembering that Hawthorne fabled his Miriam, in an air

Gateway of Palazzo Communale

146

of romance from which we are well-nigh as far today as from the building of Etruscan gates, to have given rendezvous to Kenyon at its base. Its material is a vivid green bronze, and the mantle and tiara are covered with a delicate embroidery worthy of a silversmith.

Then our leisurely friend must bestow on Perugino's frescoes in the Exchange, and on his pictures in the University, all the placid contemplation they deserve. He must go to the theatre every evening, in an orchestra-chair at twenty-two soldi, and enjoy the curious didacticism of Amore senza Stima, Severità e Debolezza, La Società Equivoca, and other popular specimens of contemporaneous Italian comedy – unless indeed the last-named be not the edifying title applied, for peninsular use, to "Le Demi-Monde" of the younger Dumas. I shall be very much surprised if, at the end of a week of this varied entertainment, he hasn't learnt how to live, not exactly in, but with, Perugia. His strolls will abound in small accidents and mercies of vision, but of which a dozen pencil-strokes would be a better memento than this poor word-sketching. From the hill on which the town is planted radiate a dozen ravines, down whose sides the houses slide and scramble with an alarming indifference to the cohesion of their little rugged blocks of flinty red stone. You ramble really nowhither without emerging on some small court or terrace that throws your view across a gulf of tangled gardens or vineyards and over to a cluster of serried black dwellings which have to hollow in their backs to keep their balance on the opposite ledge. On archways and street-staircases and dark alleys that bore through a density of massive basements, and curve and climb and plunge as they go, all to the truest mediæval tune, you may feast your fill. These are the local, the architectural, the compositional commonplaces. Some of the little streets in out-of-the-way corners are so rugged and brown and silent that you may imagine them passages long since hewn by the pick-axe in a deserted stone-quarry. The battered black houses, of the colour of buried things – things buried, that is, in accumulations of time, closer packed, even as such are, than spadefuls of earth – resemble exposed sections of natural rock; none the less so when, beyond some narrow gap, you catch the blue and silver of the sublime circle of landscape.

But I oughtn't to talk of mouldy alleys, or yet of azure distances, as if they formed the main appeal to taste in this accomplished little city. In the Sala del Cambio, where in ancient days the money-changers rattled their embossed coin and figured up their profits, you may enjoy one of the serenest æsthetic pleasures that the golden age of art anywhere offers us. Bank parlours, I believe, are always handsomely appointed, but are even those of Messrs. Rothschild such models of mural bravery as this little counting-house of a bygone fashion? The bravery is Perugino's own; for, invited clearly to do his best, he left it as a lesson to the ages, covering the four low walls and the vault with scriptural and mythological figures of extraordinary beauty. They are ranged in artless attitudes round the upper half of the room – the sybils, the prophets, the philosophers, the Greek and Roman heroes – looking down with broad serene faces, with small mild eyes and sweet mouths that commit them to nothing in particular unless to being comfortably and charmingly alive, at the incongruous proceedings of a Board of Brokers. Had finance a very high tone in those days, or were genius and faith then simply as frequent as capital and enterprise are among ourselves? The great distinction of the Sala del Cambio is that it has a friendly Yes for both these questions. There was a rigid transactional probity, it seems to say; there was also a high tide of inspiration. About the artist himself many things come up for us – more than I can attempt in their order; for he was not, I think, to an attentive observer, the mere smooth and entire and devout spirit we at first are inclined to take him for. He has that about him which leads us to wonder if he may not, after all, play a proper part enough here as the patron of the money-changers. He is the delight of a million of young ladies; but who knows whether we shouldn't find in his works, might we "go into" them a little, a trifle more of manner than of conviction and of system than of deep sincerity?

This, I allow, would put no great affront on them, and one speculates thus partly but because it's a pleasure to hang about him on any pretext, and partly because his immediate effect is to make us quite inordinately embrace the pretext of his lovely soul. His portrait, painted on the wall of the Sala (you may see it also in Rome and Florence) might at any rate serve for the likeness of Mr. Worldly-Wiseman in Bunyan's allegory. He was fond of his glass, I believe, and he made his art lucrative. This tradition is not refuted by his preserved face, and after some experience – or rather after a good deal, since you can't have a *little* of Perugino, who abounds wherever old masters congregate, so that one has constantly the sense of being "in" for all there is – you may find an echo of it in the uniform type of his creatures, their monotonous grace, their prodigious invariability. He may very well have wanted to produce figures of a substantial, yet at the same time of an impeccable innocence; but we feel that he had taught himself *how* even beyond his own belief in them, and had arrived at a process that acted at last mechanically. I confess at the same time that, so interpreted, the painter affects me as hardly less interesting, and one can't but become conscious of one's style when one's style has become, as it were, so conscious of one's, or at least of its own, fortune. If he was the inventor of a remarkably calculable *facture*, a calculation that never fails is in its way a grace of the first order, and there are things in this special appearance of perfection of practice that make him the forerunner of a mighty and more modern race. More than any of the early painters who strongly charm, you may take all his measure from a single specimen. The other samples infallibly match, reproduce unerringly the one type he had mastered, but which had the good fortune to be adorably fair, to seem to have dawned on a vision unsullied by the shadows of earth. Which truth, moreover leaves Perugino all delightful as composer and draughtsman; he has in each of these characters a sort of spacious neatness which suggests that the whole conception has been washed clean by some spiritual chemistry the last thing before reaching the canvas; after which it has been applied to that surface with a rare economy of time and means. Giotto and Fra Angelico, beside him, are full of interesting waste and irrelevant passion. In the sacristy of the charming church of San Pietro – a museum of pictures and carvings – is a row of small heads of saints formerly covering the frame of the artist's Ascension, carried off by the French. It is almost minature work, and here at least Perugino triumphs in sincerity, in apparent candour, as well as in touch. Two of the holy men are reading their breviaries, but with an air of infantine innocence quite consistent with their holding the book upside down.

Between Perugia and Cortona lies the large weedy water of Lake

Arch of Augustus, Perugia

Thrasymene, turned into a witching word forever by Hannibal's recorded victory over Rome. Dim as such records have become to us and remote such realities, he is yet a passionless pilgrim who doesn't, as he passes, of a heavy summer's day, feel the air and the light and the very faintness of the breeze all charged and haunted with them, all interfused as with the wasted ache of experience and with the vague historic haze. Processions of indistinguishable ghosts bore me company to Cortona itself, most sturdily ancient of Italian towns. It must have been a seat of ancient knowledge even when Hannibal and Flaminius came to the shock of battle, and have looked down afar from its grey ramparts on the contending swarm with something of the philosophic composure suitable to a survivor of Pelasgic and Etruscan revolutions. These grey ramparts are in great part still visible, and form the chief attraction of Cortona. It is perched on the very pinnacle of a mountain, and I wound and doubled interminably over the face of the great hill, while the jumbled roofs and towers of the arrogant little city still seemed nearer to the sky than to the railway-station. "Rather rough," Murray pronounces the local inn; and rough indeed it was; there was scarce a square foot of it that you would have cared to stroke with your hand. The landlord himself, however, was all smoothness and the best fellow in the world; he took me up into a rickety old loggia on the tip-top of his establishment and played showman as to half the kingdoms of the earth. I was free to decide at the same time whether my loss or my gain was the greater for my seeing Cortona through the medium of a festa. On the one hand the museum was closed (and in a certain sense the smaller and obscurer the town the more I like the museum); the churches – an interesting note of manners and morals – were impenetrably crowded, though, for that matter, so was the café, where I found neither an empty stool nor the edge of a table. I missed a sight of the famous painted Muse, the art-treasure of Cortona and supposedly the most precious, as it falls little short of being the only, sample of the Greek painted picture that has come down to us. On the other hand, I saw – but this is what I saw.

A part of the mountain-top is occupied by the church of St. Margaret, and this was St. Margaret's day. The houses pause roundabout it and leave a grassy slope, planted here and there with lean black cypresses. The contadini from near and far had congregated in force and were crowding into the church or winding up the slope. When I arrived they were all kneeling or uncovered; a bedizened procession, with banners and censers, bearing abroad, I believe, the relics of the saint, was re-entering the church. The scene made one of those pictures that Italy still brushes in for you with an incomparable hand and from an inexhaustible palette when you find her in the mood. The day was superb – the sky blazed overhead like a vault of deepest sapphire. The grave brown peasantry, with no great accent of costume, but with sundry small ones – decked, that is, in cheap fineries of scarlet and yellow – made a mass of motley colour in the high wind-stirred light. The procession halted in the pious hush, and the lovely land around and beneath us melted away, almost to either sea, in tones of azure scarcely less intense than the sky. Behind the church was an empty crumbling citadel, with half-a-dozen old women keeping the gate for coppers. Here were views and breezes and sun and shade and grassy corners to the heart's content, together with one couldn't say what huge seated mystic melancholy presence, the after-taste of everything the still open maw of time had consumed. I chose a spot that fairly combined all these advantages, a spot from which I seemed to look, as who should say, straight down the throat of the monster, no dark passage now, but with all the glorious day playing into it, and spent a good part of my stay at Cortona lying there at my length and observing the situation over the top of a volume that I must have brought in my pocket just for that especial wanton luxury of the resource provided and slighted. In the afternoon I came down and hustled awhile through the crowded little streets, and then strolled forth under the scorching sun and made the outer circuit of the wall. There I found tremendous uncemented blocks; they glared and twinkled in the powerful light, and I had to put on a blue eye-glass in order to throw into its proper perspective the vague Etruscan past, obtruded and magnified in such masses quite as with the effect of inadequately-withdrawn hands and feet in photographs.

I spent the next day at Arezzo, but I confess in very much the same uninvestigating fashion – taking in the "general impression", I dare say, at every pore, but rather systematically leaving the dust of the ages unfingered on the stored records: I should doubtless, in the poor time at my command, have fingered it to so little purpose. The seeker for the story of things has moreover, if he be worth his salt, a hundred insidious arts; and in that case indeed – by which I mean when his sensibility has come duly to adjust itself – the story assaults him but from too many sides. He even feels at moments that he must sneak along on tiptoe in order not to have too much of it. Besides which the case all depends on the kind of use, the range of application, his tangled consciousness, or his intelligible genius, say, may come to recognize for it. At Arezzo, however this might be, one was far from Rome, one was well within genial Tuscany, and the historic, the romantic decoction seemed to reach one's lips in less stiff doses. There at once was the "general impression" – the exquisite sense of the scarce expressible Tuscan quality, which makes immediately, for the whole pitch of one's perception, a grateful, a not at all strenuous difference, attaches to almost any coherent group of objects, to any happy aspect of the scene, for a main note, some mild recall, through pleasant friendly colour, through settled ample form, through something homely and economic too at the very heart of "style", of an identity of temperament and habit with those of the divine little Florence that one originally knew. Adorable Italy in which, for the constant renewal of interest, of attention, of affection, these refinements of variety, these so harmoniously-grouped and individually-seasoned fruits of the great garden of history, keep presenting themselves! It seemed to fall in with the cheerful Tuscan mildness for instance – sticking as I do to that ineffectual expression of the Tuscan charm, of the yellow-brown Tuscan dignity at large – that the ruined castle on the hill (with which agreeable feature Arezzo is no less furnished than Assisi and Cortona) had been converted into a great blooming, and I hope all profitable, podere or market-garden. I lounged away the half hours there under a spell as potent as the "wildest" forecast of propriety – propriety to all the particular conditions – could have figured it. I had seen Santa Maria della Pieve and its campanile of quaint colonnades, the stately, dusky cathedral – grass-plotted and residenced about almost after the fashion of an English "close" – and John of Pisa's elaborate marble shrine; I had seen the museum and its Etruscan vases and majolica platters. These were very well, but the old pacified citadel somehow, through a day of soft saturation, placed me most in relation. Beautiful hills surrounded it, cypresses cast straight shadows at its corners, while in the middle grew a wondrous Italian tangle of wheat and corn, vines and figs, peaches and cabbages, memories and images, anything and everything.

1873.

Duomo, Arezzo

152

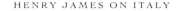

CHAPTER VIII

SIENA
EARLY AND LATE

The Red Palace, Siena

LORENCE BEING OPPRESSIVELY hot and delivered over to the mosquitoes, the occasion seemed to favour that visit to Siena which I had more than once planned and missed. I arrived late in the evening, by the light of a magnificent moon, and while a couple of benignantly-mumbling old crones were making up my bed at the inn strolled forth in quest of a first impression. Five minutes brought me to where I might gather it unhindered as it bloomed in the white moonshine. The great Piazza of Siena is famous, and though in this day of multiplied photographs and blunted surprises and profaned revelations none of the world's wonders can pretend, like Wordsworth's phantom of delight, really to "startle and waylay", yet as I stepped upon the waiting scene from under a dark archway I was conscious of no loss of the edge of a precious presented sensibility. The waiting scene, as I have called it, was in the shape of a shallow horse-shoe – as the untravelled reader who has turned over his travelled friends' portfolios will respectfully remember; or, better, of a bow in which the high wide face of the Palazzo Pubblico forms the cord and everything else the arc. It was void of any human presence that could figure to me the current year; so that, the moonshine assisting, I had half-an-hour's infinite vision of mediæval Italy. The Piazza being built on the side of a hill – or rather, as I believe science affirms, in the cup of a volcanic crater – the vast pavement converges downwards in slanting radiations of stone, the spokes of a great wheel, to a point directly before the Palazzo, which may mark the hub, though it is nothing more ornamental than the mouth of a drain. The great monument stands on the lower side and might seem, in spite of its goodly mass and its embattled cornice, to be rather defiantly out-countenanced by vast private constructions occupying the opposite eminence. This *might* be, without the extraordinary dignity of the architectural gesture with which the huge high-shouldered pile asserts itself.

On the firm edge of the palace, from bracketed base to grey-capped summit against the sky, there grows a tall slim tower which soars and soars till it has given notice of the city's greatness over the blue mountains that mark the horizon. It rises as slender and straight as a pennoned lance planted on the steel-shod toe of a mounted knight, and keeps all to itself in the blue air, far above the changing fashions of the market, the proud consciousness or rare arrogance once built into it. This beautiful tower, the finest thing in Siena and, in its rigid fashion, as permanently fine thus as a really handsome nose on a face of no matter what accumulated age, figures there still as a Declaration of Independence beside which such an affair as ours, thrown off at Philadelphia, appears to have scarce done more than helplessly give way to time. Our Independence has become a dependence on a thousand such dreadful things as the incorrupt declaration of Siena strikes us as looking for ever straight over the level of. As it stood silvered by the moonlight, while my greeting lasted, it seemed to speak, all as from soul to soul, very much indeed as some ancient worthy of a lower order, buttonholing one on the coveted chance and at the quiet hour, might have done, of a state of things long and vulgarly superseded, but to the pride and power, the once prodigious vitality, of which who could expect any one effect to testify more incomparably, more indestructibly, quite, as it were, more immortally? The gigantic houses enclosing the rest of the Piazza took up the tale and mingled with it their burden. "We are very old and a trifle weary, but we were built strong and piled high, and we shall last for many an age. The present is cold and heedless, but we keep ourselves in heart by brooding over our store of memories and traditions. We are haunted houses in every creaking timber and aching stone." Such were the gossiping connections I established with Siena before I went to bed.

Since that night I have had a week's daylight knowledge of the surface of the subject at least, and don't know how I can better present it than simply as another and a vivider page of the lesson that the ever-hungry artist has only to *trust* old Italy for her to feed him at every single step from her hand – and if not with one sort of sweetly-stale grain from that wondrous mill of history which during so many ages ground finer than any other on earth, why then always with something else. Siena has at any rate "preserved appearances" – kept the greatest number of them, that is, unaltered for the eye – about as consistently as one can imagine the thing done. Other places perhaps may treat you to as drowsy an odour of antiquity, but few exhale it from so large an area. Lying massed within her walls on a dozen clustered hilltops, she shows you at every turn in how much greater a way she once lived; and if so much of the grand manner is extinct the receptacle of the ashes still solidly rounds itself. This heavy general stress of all her emphasis on the past is what she constantly keeps in your eyes and your ears, and if you be but a casual observer and admirer the generalised response is mainly what you give her. The casual observer, however beguiled, is mostly not very learned, not over-equipped in advance with data; he hasn't specialised, his notions are necessarily vague, the chords of his imagination, for all his good-will, are inevitably muffled and weak. But such as it is, his received, his welcome impression serves his turn so far as the life of sensibility goes, and reminds him from time to time that even the lore of German doctors is but the shadow of satisfied curiosity. I have been living at the inn, walking about the streets, sitting in the Piazza; these are the simple terms of my experience. But streets and inns in Italy are the vehicles of half one's knowledge; if one has no fancy for their lessons one may burn one's note-book. In Siena everything is Sienese. The inn has an English sign over the door – a little battered plate with a rusty representation of the lion and the unicorn; but advance hopefully into the mouldy stone alley which serves as vestibule and you will find local colour enough. The landlord, I was told, had been servant in an English family, and I was curious to see how he met the

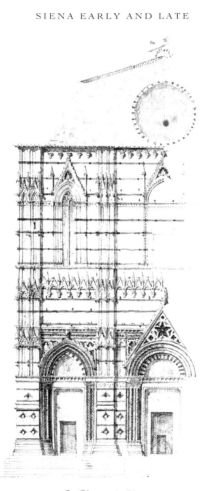

S. Giovanni, Siena

155

probable argument of the casual Anglo-Saxon after the latter's first twelve hours in his establishment. As he failed to appear I asked the waiter if he weren't at home. "Oh," said the latter, "he's a *piccolo grasso vecchiotto* who doesn't like to move." I'm afraid this little fat old man has simply a bad conscience. It's no small burden for one who likes the Italians – as who doesn't, under this restriction? – to have so much indifference even to rudimentary purifying processes to dispose of. What is the real philosophy of dirty habits, and are foul surfaces merely superficial? If unclean manners have in truth the moral meaning which I suspect in them we must love Italy better than consistency. This a number of us are prepared to do, but while we are making the sacrifice it is well we should be aware.

We may plead moreover for these impecunious heirs of the past that even if it were easy to be clean in the midst of their mouldering heritage it would be difficult to appear so. At the risk of seeming to flaunt the silly superstition of restless renovation for the sake of renovation, which is but the challenge of the infinitely precious principle of duration, one is still moved to say that the prime result of one's contemplative strolls in the dusky alleys of such a place is an ineffable sense of disrepair. Everything is cracking, peeling, fading, crumbling, rotting. No young Sienese eyes rest upon anything youthful; they open into a world battered and befouled with long use. Everything has passed its meridian except the brilliant façade of the cathedral, which is being diligently retouched and restored, and a few private palaces whose broad fronts seem to have been lately furbished and polished. Siena was long ago mellowed to the pictorial tone; the operation of time is now to deposit shabbiness upon shabbiness. But it's for the most part a patient, sturdy, sympathetic shabbiness, which soothes rather than irritates the nerves, and has in many cases doubtless as long a career to run as most of our pert and shallow freshnesses. It projects at all events a deeper shadow into the constant twilight of the narrow streets – that vague historic dusk, as I may call it, in which one walks and wonders. These streets are hardly more than sinuous flagged alleys, into which the huge black houses,

Porta Romana, Siena

between their almost meeting cornices, suffer a meagre light to filter down over rough-hewn stone, past windows often of graceful Gothic form, and great pendent iron rings and twisted sockets for torches. Scattered over their many-headed hill, they suffer the roadway often to incline to the perpendicular, becoming so impracticable for vehicles that the sound of wheels is only a trifle less anomalous than it would be in Venice. But all day long there comes up to my window an incessant shuffling of feet and clangour of voices. The weather is very warm for the season, all the world is out of doors, and the Tuscan tongue (which in Siena is reputed to have a classic purity) wags in every imaginable key. It doesn't rest even at night, and I am often an uninvited guest at concerts and *conversazioni* at two o'clock in the morning. The concerts are sometimes charming. I not only don't curse my wakefulness, but go to my window to listen. Three men come carolling by, trolling and quavering with voices of delightful sweetness, or a lonely troubadour in his shirt-sleeves draws such artful love-notes from his clear, fresh tenor, that I seem for the moment to be behind the scenes at the opera, watching some Rubini or Mario go "on" and waiting for the round of applause. In the intervals a couple of friends or enemies stop – Italians always make their points in conversation by pulling up, letting you walk on a few paces, to turn and find them standing with finger on nose and engaging your interrogative eye – they pause, by a happy instinct, directly under my window, and dispute their point or tell their story or make their confidence. One scarce is sure which it may be; everything has such an explosive promptness, such a redundancy of inflection and action. But everything for that matter takes on such dramatic life as *our* lame colloquies never know – so that almost any uttered communications here become an acted play, improvised, mimicked, proportioned and rounded, carried bravely to its *dénoûment*. The speaker seems actually to establish his stage and face his foot-lights, to create by a gesture a little scenic circumscription about him; he rushes to and fro and shouts and stamps and postures, he ranges through every phase of his inspiration. I noted the other evening a striking instance of the spontaneity of the Italian gesture, in the person of a small Sienese of I hardly know what exact age – the age of inarticulate sounds and the experimental use of a spoon. It was a Sunday evening, and this little man had accompanied his parents to the café. The Caffè Greco at Siena is a most delightful institution; you get a capital *demi-tasse* for three sous, and an excellent ice for eight, and while you consume these easy luxuries you may buy from a little hunchback the local weekly periodical, the *Vita Nuova*, for three centimes (the two centimes left from your sou, if you are under the spell of this magical frugality, will do to give the waiter). My young friend was sitting on his father's knee and helping himself to the half of a strawberry-ice with which his mamma had presented him. He had so many misadventures with his spoon that this lady at length confiscated it, there being nothing left of the ice but a little crimson liquid which he might dispose of by the common instinct of childhood. But he was no friend, it appeared, to such freedoms; he was a perfect little gentleman and he resented its being expected of him that he should drink down his remnant. He protested therefore, and it was the manner of his protest that struck me. He didn't cry audibly, though he made a very wry face. It was no stupid squall, and yet he was too young to speak. It was a penetrating concord of inarticulately pleading, accusing sounds, accompanied by gestures of the most exquisite propriety. These were perfectly mature; he did everything that a man of forty would have done if he had been pouring out a flood of sonorous eloquence. He shrugged his shoulders and wrinkled his eyebrows, tossed out his hands and folded his arms, obtruded his chin and bobbed about his head – and at last, I am happy to say, recovered his spoon. If I had had a solid little silver one I would have presented it to him as a testimonial to a perfect, though as yet unconscious, artist.

My actual tribute to him, however, has diverted me from what I had in mind – a much weightier matter – the great private palaces which are the massive majestic syllables, sentences, ·periods, of the strange message the place addresses to us. They are extraordinarily spacious and numerous, and one wonders what part they can play in the meagre economy of the actual city. The Siena of to-day is a mere shrunken semblance of the rabid little republic which in the thirteenth century waged triumphant war with Florence, cultivated the arts with splendour, planned a cathedral (though it had ultimately to curtail the design) of proportions almost unequalled, and contained a population of two hundred thousand souls. Many of these dusky piles still bear the names of the old mediæval magnates the vague mild occupancy of whose descendants has the effect of armour of proof worn over "pot" hats and tweed jackets and trousers. Half-a-dozen of them are as high as the Strozzi and Riccardi palaces in Florence; they couldn't well be higher. The very essence of the romantic and the scenic is in the way these colossal dwellings are packed together in their steep streets, in the depths of their little enclosed, agglomerated city. When we, in our day and country, raise a structure of half the mass and dignity, we leave a great space about it in the manner of a pause after a showy speech. But when a Sienese countess, as things are here, is doing her hair near a window, she is a wonderfully near neighbour to the cavalier opposite, who is being shaved by his valet. Possibly the countess doesn't object to a certain chosen publicity at her toilet; what does an Italian gentleman assure me but that the aristocracy make very free with each other? Some of the palaces are shown, but only when the occupants are at home, and now they are in *villeggiatura*. Their villaggiatura lasts eight months of the year, the waiter at the inn informs me, and they spend little more than the carnival in the city. The gossip of an inn-waiter ought perhaps to be beneath the dignity of even such thin history as this; but I confess that when, as a story-seeker always and ever, I have come in from my strolls with an irritated sense of the dumbness of stones and mortar, it has been to listen with avidity, over my dinner, to the proffered confidences of the worthy man who stands by with a napkin. His talk is really very fine, and he prides himself greatly on his cultivated tone, to which he calls my attention. He has very little good to say about the Sienese nobility. They are "proprio d'origine egoista" – whatever that may be – and there are many who can't write their names. This may be calumny; but I doubt whether the most blameless of them all could have spoken more delicately of a lady of peculiar personal appearance who had been dining near me. "She's too fat," I grossly said on her leaving the room. The waiter shook his head with a little sniff: "È troppo materiale." This lady and her companion were the party whom, thinking I might relish a little company – I had been dining alone for a week – he gleefully announced to me as newly arrived Americans. They were Americans, I found, who wore, pinned to their heads in permanence, the black lace veil or mantilla, conveyed their beans to their mouth with a knife, and spoke a strange raucous Spanish. They were in fine compatriots from Montevideo. The genius of old Siena, however, would make little of any stress of such distinctions; one representative of a far-off social platitude being about as much in order as another as he stands before the great loggia of the Casino di Nobili, the club of the best society. The nobility, which is very numerous and very rich, is still, says the apparently competent native I began by quoting, perfectly feudal and uplifted and separate. Morally and intellectually, behind the walls of its palaces, the fourteenth century, it's thrilling to think, hasn't ceased to hang on. There is no bourgeoisie to speak of;

Staircase, Siena

159

Duomo di Siena, by C. Bossoli

immediately after the aristocracy come the poor people, who are very poor indeed. My friend's account of these matters made me wish more than ever, as a lover of the preserved social specimen, of type at almost any price, that one weren't a helpless victim of the historic sense, reduced simply to staring at black stones and peeping up stately staircases; and that when one had examined the street-face of the palace, Murray in hand, one might walk up to the great drawing-room, make one's bow to the master and mistress, the old abbé and the young count, and invite them to favour one with a sketch of their social philosophy or a few first-hand family anecdotes.

The dusky labyrinth of the streets, we must in default of such initiations content ourselves with noting, is interrupted by two great candid spaces: the fan-shaped piazza, of which I just now said a word, and the smaller square in which the cathedral erects its walls of many-coloured marble. Of course since paying the great piazza my compliments by moonlight I have strolled through it often at sunnier and shadier hours. The market is held there, and wherever Italians buy and sell, wherever they count and chaffer – as indeed you hear them do right and left, at almost any moment, as you take your way among them – the pulse of life beats fast. It has been doing so on the spot just named, I suppose, for the last five hundred years, and during that time the cost of eggs and earthen pots has been gradually but inexorably increasing. The buyers nevertheless wrestle over their purchases as lustily as so many fourteenth-century burghers suddenly waking up in horror to current prices. You have but to walk aside, however, into the Palazzo Pubblico really to feel yourself a thrifty old mediævalist. The state affairs of the Republic were formerly transacted here, but it now gives shelter to modern law-courts and other prosy business. I was marched through a number of vaulted halls and chambers, which, in the intervals of the administrative sessions held in them, are peopled only by the great mouldering archaic frescoes – anything but inanimate these even in their present ruin – that cover the walls and ceiling. The chief painters of the Sienese school lent a hand in producing the works I name, and you may complete there the connoisseurship in which, possibly, you will have embarked at the Academy. I say "possibly" to be very judicial, my own observation having led me no great length. I have rather than otherwise cherished the thought that the Sienese school suffers one's eagerness peacefully to slumber – benignantly abstains in fact from whipping up a languid curiosity and a tepid faith. "A formidable rival to the Florentine," says some book – I forget which – into which I recently glanced. Not a bit of it thereupon boldly say I; the

Florentines may rest on their laurels and the lounger on his lounge. The early painters of the two groups have indeed much in common; but the Florentines had the good fortune to see their efforts gathered up and applied by a few pre-eminent spirits, such as never came to the rescue of the groping Sienese. Fra Angelico and Ghirlandaio said all their feebler *confrères* dreamt of and a great deal more beside, but the inspiration of Simone Memmi and Ambrogio Lorenzetti and Sano di Pietro has a painful air of never efflorescing into a maximum. Sodoma and Beccafumi are to my taste a rather abortive maximum. But one should speak of them all gently – and I do, from my soul; for their labour, by their lights, has wrought a precious heritage of still-living colour and rich figure-peopled shadow for the echoing chambers of their old civic fortress. The faded frescoes cover the walls like quaintly-storied tapestries; in one way or another they cast their spell. If one owes a large debt of pleasure to pictorial art one comes to think tenderly and easily of its whole evolution, as of the conscious experience of a single mysterious, striving spirit, and one shrinks from saying rude things about any particular phase of it, just as one would from referring without precautions to some error or lapse in the life of a person one esteemed. You don't care to remind a grizzled veteran of his defeats, and why should we linger in Siena to talk about Beccafumi? I by no means go so far as to say, with an amateur with whom I have just been discussing the matter, that "Sodoma is a precious poor painter and Beccafumi no painter at all"; but, opportunity being limited, I am willing to let the remark about Beccafumi pass for true. With regard to Sodoma, I remember seeing four years ago in the choir of the Cathedral of Pisa a certain small dusky specimen of the painter – an Abraham and Isaac, if I am not mistaken – which was charged with a gloomy grace. One rarely meets him in general collections, and I had never done so till the other day. He was not prolific, apparently; he had however his own elegance, and his rarity is a part of it.

Here in Siena are a couple of dozen scattered frescoes and three or four canvases; his masterpiece, among others, an harmonious Descent from the Cross. I wouldn't give a fig for the equilibrium of the figures or the ladders; but while it lasts the scene is all intensely solemn and graceful and sweet – too sweet for so bitter a subject. Sodoma's women are strangely sweet; an imaginative sense of morbid appealing attitude – as notably in the sentimental, the pathetic, but the none the less pleasant, "Swooning of Saint Catherine", the great Sienese heroine, at San Domenico – seems to me the author's finest accomplishment. His frescoes have all the same almost appealing evasion of difficulty, and a kind of mild melancholy which I am inclined to think the sincerest part of them, for it strikes me as practically the artist's depressed suspicion of his own want of force. Once he determined, however, that if he couldn't be strong he would make capital of his weakness, and painted the Christ bound to the Column, of the Academy. Here he got much nearer and I have no doubt mixed his colours with his tears; but the result can't be better described than by saying that it is pictorially, the first of the modern Christs. Unfortunately it hasn't been the last.

The main strength of Sienese art went possibly into the erection of the Cathedral, and yet even here the strength is not of the greatest strain. If, however, there are more interesting temples in Italy, there are few more richly and variously scenic and splendid, the comparative meagreness of the architectural idea being overlaid by a marvellous wealth of ingenious detail. Opposite the church – with the dull old archbishop's palace on one side and a dismantled residence of the late Grand Duke of Tuscany on the other – is an ancient hospital with a big stone bench running all along its front. Here I have sat awhile every morning for a week, like a philosophic convalescent, watching the florid façade of the cathedral glitter against the deep blue sky. It has been lavishly restored of late years, and the fresh white marble of the densely clustered pinnacles and statues and beasts and flowers flashes in the sunshine like a mosaic of jewels. There is more of this goldsmith's work in stone than I can remember or describe; it is piled up over three great doors with immense margins of exquisite decorative sculpture – still in the ancient cream-coloured marble – and beneath three sharp pediments embossed with images relieved against red marble and tipped with golden mosaics. It is in the highest degree fantastic and luxuriant – it is on the whole very lovely. As a triumph of the many-hued it prepares you for the interior, where the same parti-coloured splendour is endlessly at play – a confident complication of harmonies and contrasts and of the minor structural refinements and braveries. The internal surface is mainly wrought in alternate courses of black and white marble; but as the latter has been dimmed by the centuries to a fine mild brown the place is all a concert of relieved and dispersed glooms. Save for Pinturicchio's brilliant frescoes in the Sacristy there are no pictures to speak of; but the pavement is covered with many elaborate designs in black and white mosaic after cartoons by Beccafumi. The patient skill of these compositions makes them a rare piece of decoration; yet even here the friend whom I lately quoted rejects this over-ripe fruit of the Sienese school. The designs are nonsensical, he declares, and all his admiration is for the cunning artisans who have imitated the hatchings and

Peredos, Duomo, Siena

shadings and hair-strokes of the pencil by the finest curves of inserted black stone. But the true romance of handiwork at Siena is to be seen in the wondrous stalls of the choir, under the coloured light of the great wheel-window. Wood-carving has ever been a cherished craft of the place, and the best masters of the art during the fifteenth century lavished themselves on this prodigious task. It is the frost-work on one's window-panes interpreted in polished oak. It would be hard to find, doubtless, a more moving illustration of the peculiar patience, the sacred candour, of the great time. Into such artistry as this the author seems to put more of his personal substance than into any other; he has to wrestle not only with his subject, but with his material. He is richly fortunate when his subject is charming – when his devices, inventions and fantasies spring lightly to his hand; for in the material itself, after age and use have ripened and polished and darkened it to the richness of ebony and to a greater warmth there is something surpassingly delectable and venerable. Wander behind the altar at Siena when the chanting is over and the incense has faded, and look well at the stalls of the Barili.

1873.

II

I leave the impression noted in the foregoing pages to tell its own small story, but have it on my conscience to wonder, in this connection, quite candidly and publicly and by way of due penance, at the scantness of such first-fruits of my sensibility. I was to see Siena repeatedly in the years to follow, I was to know her better, and I would say that I was to do her an ampler justice didn't that remark seem to reflect a little on my earlier poor judgement. This judgement strikes me to-day as having fallen short – true as it may be that I find ever a value, or at least an interest, even in the moods and humours and lapses of any brooding, musing or fantasticating observer to whom the finer sense of things is *on the whole* not closed. If he has on a given occasion nodded or stumbled or strayed, this fact by itself speaks to me of him – speaks to me, that is, of his faculty and his idosyncrasies, and I care nothing for the application of his faculty unless it be, first of all, in itself interesting. Which may serve as my reply to any objection here breaking out – on the ground that if a spectator's languors are evidence, of a sort, about that personage, they are scarce evidence about the case before him, at least if the case be important. I let my perhaps rather weak expression of the sense of Siena stand, at any rate – for the sake of what I myself read into it; but I should like to amplify it by other memories, and would do so eagerly if I might here enjoy the space. The difficulty for these rectifications is that if the early vision has failed of competence or of full felicity, if initiation has thus been slow, so, with renewals and extensions, so, with the larger experience, one hindrance is exchanged for another. There is quite such a possibility as having lived into a relation too much to be able to make statement of it.

I remember on one occasion arriving very late of a summer night, after an almost unbroken run from London, and the note of that approach – I was the only person alighting at the station below the great hill of the little fortress city, under whose at once frowning and gaping gate I must have passed, in the warm darkness and the absolute stillness, very much after the felt fashion of a person of importance about to be enormously incarcerated – gives me, for preservation thus belated, the pitch, as I may call it, at various times, though always at one season, of an almost systematised æsthetic use of the place. It wasn't to be denied that the immensely better "accommodations" instituted by the multiplying, though alas more bustling, years had to be recognised as supplying a basis, comparatively prosaic if one would, to that luxury. No sooner have I written which words, however, than I find myself adding that one "wouldn't", that one doesn't – doesn't, that is, consent now to regard the then "new" hotel (pretty old indeed by this time) as anything but an aid to a free play of perception. The strong and rank old Arme d'Inghilterra, in the darker street, had passed away; but its ancient rival the Aquila Nera put forth claims to modernisation, and the Grand Hotel, the still fresher flower of modernity near the gate by which you enter from the station, takes on to my present remembrance a mellowness as of all sorts of comfort, cleanliness and kindness. The particular facts, those of the visit I began here by alluding to and those of still others, at all events, inveterately made in June or early in July, enter together into a fusion as of hot golden-brown objects seen through the practicable crevices of shutters drawn upon high, cool, darkened rooms where the scheme of the scene involved longish days of quiet work, with late afternoon emergence and contemplation waiting on the better or the worse conscience. I thus associate the compact world of the admirable hilltop, the world

Map of Siena from Baedeker's Italy *(1892)*

of a predominant golden-brown, with a general invocation of sensibility and fancy, and think of myself as going forth into the lingering light of summer evenings all attuned to intensity of the idea of compositional beauty, or in other words, freely speaking, to the question of colour, to intensity of picture. To communicate with Siena in this charming way was thus, I admit, to have no great margin for the prosecution of inquiries, but I am not sure that it wasn't, little by little, to feel the whole combination of elements better than by a more exemplary method, and this from beginning to end of the scale.

More of the elements indeed, for memory, hang about the days that were ushered in by that straight flight from the north than about any other series – if partly, doubtless, but because of my having then stayed longest. I specify it at all events for fond reminiscence as the year, the only year, at which I was present at the Palio, the earlier one, the series of furious horse-races between elected representatives of different quarters of the town taking place toward the end of June, as the second and still more characteristic exhibition of the same sort is appointed to the month of August; a spectacle that I am far from speaking of as the finest flower of my old and perhaps even a little faded cluster of impressions, but which smudges that special sojourn as with the big thumb-mark of a slightly soiled and decidedly ensanguined hand. For really, after all, the great loud gaudy romp or heated frolic, simulating ferocity if not achieving it, that is the annual pride of the town, was not intrinsically, to my view, extraordinarily impressive – in spite of its bristling with all due testimony to the passionate Italian clutch of any pretext for costume and attitude and utterance, for mumming and masquerading and raucously representing; the vast cheap vividness rather somehow refines itself, and the swarm and hubbub of the immense square melt, to the uplifted sense of a very high-placed balcony of the overhanging Chigi palace, where everything was superseded but the intenser passage, across the ages, of the great Renaissance tradition of architecture and the infinite sweetness of the waning golden day. The Palio, indubitably, was *criard* – and the more so for quite monopolising, at Siena, the note of crudity; and much of it demanded doubtless of one's patience a due respect for the long local continuity of such things; it drops into its humoured position, however, in any retrospective command of the many brave aspects of the prodigious place. Not that I am pretending here, even for the rectification, to take these at all in turn; I only go on a little with my rueful glance at the marked gaps left in my original report of sympathies entertained.

I bow my head for instance to the mystery of my not having mentioned that the coolest and freshest flower of the day was ever that of one's constant renewal of a charmed homage to Pinturicchio, coolest and freshest and signally youngest and most matutinal (as distinguished from merely primitive or crepuscular) of painters, in the library or sacristy of the Cathedral. Did I *always* find time before work to spend half-an-hour of immersion, under that splendid roof, in the clearest and tenderest, the very cleanest and "straightest", as it masters our envious credulity, of all storied fresco-worlds? This wondrous apartment, a monument in itself to the ancient pride and power of the Church, and which contains an unsurpassed treasure of gloriously illuminated missals, psalters and other vast parchment folios, almost each of whose successive leaves gives the impression of rubies, sapphires and emeralds set in gold and practically embedded in the page, offers thus to view, after a fashion splendidly sustained, a pictorial record of the career of Pope Pius II., Æneas Sylvius of the Siena Piccolomini (who gave him for an immediate successor a second of their name), most profanely literary of Pontiffs and last of would-be Crusaders, whose adventures and achievements under Pinturicchio's brush smooth themselves out for us very much to the tune of the "stories" told by some fine old man of the world, at the restful end of his life, to the cluster of his grandchildren. The end of Æneas Sylvius was not restful; he died at Ancona in troublous times, preaching war, and attempting to make it, against the then terrific Turk; but over no great worldly personal legend, among those of men of arduous affairs, arches a fairer, lighter or more pacific memorial vault than the shining Libreria of Siena. I seem to remember having it and its unfrequented enclosing precinct so often all to myself that I must indeed mostly have resorted to it for a prompt benediction on the day. Like no other strong solicitation, among artistic appeals to which one may compare it up and down the whole wonderful country, is the felt neighbouring presence of the overwrought Cathedral in its little proud possessive town: you may so often feel by the week at a time that it stands there really for your own personal enjoyment, your romantic convenience, your small wanton æsthetic use. In such a light shines for me, at all events, under such an accumulation and complication of tone flushes and darkens and richly recedes for me, across the years, the treasure-house of many-coloured marbles in the untrodden, the

*Interior of Library of Cathedral,
Siena*

drowsy, empty Sienese square. One could positively do, in the free exercise of any responsible fancy or luxurious taste, what one would with it.

But that proposition holds true, after all, for almost any mild pastime of the incurable student of loose meanings and stray relics and odd references and dim analogies in an Italian hill-city bronzed and seasoned by the ages. I ought perhaps, for justification of the right to talk, to have plunged into the Siena archives of which, on one occasion, a kindly custodian gave me, in rather dusty and stuffy conditions, as the incident vaguely comes back to me, a glimpse that was like a moment's stand at the mouth of a deep, dark mine. I didn't descend into the pit; I did, instead of this, a much idler and easier thing; I simply went every afternoon, my stint of work over, I like to recall, for a musing stroll upon the Lizza – the Lizza which had its own unpretentious but quite insidious art of meeting the lover of old stories half-way. The great and subtle thing, if you are not a strenuous specialist, in places of a heavily charged historic consciousness, is to profit by the sense of that consciousness – or in other words to cultivate a relation with the oracle – after the fashion that suits yourself; so that if the general after-taste of experience, experience at large, the fine distilled essence of the matter, seems to breathe, in such a case, from the very stones and to make a thick strong liquor of the very air, you may thus gather as you pass what is most to your purpose; which is more the indestructible mixture of lived things, with its concentrated lingering odour, than any interminable list of numbered chapters and verses. Chapters and verses, literally scanned, refuse coincidence, mostly, with the divisional proprieties of your own pile of manuscript – which is but another way of saying, in short, that if the Lizza is a mere fortified promontory of the great Sienese hill, serving at once as a stronghold for the present military garrison and as a planted and benched and band-standed walk and recreation-ground for the citizens, so I could never, toward close of day, either have enough of it or yet feel the vaguest saunterings there to be vain. They were vague with the qualification always of that finer massing, as one wandered off, of the bronzed and seasoned element, the huge rock pedestal, the bravery of walls and gates and towers and palaces and loudly asserted dominion: and then of that pervaded or mildly infested air in which one feels the experience of the ages, of which I just spoke, to be exquisitely in solution; and lastly of the wide, strange, sad, beautiful horizon, a rim of far mountains that always pictured, for the leaner on old rubbed and smoothed parapets at the sunset hour, a country not exactly blighted or deserted, but that had had its life, on an immense scale, and had gone, with all its memories and relics, into rather austere, in fact into almost grim and misanthropic, retirement. This was a manner and a mood, at any rate, in all the land, that favoured in the late afternoons the divinest landscape blues and purples — not to speak of its favouring still more my practical contention that the whole guarded headland in question, with the immense ramparts of golden brown and red that dropped into vineyards and orchards and cornfields and all the rustic elegance of the Tuscan *podere*, was knitting for me a chain of unforgettable hours; to the justice of which claim let these divagations testify.

It wasn't, however, that one mightn't without disloyalty to that scheme of profit seek impressions further afield — though indeed I may best say of such a matter as the long pilgrimage to the pictured convent of Monte Oliveto that it but played on the same fine chords as the overhanging, the far-gazing Lizza. What it came to was that one simply put to the friendly test, as it were, the mood and manner of the country. This remembrance is precious, but the demonstration of that sense as of a great heaving region stilled by some final shock and returning thoughtfully, in fact tragically, on itself, couldn't have been more pointed. The long-drawn rural road I refer to, stretching over hill and dale and to which I devoted the whole of the longest day of the year — I was in a small single-horse conveyance, of which I had already made appreciative use, and with a driver as disposed as myself ever to sacrifice speed to contemplation — is doubtless familiar now with the rush of the motor-car; the thought of whose free dealings with the solitude of Monte Oliveto makes me a little ruefully reconsider, I confess, the spirit in which I have elsewhere in these pages, on behalf of the lust, the landscape lust, of the eyes, acknowledged our general increasing debt to that vehicle. For that we met nothing whatever, as I seem at this distance of time to recall, while we gently trotted through the splendid summer hours and a dry desolation that yet somehow smiled and smiled, was part of the charm and the intimacy of the whole impression — the impression that culminated at last, before the great cloistered square, lonely, bleak and stricken, in the almost aching vision, more frequent in the Italy of to-day than anywhere in the world, of the uncalculated waste of a myriad forms of piety, forces of labour, beautiful fruits of genius. However, one gaped above all things for the impression, and what one mainly asked was that it should be strong of its kind. That was the case, I think I couldn't but feel, at every moment of the couple of hours I spent in the vast, cold, empty shell, out of which the Benedictine brotherhood sheltered there for ages had lately been turned by the strong arm of a secular State. There was but one good brother left, a very lean and

Primavera, by Adoici Tommasi

tough survivor, a dusky, elderly, friendly Abbate, of an indescribable type and a perfect manner, of whom I think I felt immediately thereafter that I should have liked to say much, but as to whom I must have yielded to the fact that ingenious and vivid commemoration was even then in store for him. Literary portraiture had marked him for its own, and in the short story of *Un Saint*, one of the most finished of contemporary French *nouvelles*, the art and the sympathy of Monsieur Paul Bourget preserve his interesting image. He figures in the beautiful tale, the Abbate of the desolate cloister and of those comparatively quiet years, as a clean, clear type of sainthood; a circumstance this in itself to cause a fond analyst of other than "Latin" race (model and painter in this case having their Latinism so strongly in common) almost endlessly to meditate. Oh, the unutterable differences in any scheme or estimate of physiognomic values, in any range of sensibility to expressional association, among observers of different, of inevitably more or less opposed, traditional and "racial" points of view! One had heard convinced Latins – or at least I had! – speak of situations of trust and intimacy in which they couldn't have endured near them a Protestant or, as who should say for instance, an Anglo-Saxon; but I was to remember my own private attempt to measure such a change of sensibility as might have permitted the prolonged close approach of the dear dingy, half-starved, very possibly all heroic, and quite ideally urbane Abbate. The depth upon depth of things, the cloud upon cloud of associations, on one side and the other, that would have had to change first!

Interior of S. Maria del Carmine, Siena

To which I may add nevertheless that since one ever supremely invoked intensity of impression and abundance of character, I feasted my fill of it at Monte Oliveto, and that for that matter this would have constituted my sole refreshment in the vast icy void of the blighted refectory if I hadn't bethought myself of bringing with me a scrap of food, too scantly apportioned, I recollect – very scantly indeed, since my *cocchiere* was to share with me – by my purveyor at Siena. Our tragic – even if so tenderly tragic – entertainer had nothing to give us; but the immemorial cold of the enormous monastic interior in which we smilingly fasted would doubtless not have had for me without that such a wealth of reference. I was to have "liked" the whole adventure, so I must somehow have liked that; by which remark I am recalled to the special treasure of the desecrated temple, those extraordinarily strong and brave frescoes of Luca Signorelli and Sodoma that adorn, in admirable conditions, several stretches of cloister wall. These creations in a manner took care of themselves; aided by the blue of the sky above the cloister-court they glowed, they insistently lived; I remember the frigid prowl through all the rest of the bareness, including that of the big dishonoured church and that even of the Abbate's abysmally resigned testimony to his mere human and personal situation; and then, with such a force of contrast and effect of relief, the great sheltered sun-flares and colour-patches of scenic composition and design where a couple of hands centuries ago turned to dust had so wrought the defiant miracle of life and beauty that the effect is of a garden blooming among ruins. Discredited somehow, since they all would, the destroyers themselves, the ancient piety, the general spirit and intention, but still bright and assured and sublime – practically, enviably immortal – the other, the still subtler, the all æsthetic good faith.

1909.

Piazza Signoria, Florence, by C. Canella

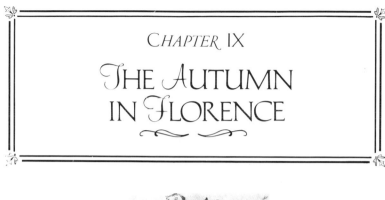

CHAPTER IX
THE AUTUMN IN FLORENCE

The Arno, Florence

LORENCE TOO HAS ITS "SEASON", not less than Rome, and I have been rejoicing for the past six weeks in the fact that this comparatively crowded parenthesis hasn't yet been opened. Coming here in the first days of October I found the summer still in almost unmenaced possession, and ever since, till within a day or two, the weight of its hand has been sensible. Properly enough, as the city of flowers, Florence mingles the elements most artfully in the spring – during the divine crescendo of March and April, the weeks when six months of steady shiver have still not shaken New York and Boston free of the long Polar reach. But the very quality of the decline of the year as we at present here feel it suits peculiarly the mood in which an undiscourageable gatherer of the sense of things, or taster at least of "charm", moves through these many-memoried streets and galleries and churches. Old things, old places, old people, or at least old races, ever strike us as giving out their secrets most freely in such moist, grey, melancholy days as have formed the complexion of the past fortnight. With Christmas arrives the opera, the only opera worth speaking of – which indeed often means in Florence the only opera worth talking through; the gaiety, the gossip, the reminders in fine of the cosmopolite and watering-place character to which the city of the Medici long ago began to bend her antique temper. Meanwhile it is pleasant enough for the tasters of charm, as I say, and for the makers of invidious distinctions, that the Americans haven't all arrived, however many may be on their way, and that the weather has a monotonous overcast softness in which, apparently, aimless contemplation grows less and less ashamed. There is no crush along the Cascine, as on the sunny days of winter, and the Arno, wandering away toward the mountains in the haze, seems as shy of being looked at as a good picture in a bad light. No light, to my eyes, nevertheless, could be better than this, which reaches us, all strained and filtered and refined, exquisitely coloured and even a bit conspicuously sophisticated, through the heavy air of the past that hangs about the place forever.

I first knew Florence early enough, I am happy to say, to have heard the change for the worse, the taint of the modern order, bitterly lamented by old haunters, admirers, lovers – those qualified to present a picture of the conditions prevailing under the good old Grand-Dukes, the two last of their line in especial, that, for its blest reflection of sweetness and mildness and cheapness and ease, of every immediate boon in life to be enjoyed quite for nothing, could but draw tears from belated listeners. Some of these survivors from the golden age – just the beauty of which indeed was in the gold, of sorts, that it poured into your lap, and not in the least in its own importunity on that head – have needfully lingered on, have seen the ancient walls pulled down and the compact and belted mass of which the Piazza della Signoria was the immemorial centre expand, under the treatment of enterprising syndics, into an ungirdled organism of the type, as they viciously say, of Chicago; one of those places of which, as their grace of a circumference is nowhere, the dignity of a centre can no longer be predicated. Florence loses itself to-day in dusty boulevards and smart *beaux quartiers*, such as Napoleon III and Baron Haussmann were to set the fashion of to a too mediæval Europe – with the effect of some precious page of antique text swallowed up in a marginal commentary that smacks of the style of the newspaper. So much for what has happened on this side of that line of demarcation which, by an odd law, makes us, with our preference for what we are pleased to call the picturesque, object to such occurrences even *as* occurrences. The real truth is that objections are too vain, and that he would be too rude a critic here, just now, who shouldn't be in the humour to take the thick with the thin and to try at least to read something of the old soul into the new forms.

There is something to be said moreover for your liking a city (once it's a question of your actively circulating) to pretend to comfort you more by its extent than by its limits; in addition to which Florence was anciently, was in her palmy days peculiarly, a daughter of change and movement and variety, of shifting moods, policies and *régimes* – just as the Florentine character, as we have it to-day, is a character that takes all things easily for having seen so many come and go. It saw the national capital, a few years since, arrive and sit down by the Arno, and took no further thought than sufficed for the day; then it saw the odd visitor depart and whistled her cheerfully on her way to Rome. The new boulevards of the Sindaco Peruzzi come, it may be said, but they don't go; which, after all, it isn't from the æsthetic point of view strictly necessary they should. A part of the essential amiability of Florence, of her genius for making you take to your favour on easy terms everything that in any way belongs to her, is that she has already flung an element of her grace over all their undried mortar and plaster. Such modern arrangements as the Piazza d'Azeglio and the *viale* or Avenue of the Princess Margaret please not a little, I think – for what

Piazza, Florence

177

Florence from Fiesole

they are! – and do so even in a degree, by some fine local privilege, just because they are Florentine. The afternoon lights rest on them as if to thank them for not being worse, and their vistas are liberal where they look toward the hills. They carry you close to these admirable elevations, which hang over Florence on all sides, and if in the foreground your sense is a trifle perplexed by the white pavements dotted here and there with a policeman or a nursemaid, you have only to reach beyond and see Fiesole turn to violet, on its ample eminence, from the effect of the opposite sunset.

Facing again then to Florence proper you have local colour enough and to spare – which you enjoy the more, doubtless, from standing off to get your light and your point of view. The elder streets abutting on all this newness bore away into the heart of the city in narrow, dusky perspectives that quite refine, in certain places, by an art of their own, on the romantic appeal. There are temporal and other accidents thanks to which, as you pause to look down them and to penetrate the deepening shadows that accompany their retreat, they resemble little corridors leading out from the past, mystical like the ladder in Jacob's dream; so that when you see a single figure advance and draw nearer you are half afraid to wait till it arrives – it must be too much of the nature of a ghost, a messenger from an underworld. However this may be, a place paved with such great mosaics of slabs and lined with palaces of so massive a tradition, structures which, in their large dependence on pure proportion for interest and beauty, reproduce more than other modern styles the simple nobleness of Greek architecture, must ever have placed dignity first in the scale of invoked effect and laid up no great treasure of that ragged picturesqueness – the picturesqueness of large poverty – on which we feast our idle eyes at Rome and Naples. Except in the unfinished fronts of the churches, which, however, unfortunately, are mere ugly blankness, one finds less of the poetry of ancient over-use, or in other words less romantic southern shabbiness, than in most Italian cities. At two or three points, none the less, this sinister grace exists in perfection – just such perfection as so often proves that what is literally hideous may be constructively delightful and what is intrinsically tragic play on the finest chords of appreciation. On the north side of the Arno, between Ponte Vecchio and Ponte Santa Trinità, is a row of immemorial houses that back on the river, in whose yellow flood they bathe their sore old feet. Anything more battered

Map of Florence from Baedeker's Italy *(1892)*

and befouled, more cracked and disjointed, dirtier, drearier, poorer, it would be impossible to conceive. They look as if fifty years ago the liquid mud had risen over their chimneys and then subsided again and left them coated forever with its unsightly slime. And yet forsooth, because the river is yellow, and the light is yellow, and here and there, elsewhere, some mellow mouldering surface, some hint of colour, some accident of atmosphere, takes up the foolish tale and repeats the note – because, in short, it is Florence, it is Italy, and the fond appraiser, the infatuated alien, may have had in his eyes, at birth and afterwards, the micaceous sparkle of brown-stone fronts no more interesting than so much sand-paper, these miserable dwellings, instead of suggesting mental invocations to an enterprising board of health, simply create their own standard of felicity and shamelessly live in it. Lately, during the misty autumn nights, the moon has shone on them faintly and refined their shabbiness away into something ineffably strange and spectral. The turbid stream sweeps along without a sound, and the pale tenements hang above it like a vague miasmatic exhalation. The dimmest back-scene at the opera, when the tenor is singing his sweetest, seems hardly to belong to a world more detached from responsibility.

What it is that infuses so rich an interest into the general charm is difficult to say in a few words; yet as we wander hither and thither in quest of sacred canvas and immortal bronze and stone we still feel the genius of the place hang about. Two industrious English ladies, the Misses Horner, have lately published a couple of volumes of "Walks" by the Arno-side, and their work is a long enumeration of great artistic deeds. These things remain for the most part in sound preservation, and, as the weeks go by and you spend a constant portion of your days among them the sense of one of the happiest periods of human Taste – to put it only at that – settles upon your spirit. It was not long; it lasted, in its splendour, for less than a century; but it has stored away in the palaces and churches of Florence a heritage of beauty that these three enjoying centuries since haven't yet exhausted. This forms a clear intellectual atmosphere into which you may turn aside from the modern world and fill your lungs as with the breath of a forgotten creed. The memorials of the past here address us moreover with a friendliness, win us by we scarcely know what sociability, what equal amenity, that we scarce find matched in other great æsthetically endowed communities and periods. Venice, with her old palaces cracking under the weight of their treasures, is, in her influence, insupportably sad; Athens, with her maimed marbles and dishonoured memories, transmutes the consciousness of sensitive observers, I am told, into a chronic heartache; but in one's impression of old Florence the abiding felicity, the sense of saving sanity, of something sound and human, predominates, offering you a medium still conceivable for life. The reason of this is partly, no doubt, the "sympathetic" nature, the temperate joy, of Florentine art in general – putting the sole Dante, greatest of literary artists, aside; partly the tenderness of time, in its lapse, which, save in a few cases, has been as sparing of injury as if it knew that when it should have dimmed and corroded these charming things it would have nothing so sweet again for its tooth to feed on. If the beautiful Ghirlandaios and Lippis are fading this generation will never know it. The large Fra Angelico in the Academy is as clear and keen as if the good old monk stood there wiping his brushes; the colours seem to *sing*, as it were, like new-fledged birds in June. Nothing is more characteristic of early Tuscan art than the high-reliefs of Luca della Robbia; yet there isn't one of them that, except for the unique mixture of freshness with its wisdom, of candour with its expertness, mightn't have been modelled yesterday.

But perhaps the best image of the absence of stale melancholy or wasted splendour, of the positive presence of what I have called temperate joy, in the Florentine impression and genius, is the bell-tower of Giotto, which rises beside the Cathedral. No beholder of it will have forgotten how straight and slender it stands there, how strangely rich in the common street, plated with coloured marble patterns, and yet so far from simple or severe in design that we easily wonder how its author, the painter of exclusively and portentously grave little pictures, should have fashioned a building which in the way of elaborate elegance, of the true play of taste, leaves a jealous modern criticism nothing to miss. Nothing can be imagined at once more lightly and more pointedly fanciful; it might have been handed over to the city, as it stands, by some Oriental genie tired of too much detail. Yet for all that suggestion it seems of no particular time – not grey and hoary like a Gothic steeple, not cracked and despoiled like a Greek temple; its marbles shining so little less freshly than when they were laid together, and the sunset lighting up its cornice with such a friendly radiance, that you come at last to regard it simply as the graceful, indestructible soul of the place made visible. The Cathedral, externally, for all its solemn hugeness, strikes the same note of would-be reasoned elegance and cheer; it has conventional grandeur, of course, but a grandeur so frank and ingenuous even in its *parti-pris*. It has seen so much, and outlived so much, and served so many sad purposes, and yet remains in aspect so full of the fine Tuscan geniality, the feeling for life, one may almost say the feeling for amusement, that inspired it. Its vast many-coloured marble walls become at any rate, with this, the friendliest note of all Florence; there is an unfailing charm in walking past them while they lift their great acres of geometrical mosaic higher in the air than you have time or other occasion to look. You greet them from the deep street as you greet the side of a mountain when you move in the gorge – not twisting back your head to keep looking at the top, but content with the minor accidents, the nestling hollows and soft cloud-shadows, the general protection of the valley.

Florence is richer in pictures than we really know till we have begun to look for them in outlying corners. Then, here and there, one comes upon lurking values and hidden gems that it quite seems one might as a good New Yorker quietly "bag" for the aspiring Museum of that city without their being missed. The Pitti Palace is of course a collection of masterpieces; they jostle each other in their splendour, they perhaps even, in their merciless multitude, rather fatigue our admiration. The Uffizi is almost as fine a show, and together with that long serpentine artery which crosses the Arno and connects them, making you ask yourself, whichever way you take it, what goal can be grand enough to crown such a journey, they form the great central treasure-chamber of the town. But I have been neglecting them of late for love of the Academy, where there are fewer copyists and tourists, above all fewer pictorial lions, those whose roar is heard from afar and who strike us as expecting overmuch to have it their own way in the jungle. The pictures at the Academy are all, rather, doves – the whole impression is less pompously

Piazza dell' Annunciata, Florence

Florence, by Oswald Achenbach

tropical. Selection still leaves one too much to say, but I noted here, on my last occasion, an enchanting Botticelli so obscurely hung, in one of the smaller rooms, that I scarce knew whether most to enjoy or to resent its relegation. Placed, in a mean black frame, where you wouldn't have looked for a masterpiece, it yet gave out to a good glass every characteristic of one. Representing as it does the walk of Tobias with the angel, there are really parts of it that an angel might have painted; but I doubt whether it is observed by half-a-dozen persons a year. That was my excuse for my wanting to know, on the spot, though doubtless all sophistically, what dishonour, could the transfer be artfully accomplished, a strong American light and a brave gilded frame would, comparatively speaking, do it. There and then it would shine with the intense authority that we claim for the fairest things – would exhale its wondrous beauty as a sovereign example. What it comes to is that this master is the most interesting of a great band – the only Florentine save Leonardo and Michael in whom the impulse was original and the invention rare.

His imagination is of things strange, subtle and complicated – things it at first strikes us that we moderns have reason to know, and that it has taken us all the ages to learn; so that we permit ourselves to wonder how a "primitive" could come by them. We soon enough reflect, however, that we ourselves have come by them almost only *through* him, exquisite spirit that he was, and that when we enjoy, or at least when we encounter, in our William Morrises, in our Rossettis and Burne-Joneses, the note of the haunted or over-charged consciousness, we are but treated, with other matters, to repeated doses of diluted Botticelli. He practically set with his own hand almost all the copies to almost all our so-called pre-Raphaelites, earlier and later, near and remote.

Let us at the same time, none the less, never fail of response to the great Florentine geniality at large. Fra Angelico, Filippo Lippi, Ghirlandaio, were not "subtly" imaginative, were not even riotously so; but what other three were ever more gladly observant, more vividly and richly true? If there should some time be a weeding out of the world's possessions the best works of the early Florentines will certainly be counted among the

Palazzo Gandi, Florence

flowers. With the ripest performances of the Venetians – by which I don't mean the over-ripe – we can but take them for the most valuable things in the history of art. Heaven forbid we should be narrowed down to a cruel choice; but if it came to a question of keeping or losing between half-a-dozen Raphaels and half-a-dozen things it would be a joy to pick out at the Academy, I fear that, for myself, the memory of the Transfiguration, or indeed of the other Roman relics of the painter wouldn't save the Raphaels. And yet this was so far from the opinion of a patient artist whom I saw the other day copying the finest of Ghirlandaios – a beautiful Adoration of the Kings at the Hospital of the Innocenti. Here was another sample of the buried art-wealth of Florence. It hangs in an obscure chapel, far aloft, behind an altar, and though now and then a stray tourist wanders in and puzzles awhile over the vaguely-glowing forms, the picture is never really seen and enjoyed. I found an aged Frenchman of modest mien perched on a little platform beneath it, behind a great hedge of altar-candlesticks, with an admirable copy all completed. The difficulties of his task had been well-nigh insuperable, and his performance seemed to me a real feat of magic. He could scarcely move or turn, and could find room for his canvas but by rolling it together and painting a small piece at a time, so that he never enjoyed a view of his *ensemble*. The original is gorgeous with colour and bewildering with decorative detail, but not a gleam of the painter's crimson was wanting, not a curl in his gold arabesques. It seemed to me that if I had copied a Ghirlandaio in such conditions I would at least maintain for my own credit that he was the first painter in the world. "Very good of its kind," said the weary old man with a shrug of reply for my raptures; "but oh how far short of Raphael!" However that may be, if the reader chances to observe this consummate copy in the so commendable Museum devoted in Paris to such works, let him stop before it with a due reverence; it is one of the patient things of art. Seeing it wrought there, in its dusky nook, under such scant convenience, I found no bar in the painter's foreignness to a thrilled sense that the old art-life of Florence isn't yet extinct. It still at least works spells and almost miracles.

1873.

Une Fonte à Livorno, by A. Belimbau

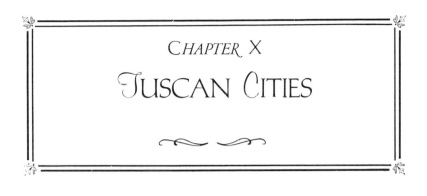

CHAPTER X
TUSCAN CITIES

The Loggia, Lucca

HE CITIES I REFER TO are Leghorn, Pisa, Lucca and Pistoia, among which I have been spending the last few days. The most striking fact as to Leghorn, it must be conceded at the outset, is that, being in Tuscany, it should be so scantily Tuscan. The traveller curious in local colour must content himself with the deep blue expanse of the Mediterranean. The streets, away from the docks, are modern, genteel and rectangular; Liverpool might acknowledge them if it weren't for their clean-coloured, sun-bleached stucco. They are the offspring of the new industry which is death to the old idleness. Of interesting architecture, fruit of the old idleness or at least of the old leisure, Leghorn is singularly destitute. It has neither a church worth one's attention, nor a municipal palace, nor a museum, and it may claim the distinction, unique in Italy, of being the city of no pictures. In a shabby corner near the docks stands a statue of one of the elder Grand-Dukes of Tuscany, appealing to posterity on grounds now vague – chiefly that of having placed certain Moors under tribute. Four colossal negroes, in very bad bronze, are chained to the base of the monument, which forms with their assistance a sufficiently fantastic group; but to patronise the arts is not the line of the Livornese, and for want of the slender annuity which would keep its precinct sacred this curious memorial is buried in dockyard rubbish. I must add that on the other hand there is a very well-conditioned and, in attitude and gesture, extremely natural and familiar statue of Cavour in one of the city squares, and in another a couple of effigies of recent Grand-Dukes, represented, that is dressed, or rather undressed, in the character of heroes of Plutarch. Leghorn is a city of magnificent spaces, and it was so long a journey from the sidewalk to the pedestal of these images that I never took the time to go and read the inscriptions. And in truth, vaguely, I bore the originals a grudge, and wished to know as little about them as possible; for it seemed to me that as *patres patriæ*, in their degree, they might have decreed that the great blank, ochre-faced piazza should be a trifle less ugly. There is a distinct amenity, however, in any experience of Italy almost anywhere, and I shall probably in the future not be above sparing a light regret to several of the hours of which the one I speak of was composed. I shall remember a large cool bourgeois villa in the garden of a noiseless suburb – a middle-aged Villa Franco (I owe it as a genial pleasant *pension* the tribute of recognition), roomy and stony, as an Italian villa should be. I shall remember that, as I sat in the garden and, looking up from my book, saw through a gap in the shrubbery the red house-tiles against the deep blue sky and the grey underside of the ilex-leaves turned up by the Mediterranean breeze, it was all still quite Tuscany, if Tuscany in the minor key.

If you should naturally desire, in such conditions, a higher intensity, you have but to proceed, by a very short journey, to Pisa – where, for that matter, you will seem to yourself to have hung about a good deal already, and from an early age. Few of us can have had a childhood so unblessed by contact with the arts as that one of its occasional diversions shan't have been a puzzled scrutiny of some alabaster model of the Leaning Tower under a glass cover in a back-parlour. Pisa and its monuments have, in other words, been industriously vulgarised, but it is astonishing how well they have survived the process. The charm of the place is in fact of a high order and but partially foreshadowed by the famous crookedness of its campanile. I felt it irresistibly and yet almost inexpressibly the other afternoon, as I made my way to the classic corner of the city through the warm drowsy air which nervous people come to inhale as a sedative. I was with an invalid companion who had had no sleep to speak of for a fortnight. "Ah! stop the carriage," she sighed, or yawned, as I could feel, deliciously, "in the shadow of this old slumbering palazzo, and let me sit here and close my eyes, and taste for an hour of oblivion." Once strolling over the grass, however, out of which the quartette of marble monuments rises, we awaked responsively enough to the present hour. Most people remember the happy remark of tasteful, old-fashioned Forsyth (who touched a hundred other points in his "Italy" scarce less happily) as to the fact that the four famous objects are "fortunate alike in their society and their solitude." It must be admitted that they are more fortunate in their society than we felt ourselves to be in ours; for the scene presented the animated appearance for which, on any fine spring day, all the choicest haunts of ancient quietude in Italy are becoming yearly more remarkable. There were clamorous beggars at all the sculptured portals, and bait for beggars, in abundance, trailing in and out of them under convoy of loquacious ciceroni. I forget just how I apportioned the responsibility of intrusion, for it was not long before fellow-tourists and fellow-countrymen became a vague, deadened, muffled presence, that of the dentist's last words when he is giving you ether. They suffered mystic disintegration in the dense, bright, tranquil air, so charged with its own messages. The Cathedral and its companions are fortunate indeed in everything – fortunate in the spacious angle of grey old city-wall which folds about them in their sculptured elegance like a strong protecting arm; fortunate in the broad greensward which stretches from the marble base of Cathedral and cemetery to the rugged foot of the rampart; fortunate in the little vagabonds who dot the grass, plucking daisies and exchanging Italian cries; fortunate in the pale-gold tone to which time and the soft sea-damp have mellowed and darkened their marble plates; fortunate, above all, in an indescribable grace of grouping, half hazard, half design, which insures them, in one's memory of things admired, very much the same isolated corner that they occupy in the charming city.

Of the smaller cathedrals of Italy I know none I prefer to that of

The Cathedral, Pisa

Pisa; none that, on a moderate scale, produces more the impression of a great church. It has without so modest a measurability, represents so clean and compact a mass, that you are startled when you cross the threshold at the apparent space it encloses. An architect of genius, for all that he works with colossal blocks and cumbrous pillars, is certainly the most cunning of conjurors. The front of the Duomo is a small pyramidal screen, covered with delicate carvings and chasings, distributed over a series of short columns upholding narrow arches. It might be a sought imitation of goldsmith's work in stone, and the area covered is apparently so small that extreme fineness had been prescribed. How is it therefore that on the inner side of this facade the wall should appear to rise to a splendid height and to support one end of a ceiling as remote in its gilded grandeur, one could almost fancy, as that of St Peter's; how it is that the nave should stretch away in such solemn vastness, the shallow transepts emphasise the grand impression and the apse of the choir hollow itself out like a dusky cavern fretted with golden stalactites, is all matter for exposition by a keener architectural analyst than I. To sit somewhere against a pillar where the vista is large and the incidents cluster richly, and vaguely revolve these mysteries without answering them, is the best of one's usual enjoyment of a great church. It takes no deep sounding to conclude indeed that a gigantic Byzantine Christ in mosaic, on the concave roof of the choir, contributes largely to the particular impression here as of very old and choice and original and individual things. It has even more of stiff solemnity than is common to works of its school, and prompts to more wonder than ever on the nature of the human mind at a time when such unlovely shapes could satisfy its conception of holiness. Truly pathetic is the fate of these huge mosaic idols, thanks to the change that has overtaken our manner of acceptance of them. Strong the contrast between the original sublimity of their pretensions and the way in which they flatter that free sense of the grotesque which the modern imagination has smuggled even into the appreciation of religious forms. They were meant to yield scarcely to the Deity itself in grandeur, but the only part they play now is to stare helplessly at our critical, our æsthetic patronage of them. The spiritual refinement marking the hither end of a progress hadn't, however, to wait for us to signalise it; it found expression three centuries ago in the beautiful specimen of the painter Sodoma on the wall of the choir. This latter, a small Sacrifice of Isaac, is one of the best examples of its exquisite author, and perhaps, as chance has it, the most perfect opposition that could be found in the way of the range of taste to the effect of the great mosaic. There are many painters more powerful than Sodoma –

painters who, like the author of the mosaic, attempted and compassed grandeur; but none has a more persuasive grace, none more than he was to sift and chasten a conception till it should affect one with the sweetness of a perfectly distilled perfume.

Of the patient successive efforts of painting to arrive at the supreme refinement of such a work as the Sodoma the Campo Santo hard by offers a most interesting memorial. It presents a long, blank marble wall to the relative profaneness of the Cathedral close, but within it is a perfect treasure-house of art. This quadrangular defence surrounds an open court where weeds and wild roses are tangled together and a sunny stillness seems to rest consentingly, as if Nature had been won to consciousness of the precious relics committed to her. Something in the quality of the place recalls the collegiate cloisters of Oxford, but it must be added that this is the handsomest compliment to that seat of learning. The open arches of the quadrangles of Magdalen and Christ Church are not of mellow Carrara marble, nor do they offer to sight columns, slim and elegant, that seem to frame the unglazed windows of a cathedral. To be buried in the Campo Santo of Pisa, I may however further qualify, you need only be, or to have more or less anciently been, illustrious, and there is a liberal allowance both as to the character and degree of your fame. The most obtrusive object in one of the long vistas is a most complicated monument to Madame Catalani, the singer, recently erected by her possibly too-appreciative heirs. The wide pavement is a mosaic of sepulchral slabs, and the walls, below the base of the paling frescoes, are encrusted with inscriptions and encumbered with urns and antique sarcophagi. The place is at once a cemetery and a museum, and its especial charm is its strange mixture of the active and the passive, of art and rest, of life and death. Originally its walls were one vast continuity of closely pressed frescoes; but now the great capricious scars and stains have come to outnumber the

Church of La Spina sul Arno, Pisa

pictures, and the cemetery has grown to be a burial-place of pulverised masterpieces as well as of finished lives. The fragments of painting that remain are fortunately the best; for one is safe in believing that a host of undimmed neighbours would distract but little from the two great works of Orcagna. Most people know the "Triumph of Death" and the "Last Judgment" from descriptions and engravings; but to measure the possible good faith of imitative art one must stand there and see the painter's howling potentates dragged into hell in all the vividness of his bright hard colouring; see his feudal courtiers, on their palfreys, hold their noses at what they are so fast coming to; see his great Christ, in judgement, refuse forgiveness with a gesture commanding enough, really inhuman enough, to make virtue merciless forever. The charge that Michael Angelo borrowed his cursing Saviour from this great figure of Orcagna is more valid than most accusations of plagiarism; but of the two figures one at least could be spared. For direct, triumphant expressiveness these two superb frescoes have probably never been surpassed. The painter aims at no very delicate meanings, but he drives certain gross ones home so effectively that for a parallel to his process one must look to the art of the actor, the emphasising "point"-making mime. Some of his female figures are superb – they represent creatures of a formidable temperament.

There are charming women, however, on the other side of the cloister – in the beautiful frescoes of Benozzo Gozzoli. If Orcagna's work was appointed to survive the ravage of time it is a happy chance that it should be balanced by a group of performances of such a different temper. The contrast is the more striking that in subject the inspiration of both painters is strictly, even though superficially, theological. But Benozzo cares, in his theology, for nothing but the story, the scene and the drama – the chance to pile up palaces and spires in his backgrounds against pale blue skies cross-barred with pearly, fleecy clouds, and to scatter sculptured arches and shady trellises over the front, with every incident of human life going forward lightly and gracefully beneath them. Lightness and grace are the painter's great

Pisa

qualities, marking the hithermost limit of unconscious elegance, after which "style" and science and the wisdom of the serpent set in. His charm is natural fineness; a little more and we should have refinement – which is a very different thing. Like all *les délicats* of this world, as M. Renan calls them, Benozzo has suffered greatly. The space on the walls he originally covered with his Old Testament stories is immense; but his exquisite handiwork has peeled off by the acre, as one may almost say, and the latter compartments of the series are swallowed up in huge white scars, out of which a helpless head or hand peeps forth like those of creatures sinking into a quicksand. As for Pisa at large, although it is not exactly what one would call a mouldering city – for it has a certain well-aired cleanness and brightness, even in its supreme tranquillity – it affects the imagination very much in the same way as the Campo Santo. And, in truth, a city so ancient and deeply historic as Pisa is at every step but the burial-ground of a larger life than its present one. The wide empty streets, the goodly Tuscan palaces – which look as if about all of them there were a genteel private understanding, independent of placards, that they are to be let extremely cheap – the delicious relaxing air, the full-flowing yellow river, the lounging Pisani, smelling, metaphorically, their poppy-flowers, seemed to me all so many admonitions to resignation and oblivion. And this is what I mean by saying that the charm of Pisa (apart from its cluster of monuments) is a charm of a high order. The architecture has but a modest dignity; the lions are few; there are no fixed points for stopping and gaping. And yet the impression is profound; the charm is a moral charm. If I were ever to be incurably disappointed in life, if I had lost my health, my money, or my friends, if I were resigned forevermore to pitching my expectations in a minor key, I should go and invoke the Pisan peace. Its quietude would seem something more than a stillness – a hush. Pisa may be a dull place to live in, but it's an ideal place to wait for death.

Nothing could be more charming than the country between Pisa and Lucca – unless possibly the country between Lucca and Pistoia. If Pisa is dead Tuscany Lucca is Tuscany still living and enjoying, desiring and intending. The town is a charming mixture of antique "character" and modern inconsequence; and not only the town, but the country – the blooming romantic country which you admire from the famous promenade on the city-wall. The wall is of superbly solid

West Porch of Cathedral, Pistoia

and intensely "toned" brickwork and of extraordinary breadth, and its summit, planted with goodly trees and swelling here and there into bastions and outworks and little open gardens, surrounds the city with a circular lounging-place of a splendid dignity. This well-kept, shady, ivy-grown rampart reminded me of certain mossy corners of England; but it looks away to a prospect of more than English loveliness – a broad green plain where the summer yields a double crop of grain, and a circle of bright blue mountains speckled with high-hung convents and profiled castles and nestling villas, and traversed by valleys of a deeper and duskier blue. In one of the deepest and shadiest of these recesses one of the most "sympathetic" of small watering-places is hidden away yet awhile longer from easy invasion – the Baths to which Lucca has lent its name. Lucca is pre-eminently a city of churches; ecclesiastical architecture being indeed the only one of the arts to which it seems to have given attention. There are curious bits of domestic architecture, but no great palaces, and no importunate frequency of pictures. The Cathedral, however, sums up the merits of its companions and is a singularly noble and interesting church. Its peculiar boast is a wonderful inlaid front, on which horses and hounds and hunted beasts are lavishly figured in black marble over a white ground. What I chiefly appreciated in the grey solemnity of the nave and transepts was the superb effect of certain second-storey Gothic arches – those which rest on the pavement being Lombard. These arches are delicate and slender, like those of the cloister at Pisa, and they play their part in the dusky upper air with real sublimity.

At Pistoia there is of course a Cathedral, and there is nothing unexpected in its being, externally at least, highly impressive; in its having a grand campanile at its door, a gaudy baptistery, in alternate layers of black and white marble, across the way, and a stately civic palace on either side. But even had I the space to do otherwise I should prefer to speak less of the particular objects of interest in the place than of the pleasure I found it to lounge away in the empty streets the quiet hours of a warm afternoon. To say where I lingered longest would be to tell of a little square before the hospital, out of which you look up at the beautiful frieze in coloured earthenware by the brothers Della Robbia, which runs across the front of the building. It represents the seven orthodox offices of charity and, with its brilliant blues and yellows and its tender expressiveness, brightens up amazingly, to the sense and soul, this little grey corner of the mediæval city. Pistoia is still mediæval. How grass-grown it seemed, how full of idle vistas and melancholy nooks! If nothing was supremely wonderful, everything was delicious.

1874.

CHAPTER XI

RAVENNA

San Apollinare Nuovo, Ravenna

 WRITE THESE LINES on a cold Swiss mountain-top, shut in by an intense white mist from any glimpse of the under-world of lovely Italy; but as I jotted down the other day in the ancient capital of Honorius and Theodoric the few notes of which they are composed, I let the original date stand for local colour's sake. Its mere look, as I transcribe it, emits a grateful glow in the midst of the Alpine rawness, and gives a depressed imagination something tangible to grasp while awaiting the return of fine weather. For Ravenna was glowing, less than a week since, as I edged along the narrow strip of shadow binding one side of the empty, white streets. After a long, chill spring the summer this year descended upon Italy with a sudden jump and an ominous hot breath. I stole away from Florence in the night, and even on top of the Apennines, under the dull starlight and in the rushing train, one could but sit and pant perspiringly.

At Bologna I found a festa, or rather two festas, a civil and a religious, going on in mutual mistrust and disparagement. The civil, that of the Statuto, was the one fully national Italian holiday as by law established – the day that signalises everywhere over the land at once its achieved and hard-won unification; the religious was a jubilee of certain local churches. The latter is observed by the Bolognese parishes in couples, and comes round for each couple but once in ten years – an arrangement by which the faithful at large insure themselves a liberal recurrence of expensive processions. It wasn't my business to distinguish the sheep from the goats, the pious from the profane, the prayers from the scoffers; it was enough that, melting together under the scorching sun, they filled the admirably solid city with a flood of spectacular life. The combination at one point was really dramatic. While a long procession of priests and young virgins in white veils, bearing tapers, marshalled itself in one of the streets, a review of the King's troops went forward outside the town. On its return a large detachment of cavalry passed across the space where the incense was burning, the pictured banners swaying and the litany being droned, and checked the advance of the little ecclesiastical troop. The long vista of the street, between the porticoes, was festooned with garlands and scarlet and tinsel; the robes and crosses and canopies of the priests, the clouds of perfumed smoke and the white veils of the maidens, were resolved by the hot bright air into a gorgeous medley of colour, across which the mounted soldiers rattled and flashed as if it had been a conquering army trampling on an embassy of propitiation. It was, to tell the truth, the first time an Italian festa had really exhibited to my eyes the genial glow and the romantic particulars promised by song and story; and I confess that those eyes found more pleasure in it than they were to find an hour later in the picturesque on canvas as one observes it in the Pinacoteca. I found myself scowling most unmercifully at Guido and Domenichino.

For Ravenna, however, I had nothing but smiles – grave, reflective, philosophic smiles, I hasten to add, such as accord with the historic dignity, not to say the mortal sunny sadness, of the place. I arrived there in the evening, before, even at drowsy

Baldachino, Bologna Cathedral

196

Ravenna, the festa of the Statuto had altogether put itself to bed. I immediately strolled forth from the inn, and found it sitting up awhile longer on the piazza, chiefly at the café door, listening to the band of the garrison by the light of a dozen or so of feeble tapers, fastened along the front of the palace of the Government. Before long, however, it had dispersed and departed, and I was left alone with the grey illumination and with an affable citizen whose testimony as to the manners and customs of Ravenna I had aspired to obtain. I had, borrowing confidence from prompt observation, suggested deferentially that it wasn't the liveliest place in the world, and my friend admitted that it was in fact not a seat of ardent life. But had I seen the Corso? Without seeing the Corso one didn't exhaust the possibilities. The Corso of Ravenna, of a hot summer night, had an air of surprising seclusion and repose. Here and there in an upper closed window glimmered a light; my companion's footsteps and my own were the only sounds; not a creature was within sight. The suffocating air helped me to believe for a moment that I walked in the Italy of Boccaccio, hand-in-hand with the plague, through a city which had lost half its population by pestilence and the other half by flight. I turned back into my inn profoundly satisfied. This at last was the old-world dulness of a prime distillation; this at last was antiquity, history, repose.

The impression was largely confirmed and enriched on the following day; but it was obliged at an early stage of my visit to give precedence to another – the lively perception, namely, of the thinness of my saturation with Gibbon and the other sources of legend. At Ravenna the waiter at the café and the coachman who drives you to the Pine-Forest allude to Galla Placidia and Justinian as to any attractive topic of the hour; wherever you turn you encounter some fond appeal to your historic presence of mind. For myself I could only attune my spirit vaguely to so ponderous a challenge, could only feel I was breathing an air of prodigious records and relics. I conned my guide-book and looked up at the great mosaics, and then fumbled at poor Murray again for some intenser light on the court of Justinian; but I can imagine that to a visitor more intimate with the originals of the various great almond-eyed mosaic portraits in the vaults of the churches these extremely curious works of art may have a really formidable interest. I found in the place at large, by daylight, the look of a vast straggling depopulated village. The streets with hardly an exception are grass-grown, and though I walked about all day I failed to encounter a single wheeled vehicle. I remember no shop but the little establishment of an urbane photographer, whose views of the Pineta, the great legendary pine-forest just without the town, gave me an irresistible desire to seek that refuge. There was no architecture to speak of; and though there are a great many large domiciles with aristocratic names they stand cracking and baking in the sun in no very comfortable fashion. The houses have for the most part an all but rustic rudeness; they are low and featureless and shabby, as well as interspersed with high garden walls over which the long arms of tangled vines hang motionless into the stagnant streets. Here and there in all this dreariness, in some particularly silent and grassy corner, rises an old brick church with a front more or less spoiled by cheap modernisation, and a strange cylindrical campanile pierced with small arched windows and extremely suggestive of the fifth century. These churches constitute the palpable interest of Ravenna, and their own principal interest, after thirteen centuries of well-intentioned spoliation, resides in their unequalled collection of early Christian mosaics. It is an interest simple, as who should say, almost to harshness, and leads one's attention along a straight and narrow way. There are older churches in Rome, and churches which, looked at as museums, are more variously and richly informing; but in Rome you stumble at every step on some curious pagan memorial, often beautiful enough to make your thoughts wander far from the strange stiff primitive Christian forms.

Ravenna, on the other hand, began with the Church, and all her monuments and relics are harmoniously rigid. By the middle of the first century she possessed an exemplary saint, Apollinaris, a disciple of Peter, to whom her two finest places of worship are dedicated. It was to one of these, jocosely entitled the "new", that I first directed my steps. I lingered outside awhile and looked at the great red, barrel-shaped bell-towers, so rusty, so crumbling, so archaic, and yet so resolute to ring in another century or two, and then went in to the coolness, the shining marble columns, the queer old sculptured slabs and sarcophagi and the long mosaics that scintillated, under the roof, along the wall of the nave. San Apollinare Nuovo, like most of its companions, is a magazine of early Christian odds and ends; fragments of yellow marble encrusted with quaint sculptured emblems of primitive dogma;

Remains of the Palace of Theodorii and Campanile of S. Apollinare

great rough troughs, containing the bones of old bishops; episcopal chairs with the marble worn narrow by centuries of pressure from the solid episcopal person; slabs from the fronts of old pulpits, covered with carven hieroglyphics of an almost Egyptian abstruseness – lambs and stags and fishes and beasts of theological affinities even less apparent. Upon all these strange things the strange figures in the great mosaic panorama look down, with coloured cheeks and staring eyes, lifelike enough to speak to you and answer your wonderment and tell you in bad Latin of the decadence that it was in such and such a fashion they believed and worshipped. First, on each side, near the door, are houses and ships and various old landmarks of Ravenna; then begins a long procession, on one side, of twenty-two white-robed virgins and three obsequious magi, terminating in a throne bearing the Madonna and Child, surrounded by four angels; on the other side, of an equal number of male saints (twenty-five, that is) holding crowns in their hands and leading to a Saviour enthroned between angels of singular expressiveness. What it is these long slim seraphs express I cannot quite say, but they have an odd, knowing, sidelong look out of the narrow ovals of their eyes which, though not without sweetness, would certainly make me murmur a defensive prayer or so were I to find myself alone in the church towards dusk. All this work is of the latter part of the sixth century and brilliantly preserved. The gold backgrounds twinkle as if they had been inserted yesterday, and here and there a figure is executed almost too much in the modern manner to be interesting; for the charm of mosaic work is, to my sense, confined altogether to the infancy of the art. The great Christ, in the series of which I speak, is quite an elaborate picture, and yet he retains enough of the orthodox stiffness to make him impressive in the simpler, elder sense. He is clad in a purple robe, even as an emperor, his hair and beard are artfully curled, his eyebrows arched, his complexion brilliant, his whole aspect such a one as the popular mind may have attributed to Honorius or Valentinian. It is all very Byzantine, and yet I found in it much of that interest which is inseparable, to a facile imagination, from all early representations of our Lord. Practically they are no more authentic than the more or less plausible inventions of Ary Scheffer and Holman Hunt; in spite of which they borrow a certain value, factitious perhaps but irresistible, from the mere fact that they are twelve or thirteen centuries less distant from the original. It is something that this was the way the people in the sixth century imagined Jesus to have looked; the image has suffered by so many the fewer accretions. The great purple-robed monarch on the wall of Ravenna is at least a very potent and positive

Christ, and the only objection I have to make to him is that though in this character he must have had a full apportionment of divine foreknowledge he betrays no apprehension of Dr. Channing and M. Renan. If one's preference lies, for distinctness' sake, between the old plainness and the modern fantasy, one must admit that the plainness has here a very grand outline.

I spent the rest of the morning in charmed transition between the hot yellow streets and the cool grey interiors of the churches. The greyness everywhere was lighted up by the scintillation, on vault and entablature, of mosaics more or less archaic, but always brilliant and elaborate, and everywhere too by the same deep amaze of the fact that, while centuries had worn themselves away and empires risen and fallen, these little cubes of coloured glass had stuck in their allotted places and kept their freshness. I have no space for a list of the various shrines so distinguished, and, to tell the truth, my memory of them has already become a very generalised and undiscriminated record. The total aspect of the place, its sepulchral stillness, its absorbing perfume of evanescence and decay and mortality, confounds the distinctions and blurs the details. The Cathedral, which is vast and high, has been excessively modernised, and was being still more so by a lavish application of tinsel and cotton-velvet in preparation for the centenary feast of Saint Apollinaris, which befalls next month. Things on this occasion are to be done handsomely, and a fair Ravennese informed me that a single family had contributed three thousand francs towards a month's vesper-music. It seemed to me hereupon that I should like in the August twilight to wander into the quiet nave of San Appollinare, and look up at the great mosaics through the resonance of some fine chanting. I remember distinctly enough, however, the tall basilica of San Vitale, of octagonal shape, like an exchange or custom-house – modelled, I believe, upon Saint Sophia at Constantinople. It has a great span of height and a great solemnity, as well as a choir densely pictured over on arch and apse with mosaics of the time of Justinian. These are regular pictures, full of movement, gesture and perspective, and just enough sobered in hue by time to bring home their remoteness. In the middle of the church, under the great dome, sat an artist whom I envied, making at an effective angle a study of the choir and its broken lights, its decorated altar and its encrusted twinkling walls. The picture, when finished, will hang, I suppose, on the library wall of some person of taste; but even if it is much better than is probable – I didn't look at it – all his taste won't tell the owner, unless he has been there, in just what a soundless, mouldering, out-of-the-way corner of old Italy it was painted. An even better place for an artist fond of dusky architectural nooks, except that here the dusk is excessive and he would hardly be able to tell his green from his red, is the extraordinary little church of the Santi Nazaro e Celso, otherwise known as the mausoleum of Galla Placidia. This is perhaps on the whole the spot in Ravenna where the impression is of most sovereign authority and most thrilling force. It consists of a narrow low-browed cave, shaped like a Latin cross, every inch of which except the floor is covered with dense symbolic mosaics. Before you and on each side, through the thick brown light, loom three enormous barbaric sarcophagi, containing the remains of potentates of the Lower Empire. It is as if history had burrowed under ground to escape from research and you had fairly run it to earth. On the right lie the ashes of the Emperor Honorius, and in the middle those of his sister, Galla Placidia, a lady who, I believe, had great adventures. On the other side rest the bones of Constantius III. The place might be a small natural grotto lined with glimmering mineral substances, and there is something quite tremendous in being shut up so closely with these three imperial ghosts. The shadow of the great Roman name broods upon the huge sepulchres and abides forever within the narrow walls.

But still other memories hang about than those of primitive bishops and degenerate emperors. Byron lived here and Dante died here, and the tomb of the one poet and the dwelling of the other are among the advertised appeals. The grave of Dante, it must be said, is anything but Dantesque, and the whole precinct is disposed with that odd vulgarity of taste which distinguishes most modern Italian tributes to greatness. The author of *The Divine Comedy* commemorated in stucco, even in a slumbering corner of Ravenna, is not "sympathetic". Fortunately of all poets he least needs a monument, as he was pre-eminently an architect in diction and built himself his temple of fame in verses more solid than Cyclopean blocks. If Dante's tomb is not Dantesque, so neither is Byron's house Byronic, being a homely, shabby, two-storeyed dwelling, directly on the street, with as little as possible of isolation and mystery. In Byron's time it was an inn, and it is rather a curious reflection that "Cain" and the "Vision of Judgment" should have been written at an hotel. The fact supplies a commanding precedent for self-abstraction to tourists at once sentimental and literary. I must declare indeed that my acquaintance with Ravenna considerably increased my esteem for Byron and helped to renew my faith in the sincerity of his inspiration. A man so much *de son temps* as the author

Dante's Tomb, Ravenna

of the above-named and other pieces can have spent two long years in this stagnant city only by the help of taking a great deal of disinterested pleasure in his own genius. He had indeed a notable pastime – the various churches are adorned with monuments of ancestral Guicciolis – but it is none the less obvious that Ravenna, fifty years ago, would have been an intolerably dull residence to a foreigner of distinction unequipped with intellectual resources. The hour one spends with Byron's memory then is almost compassionate. After all, one says to one's self as one turns away from the grandiloquent little slab in front of his house and looks down the deadly provincial vista of the empty, sunny street, the author of so many superb stanzas asked less from the world than he gave it. One of his diversions was to ride in the Pineta, which, beginning a couple of miles from the city, extends some twenty-five miles along the sands of the Adriatic. I drove out to it for Byron's sake, and Dante's, and Boccaccio's, all of whom have interwoven it with their fictions, and for that of a possible whiff of coolness from the sea. Between the city and the forest, in the midst of malarious rice-swamps, stands the finest of the Ravennese churches, the stately temple of San Appollinare in Classe. The Emperor Augustus constructed hereabouts a harbour for fleets, which the ages have choked up, and which survives only in the title of this ancient church. Its extreme loneliness makes it doubly impressive. They opened the great doors for me, and let a shaft of heated air go wander up the beautiful nave between the twenty-four lustrous, pearly columns of cipollino marble, and mount the wide staircase of the choir and spend itself beneath the mosaics of the vault. I passed a memorable half-hour sitting in this wave of tempered light, looking down the cool grey avenue of the nave, out of the open door, at the vivid green swamps, and listening to the melancholy stillness. I rambled for an hour in the Wood of Associations, between the tall smooth, silvery stems of the pines, and beside a creek which led me to the outer edge of the wood and a view of white sails, gleaming and gliding behind the sand-hills. It was infinitely, it was nobly "quaint", but, as the trees stand at wide intervals and bear far aloft in the blue air but a little parasol of foliage, I suppose that, of a glaring summer day, the forest itself was only the more characteristic of its clime and country for being perfectly shadeless.

1873.

CHAPTER XII

THE SAINT'S AFTERNOON AND OTHERS

Terracina

EFORE AND ABOVE ALL was the sense that, with the narrow limits of past adventure, I had never yet had such an impression of what the summer could be in the south or the south in the summer; but I promptly found it, for the occasion, a good fortune that my terms of comparison were restricted. It was really something, at a time when the stride of the traveller had become as long as it was easy, when the seven-league boots positively hung, for frequent use, in the closet of the most sedentary, to have kept one's self so innocent of strange horizons that the Bay of Naples in June might still seem quite final. That picture struck me – a particular corner of it at least, and for many reasons – as the last word; and it is this last word that comes back to me, after a short interval, in a green, grey northern nook, and offers me again its warm, bright golden meaning before it also inevitably catches the chill. Too precious, surely, for us not to suffer it to help us as it may is the faculty of putting together again in an order the sharp minutes and hours that the wave of time has been as ready to pass over as the salt sea to wipe out the letters and words your stick has traced in the sand. Let me, at any rate, recover a sufficient number of such signs to make a sort of sense.

I

CAPRI

Far aloft on the great rock was pitched, as the first note, and indeed the highest, of the wondrous concert, the amazing creation of the friend who had offered me hospitality, and whom, more almost than I had ever envied any one anything, I envied the privilege of being able to reward a heated, artless pilgrim with a revelation of effects so incalculable. There was none but the loosest prefigurement as the creaking and puffing little boat, which had conveyed me only from Sorrento, drew closer beneath the prodigious island – beautiful, horrible and haunted – that does most, of all the happy elements and accidents, towards making the Bay of Naples, for the study of composition, a lesson in the grand style. There was only, above and below, through the blue of the air and sea, a great confused shining of hot cliffs and crags and buttresses, a loss, from nearness, of the splendid couchant outline and the more comprehensive mass, and an opportunity – oh, not lost, I assure you – to sit and meditate, even moralise, on the empty deck, while a happy brotherhood of American and German tourists, including, of course, many sisters, scrambled down into little waiting, rocking tubs and, after a few strokes, popped systematically into the small orifice of the Blue Grotto. There was an appreciable moment when they were all lost to view in that receptacle, the daily "psychological" moment during which it must so often befall the recalcitrant observer on the deserted deck to find himself aware of how delightful it might be if none of them should come out again. The charm, the fascination of the idea is not a little – though also not wholly – in the fact that, as the wave rises over the aperture, there is the most encouraging appearance that they perfectly

Fuori Grotta, Naples

may not. There it is. There is no more of them. It is a case to which nature has, by the neatest stroke and with the best taste in the world, just quietly attended.

Beautiful, horrible, haunted: that is the essence of what, about itself, Capri says to you – dip again into your Tacitus and see why; and yet, while you roast a little under the awning and in the vaster shadow, it is not because the trail of Tiberius is ineffaceable that you are most uneasy. The trail of Germanicus in Italy to-day ramifies further and bites perhaps even deeper; a proof of which is, precisely, that his eclipse in the Blue Grotto is inexorably brief, that here he is popping out again, bobbing enthusiastically back and scrambling triumphantly back. The spirit, in truth, of his effective appropriation of Capri has a broad-faced candour against which there is no standing up, supremely expressive as it is of the well-known "love that kills", of Germanicus's fatal susceptibility. If I were to let myself, however, incline to *that* aspect of the serious case of Capri I should embark on strange depths. The straightness and simplicity, the classic, synthetic directness of the German passion for Italy, make this passion probably the sentiment in the world that is in the act of supplying enjoyment in the largest, sweetest mouthfuls; and there is something unsurpassably marked in the way that on this irresistible shore it has seated itself to ruminate and digest. It keeps the record in its own loud accents; it breaks out in the folds of the hills and on the crests of the crags into every manner of symptom and warning. Huge advertisements and portents stare across the bay; the acclivities bristle with breweries and "restorations" and with great ugly Gothic names. I hasten, of course, to add that some such general consciousness as this may well oppress, under any sky, at the century's end, the brooding tourist who makes himself a prey by staying anywhere, when the gong sounds, "behind". It is behind, in the track and the reaction, that he least makes out the end of it all, perceives that to visit any one's country for any one's sake is more and more to find someone quite other in possession. No one, least of all the brooder himself, is in his own.

Sorrento with Vesuvius in the Distance

II

I certainly, at any rate, felt the force of this truth when, on scaling the general rock with the eye of apprehension, I made out at a point much nearer its summit than its base the gleam of a dizzily-perched white sea-gazing front which I knew for my particular landmark and which promised so much that it would have been welcome to keep even no more than half. Let me instantly say that it kept still more than it promised, and by no means least in the way of leaving far below it the worst of the outbreak of restorations and breweries. There is a road at present to the upper village, with which till recently communication was all by rude steps cut in the rock and diminutive donkeys scrambling on the flints; one of those fine flights of construction which the great road-making "Latin races" take, wherever they prevail, without advertisement or bombast; and even while I followed along the face of the cliff its climbing consolidated ledge, I asked myself how I could think so well of it without consistently thinking better still of the temples of beer so obviously destined to enrich its terminus. The perfect answer to that was of course that the brooding tourist is never bound to be consistent. What happier law for him than this very one, precisely, when on at last alighting, high up in the blue air, to stare and gasp and almost disbelieve, he embraced little by little the beautiful truth particularly, on this occasion, reserved for himself, and took in the stupendous picture? For here above all had the thought and the hand come from far away – even from *ultima Thule*, and yet were in possession triumphant and acclaimed. Well, all one could say was that the way they had felt their opportunity, the divine conditions of the place, spoke of the advantage of some such intellectual perspective as a remote original standpoint alone perhaps can give. If what had finally, with infinite patience, passion, labour, taste, got itself done there, was like some supreme reward of an old dream of Italy, something perfect after long delays, was it not verily in *ultima Thule* that the vow would have been piously enough made and the germ tenderly enough nursed? For a certain art of asking of Italy all she can give, you must doubtless either be a rare *raffiné* or a rare genius, a sophisticated Norseman or just a Gabriele d'Annunzio.

All she can give appeared to me, assuredly, for that day and the following, gathered up and enrolled there: in the wondrous cluster and dispersal of chambers, corners, courts, galleries, arbours, arcades, long white ambulatories and vertiginous points of view. The greatest charm of all perhaps was that, thanks to the particular conditions, she seemed to abound, to overflow, in directions in which I had never yet enjoyed the chance to find her so free. The indispensable thing was therefore, in observation, in reflection, to press the opportunity hard, to recognise that as the abundance was splendid, so, by the same stroke, it was immensely suggestive. It dropped into one's lap, naturally, at the end of an hour or two, the little white flower of its formula: the brooding tourist, in other words, could only continue to brood till he had made out in a measure, as I may say, what was so wonderfully the matter with him. He was simply then in the presence, more than ever yet, of the possible poetry of the personal and social life of the south, and the fun would depend much – as occasions are fleeting – on his arriving in time, in the interest of that imagination which is his only field of sport, at adequate new notations of it. The sense of all this, his obscure and special fun in the general bravery, mixed, on the morrow, with the long, human hum of the bright, hot day and filled up the golden cup with questions and answers. The feast of St. Antony, the patron of the upper town, was the one thing in the air, and of the private beauty of the place, there on the narrow shelf, in the shining, shaded loggias and above the blue gulfs, all comers were to be made free.

III

The church-feast of its saint is of course for Anacapri, as for any self-respecting Italian town, the great day of the year, and the smaller the small "country", in native parlance, as well as the simpler, accordingly, the life, the less the chance for leakage, on other pretexts, of the stored wine of loyalty. This pure fluid, it was easy to feel overnight, had not sensibly lowered its level; so that nothing indeed, when the hour came, could well exceed the outpouring. All up and down the Sorrentine promontory the early summer happens to be the time of the saints, and I had just been witness there of a week on every day of which one might have travelled, through kicked-up clouds and other

Capri

207

View of Amalfi Harbour, by Thomas Ender

demonstrations, to a different hot holiday. There had been no bland evening that, somewhere or other, in the hills or by the sea, the white dust and the red glow didn't rise to the dim stars. Dust, perspiration, illumination, conversation – these were the regular elements. "They're very civilised," a friend who knows them as well as they can be known had said to me of the people in general; "plenty of fireworks and plenty of talk - that's all they ever want." That they were "civilised" – on the side on which they were most to show – was therefore to be the word of the whole business, and nothing could have, in fact, had more interest than the meaning that for the thirty-six hours I read into it.

Seen from below and diminished by distance, Anacapri makes scarce a sign, and the road that leads to it is not traceable over the rock; but it sits at its ease on its high, wide table, of which it covers – and with picturesque southern culture as well – as much as it finds convenient. As much of it as possible was squeezed all the morning, for St. Antony, into the piazzetta before the church, and as much more into that edifice as the robust odour mainly prevailing there allowed room for. It was the odour that was in prime occupation, and one could only wonder how so many men, women and children could cram themselves into so much smell. It was surely the smell, thick and resisting, that was least successfully to be elbowed. Meanwhile the good saint, before he could move into the air, had, among the tapers and the tinsel, the opera-music and the pulpit poundings, bravely to snuff it up. The shade outside was hot, and the sun was hot; but we waited as densely for him to come out, or rather to come "on", as the pit at the opera waits for the great tenor. There were people from below and people from the mainland and people from Pomerania and a brass band from Naples. There were other figures at the end of longer strings - strings that, some of them indeed, had pretty well given way and were now but little snippets trailing in the dust. Oh, the queer sense of the good old Capri of artistic legend, of which the name itself was, in the more benighted years – years of the contadina and the pifferaro – a bright evocation! Oh, the echo, on the spot, of each romantic tale. Oh, the loafing painters, so bad and so happy, the conscious models, the vague personalities! The "beautiful Capri girl" was of course not missed, though not perhaps so beautiful as in her ancient glamour, which none the less didn't at all exclude the probable presence – with *his* legendary light quite undimmed – of the English lord in disguise who will at no distant date marry her. The whole thing was there; one held it in one's hand.

The saint comes out at last, borne aloft in long procession and under a high canopy: a rejoicing, staring, smiling saint, openly delighted with the one happy hour in the year on which he may take his own walk. Frocked and tonsured, but not at all macerated, he holds in his hand a small wax puppet of an infant Jesus and shows him to all their friends, to whom he nods and bows: to whom, in the dazzle of the sun he literally seems to grin and wink, while his litter sways and his banners flap and every one gaily greets him. The ribbons and draperies flutter, and the white veils of the marching maidens, the music blares and the guns go off and the chants resound, and it is all as holy and merry and noisy as possible. The procession – down to the delightful little tinselled and bare-bodied babies, miniature St. Antonys irrespective of sex, led or carried by proud papas or brown grandsires – includes so much of the population that you marvel there is such a muster to look on – like the charades given in a family in which every one wants to act. But it is all indeed in a manner one house, the little high-niched island community, and nobody therefore, even in the presence of the head of it, puts on an air of solemnity. Singular and suggestive before everything else is the absence of any approach to our notion of the posture of respect, and this among people whose manners in general struck one as so good and, in particular, as so cultivated. The office of the saint – of which the festa is but the annual reaffirmation – involves not the faintest attribute of remoteness or mystery.

While, with my friend, I waited for him, we went for coolness into the second church of the place, a considerable and bedizened structure, with the rare curiosity of a wondrous pictured pavement of majolica, the garden of Eden done in large coloured tiles or squares, with every beast, bird and river, and a brave *diminuendo*, in especial, from portal to altar, of perspective, so that the animals and objects of the foreground are big and those of the successive distances differ with much propriety. Here in the sacred shade the old women were knitting, gossiping, yawning, shuffling about; here the children were romping and "larking"; here, in a manner, were the open parlour, the nursery, the kindergarten and the conversazione of the poor. This is everywhere the case by the southern sea. I remember near Sorrento a wayside chapel that seemed the scene of every function of domestic

View near the Dogana Nuova, Naples

life, including cookery and others. The odd thing is that it all appears to interfere so little with that special civilised note – the note of manners – which is so constantly touched. It is barbarous to expectorate in the temple of your faith, but that doubtless is an extreme case. Is civilisation really measured by the number of things people do respect? There would seem to be much evidence against it. The oldest societies, the societies with most traditions, are naturally not the least ironic, the least *blasées*, and the African tribes who take so many things into account that they fear to quit their huts at night are not the fine flower.

IV

Where, on the other hand, it was impossible not to feel to the full all the charming *riguardi* – to use their own good word – in which our friends *could* abound, was, that afternoon, in the extraordinary temple of art and hospitality that had been benignantly opened to me. Hither, from three o'clock to seven, all the world, from the small in particular to the smaller and the smallest, might freely flock, and here, from the first hour to the last, the huge straw-bellied flasks of purple wine were tilted for all the thirsty. They were many, the thirsty, they were three hundred, they were unending; but the draughts they drank were neither countable nor counted. This boon was dispensed in a long, pillared portico, where everything was white and light save the blue of the great bay as it played up from far below or as you took it in, between shining columns, with your elbows on the parapet. Sorrento and Vesuvius were over against you; Naples furthest off, melted, in the middle of the picture, into shimmering vagueness and innocence; and the long arm of Posilippo and the presence of the other islands, Procida, the stricken Ischia, made themselves felt to the left. The grand air of it all was in one's very nostrils and seemed to come from sources too numerous and too complex to name. It was antiquity in solution, with every brown, mild figure, every note of the old speech, every tilt of the great flask, every shadow cast by every classic fragment, adding its touch to the impression. What was the secret of the surprising amenity? – to the essence of which one got no nearer than simply by feeling afresh the old story of the deep interfusion of the present with the past. You had felt that often before, and all that could, at the most, help you now was that, more than ever yet, the

Entrance to the Grotto of Posillipo

211

present appeared to become again really classic, to sigh with strange elusive sounds of Virgil and Theocritus. Heaven only knows how little they would in truth have had to say to it, but we yield to these visions as we must, and when the imagination fairly turns in its pain almost any soft name is good enough to soothe it.

It threw such difficulties but a step back to say that the secret of the amenity was "style"; for what in the world was the secret of style, which you might have followed up and down the abysmal old Italy for so many a year only to be still vainly calling for it? Everything, at any rate, that happy afternoon, in that place of poetry, was bathed and blessed with it. The castle of Barbarossa had been on the height behind; the villa of black Tiberius had overhung the immensity from the right; the white arcades and the cool chambers offered to every step some sweet old "piece" of the past, some rounded porphyry pillar supporting a bust, some shaft of pale alabaster upholding a trellis, some mutilated marble image, some bronze that had roughly resisted. Our host, if we came to that, had the secret; but he could only express it in grand practical ways. One of them was precisely this wonderful "afternoon tea", in which tea only – *that*, good as it is, has never the note of style – was not to be found. The beauty and the poetry, at all events, were clear enough, and the extraordinary uplifted distinction; but where, in all this, it may be asked, was the element of "horror" that I have spoken of as sensible? – what obsession that was not charming could find a place in that splendid light, out of which the long summer squeezes every secret and shadow? I'm afraid I'm driven to plead that these evils were exactly in one's imagination, a predestined victim always of the cruel, the fatal historic sense. To make so much distinction, how much history had been needed! – so that the whole air still throbbed and ached with it, as with an accumulation of ghosts to whom the very climate was pitiless, condemning them to blanch for ever in the general glare and grandeur, offering them no dusky northern nook, no place at the friendly fireside, no shelter of legend or song.

Fountain in the Villa Reale, Naples

My friend had, among many original relics, in one of his white galleries – and how he understood the effect and the "value" of whiteness! – two or three reproductions of the finest bronzes of the Naples museum, the work of a small band of brothers whom he had found himself justified in trusting to deal with their problem honourably and to bring forth something as different as possible from the usual compromise of commerce. They had brought forth, in especial, for him, a copy of the young resting, slightly-panting Mercury which it was a pure delight to live with, and they had come over from Naples on St. Antony's eve, as they had done the year before, to report themselves to their patron, to keep up good relations, to drink Capri wine and to join in the tarantella. They arrived late, while we were at supper; they received their welcome and their billet, and I am not sure it was not the conversation and the beautiful manners of these obscure young men that most fixed in my mind for the time the sense of the side of life that, all around, was to come out strongest. It would be artless, no doubt, to represent them as high types of innocence or even of energy – at the same time that, weighing them against *some* ruder folk of our own race, we might perhaps have made bold to place their share even of these qualities in the scale. It was an impression indeed never infrequent in Italy, of which I might, in these days, first have felt the force during a stay, just earlier, with a friend at Sorrento – a friend who had good-naturedly "had in", on his wondrous terrace, after dinner, for the pleasure of the gaping alien, the usual local quartette, violins, guitar and flute, the musical barber, the musical tailor, saddler, joiner, humblest sons of the people and exponents of Neapolitan song. Neapolitan song, as we know, has been blown well about the world, and it is late in the day to arrive with a ravished ear for it. That, however, was scarcely at all, for me, the question: the question, on the Sorrento terrace, so high up in the cool Capri night, was of the present outlook, in the world, for the races with whom it has been a tradition, in intercourse, positively to please.

The personal civilisation, for intercourse, of the musical barber and tailor, of the pleasant young craftsmen of my other friend's company, was something that could be trusted to make the brooding tourist brood afresh – to say more to him in fact, all the rest of the second occasion, than everything else put together. The happy address, the charming expression, the indistinctive discretion, the complete eclipse, in short, of vulgarity and brutality – these things easily became among these people the supremely suggestive note, begetting a hundred hopes and fears as to the place that, with the present general turn of affairs about the globe, is being kept for them. They are perhaps what the races politically feeble have still most to contribute – but what appears to be the happy prospect for the races politically feeble? And so the afternoon waned, among the mellow marbles and the pleasant folk – the purple wine flowed, the golden light faded, song and dance grew free and circulation slightly embarrassed. But the great impression remained and finally was exquisite. It was all purple wine, all art and song, and nobody a grain the worse. It was fireworks and conversation – the former, in the piazzetta, were to come later; it was civilisation and amenity. I took in the greater picture, but I lost nothing else; and I talked with the contadini about antique sculpture. No, nobody was a grain the worse; and I had plenty to think of. So it was I was quickened to remember that we others, we of my own country, as a race politically *not* weak, had – by what I had somewhere just heard – opened "three hundred 'saloons'" at Manilla.

VI

The "other" afternoons I here pass on to – and I may include in them, for that matter, various mornings scarce less charmingly sacred to memory – were occasions of another and a later year; a brief but all felicitous impression of Naples itself, and of the approach to it from Rome, as well as of the return to Rome by a different wonderful way, which I feel I shall be wise never to attempt to "improve on". Let me muster assurance to confess that this comparatively recent and superlatively rich reminiscence gives me for its first train of ineffable images those of a motor-run that, beginning betimes of a splendid June day, and seeing me, with my genial companions, blissfully out of Porta San Paolo, hung over us thus its benediction till the splendour had faded in the lamplit rest of the Chiaja. "We'll go by the mountains," my friend, of the winged chariot, had said, "and we'll come back, after three days, by the sea"; which handsome promise flowered into such flawless performance that I could but feel it to have closed and rounded for me, beyond any further rehandling, the long-drawn rather indeed than thick-studded chaplet of my visitations of Naples – from the first, seasoned with the highest sensibility of youth, forty years ago, to this last the other day. I find myself noting with interest – and just to be able to emphasise it is what inspires me with these remarks – that, in spite of the milder and smoother and perhaps, pictorially speaking, considerably emptier, Neapolitan face of things, things in general, of our later time, I recognised in my final impression a grateful, a beguiling serenity. The place is at the best wild and weird and sinister, and yet seemed on this occasion to be seated more at her ease in her immense natural dignity. My disposition to feel that, I hasten to add, was doubtless my own secret; my three beautiful days, at any rate, filled themselves with the splendid harmony, several of the minor notes of which ask for a place, such as it may be, just here.

Wondrously, it was a clean and cool and, as who should say, quiet and amply interspaced Naples – in tune with itself, no harsh jangle of *forestieri* vulgarising the concert. I seemed in fact, under the blaze of summer, the only stranger – though the blaze of summer itself was, for that matter, everywhere but a higher pitch of light and colour and tradition, and a lower pitch of everything else; even, it struck me, of sound and fury. The appeal in short was genial, and, faring out to Pompeii of a Sunday afternoon, I enjoyed there, for the only time I can recall, the sweet chance of a late hour or two, the hour of the lengthening shadows, absolutely alone. The impression remains ineffaceable – it was to supersede half-a-dozen other mixed memories, the sense that had remained with me, from far back, of a pilgrimage always here beset with traps and shocks and vulgar importunities, achieved under fatal discouragements. Even Pompeii, in fine, haunt of *all* the cockneys of creation burned itself, in the warm still eventide, as clear as glass, or as the glow of a pale topaz, and the particular cockney who roamed without a plan and at his ease, but with his feet on Roman slabs, his hands on Roman stones, his eyes on the Roman void, his consciousness really at last of some good to him, could open himself as never before to the fond luxurious fallacy of a close communion, a direct revelation. With which there were other moments for him not less the fruit of the slow unfolding of time; the clearest of these again being those enjoyed on the terrace of a small island-villa – the island a rock and the villa a wondrous little rock-garden, unless a better term would be perhaps rock-salon, just off the extreme point of Posilippo and where, thanks to a friendliest hospitality, he was to hang ecstatic, through another sublime afternoon, on the wave of a magical wand. Here, as happened, were charming wise, original people even down to delightful amphibious American children, enamelled by the sun of the Bay as for figures of miniature Tritons and Nereids on a Renaissance plaque; and above all, on the part of the general prospect, a demonstration of the grand style of composition and effect that one was never to wish to see bettered. The way in which the Italian scene on such occasions as this seems to purify itself to the

Pompeii

transcendent and perfect *idea* alone – idea of beauty, of dignity, of comprehensive grace, with all accidents merged, all defects disowned, all experience outlived, and to gather itself up into the mere mute eloquence of what has just incalculably *been*, remains forever the secret and the lesson of the subtlest daughter of History. All one could do, at the heart of the overarching crystal, and in presence of the relegated City, the far-trailing Mount, the grand Sorrentine headland, the islands incomparably stationed and related, was to wonder what may well become of the so many other elements of any poor human and social complexus, what might become of any successfully-working or only struggling and floundering civilisation at all, when high Natural Elegance proceeds to take such exclusive charge and recklessly assume, as it were, *all* the responsibilities.

VII

This indeed had been quite the thing I was asking myself all the wondrous way down from Rome, and was to ask myself afresh, on the return, largely within sight of the sea, as our earlier course had kept to the ineffably romantic inland valleys, the great decorated blue vistas in which the breasts of the mountains shine vaguely with strange high-lying city and castle and church and convent, even as shoulders of no diviner line might be hung about with dim old jewels. It was odd, at the end of time, long after those initiations, of comparative youth, that had then struck one as extending the very field itself of felt charm, as exhausting the possibilities of fond surrender, it was odd to have positively a new basis of enjoyment, a new gate of triumphant passage, thrust into one's consciousness and opening to one's use; just as I confess I have to brace myself a little to call by such fine names our latest, our ugliest and most monstrous aid to motion. It is true of the monster, as we have known him up to now, that one can neither quite praise him nor quite blame him without a blush – he reflects so the nature of the company he's condemned to keep. His splendid easy power addressed to noble aims make him assuredly on occasion a purely beneficent creature. I parenthesise at any rate that I know him in no other light – counting out of course the acquaintance that consists of a dismayed arrest in the road, with back flattened against wall or hedge, for the dusty, smoky, stenchy shock of his passage. To no end is his easy power more blest than to that of ministering to the ramifications, as it were, of curiosity, or to that, in other words, of achieving for us, among the kingdoms of the earth, the grander and more genial, the comprehensive and *complete* introduction. Much as

Marina di Napoli, by Gaetano Esposito

was ever to be said for our old forms of pilgrimage – and I am convinced that they are far from wholly superseded – they left, they had to leave, dreadful gaps in our yearning, dreadful lapses in our knowledge, dreadful failures in our energy; there were always things off and beyond, goals of delight and dreams of desire, that dropped as a matter of course into the unattainable, and over to which our wonder-working agent now flings the firm straight bridge. Curiosity has lost, under this amazing extension, its salutary renouncements perhaps; contemplation has become one with action and satisfaction one with desire – speaking always in the spirit of the inordinate lover of an enlightened use of our eyes. That may represent, for all I know, an insolence of advantage on which there will be eventual heavy charges, as yet obscure and incalculable, to pay, and I glance at the possibility only to avoid all thought of the lesson of the long run, and to insist that I utter this dithyramb but in the immediate flush and fever of the short. For such a beat of time as our fine courteous and contemplative advance upon Naples, and for such another as our retreat northward under the same fine law of observation and homage, the bribed consciousness could only decline to question its security. The sword of Damocles suspended over that presumption, the skeleton at the banquet of extravagant ease, would have been that even at our actual inordinate rate – leaving quite apart "improvements" to come – such savings of trouble begin to use up the world; some hard grain of difficulty being always a necessary part of the composition of pleasure. The hard grain in our old comparatively pedestrian mixture, before this business of our learning not so much even to fly (which might indeed involve trouble) as to be mechanically and prodigiously flown, quite another matter, was the element of uncertainty, effort and patience; the handful of silver nails which, I admit, drove many an impression home. The seated motorist misses the silver nails, I fully acknowledge, save in so far as his æsthetic (let alone his moral) conscience may supply him with some artful subjective substitute; in which case the thing becomes a precious secret of his own.

However, I wander wild – by which I mean I look too far ahead; my intention having been only to let my sense of the merciless June beauty of Naples Bay at the sunset hour and on the island terrace associate itself with the whole inexpressible taste of our two motor-days' feast of scenery. That queer question of the exquisite grand manner as the most emphasised *all* of things – of what it may, seated so predominant in nature, insidiously, through the centuries, let generations and populations "in for", hadn't in the least waited for the special emphasis I speak of to hang about me. I must have found myself more or less consciously entertaining it by the way – since how couldn't it be of the very essence of the truth, constantly and intensely before us, that Italy is really so much the most beautiful country in the world, taking all things together, that others must stand off and be hushed while she speaks? Seen thus in great comprehensive iridescent stretches, it is the incomparable wrought *fusion*, fusion of human history and mortal passion with the elements of earth and air, of colour, composition and form, that constitute her appeal and give it the supreme heroic grace. The chariot of fire favours fusion rather than promotes analysis, and leaves much of that first June picture for me, doubtless, a great accepted blur of violet and silver. The various hours and successive aspects, the different strong passages of our reverse process, on the other hand, still figure for me even as some series of sublime landscape-frescoes – if the great Claude, say, had ever used that medium – in the immense gallery of a palace; the homeward run by Capua, Terracina, Gaeta and its storeyed headland fortress, across the deep, strong, indescribable Pontine Marshes, white-cattled, strangely pastoral, sleeping in the afternoon glow, yet stirred by the near sea-breath. Thick somehow to the imagination as some full-bodied sweetness of syrup is thick to the palate the atmosphere of that region – thick with the sense of history and the very taste of time; as if the haunt and home (which indeed it is) of some great fair bovine aristocracy attended and guarded by halberdiers in the form of the mounted and long-lanced herdsmen, admirably congruous with the whole picture at every point, and never more so than in their manner of gaily taking up, as with bell-voices of golden bronze, the offered wayside greeting.

There had been this morning among the impressions of our first hour an unforgettable specimen of that general type – the image of one of those human figures on which our perception of the romantic so often pounces in Italy as on the genius of the scene personified; with this advantage, that as the scene there has, at its best, an unsurpassable distinction, so the physiognomic representative, standing for it all, and with an animation, a complexion, an expression, a fineness and fulness of humanity that appear to have gathered it in and to sum it up, becomes beautiful by the same simple process, very much, that makes the heir to a great capitalist rich. Our early start, our roundabout descent from Posilippo by shining Baiae for avoidance of the city, had been an hour of enchantment beyond any notation I can here recover; all lustre and azure, yet all composition and classicism, the prospect developed and spread, till after extraordinary upper reaches of radiance and horizons of pearl we came at the turn of a descent upon a stalwart young gamekeeper, or perhaps substantial young farmer, who, well-appointed and blooming, had unslung his gun and, resting on it beside a hedge, just lived for us, in the rare felicity of his whole look, during that moment and while, in recognition, or almost, as we felt, in homage, we instinctively checked our speed. He pointed, as it were, the lesson, giving the supreme right accent or final exquisite turn to the immense magnificent phrase; which from those moments on, and on and on, resembled doubtless nothing so much as a page written, by a consummate verbal economist and master of style, in the noblest of all tongues. Our splendid human plant by the wayside had flowered thus into style – and there wasn't to be, all day, a lapse of eloquence, a wasted word or a cadence missed.

These things are personal memories, however, with the logic of certain insistences of that sort often difficult to seize. Why should I have kept so sacredly uneffaced, for instance, our small afternoon wait at tea-time or, as we made it, coffee-time, in the little brown piazzetta of Velletri, just short of the final push on through the flushed Castelli Romani and the drop and home-stretch across the darkening Campagna? We had been dropped into the very lap of the ancient civic family, after the inveterate fashion of one's sense of such stations in small Italian towns. There was a narrow raised terrace, with steps, in front of the best of the two or three local cafés, and in the soft enclosed, the warm waning light of June various benign contemplative worthies sat at disburdened tables and, while they smoked long black weeds, enjoyed us under those probable workings of subtlety with which we invest so many quite unimaginably blank (I dare say) Italian simplicities. The charm was, as always in Italy, in the tone and the air and the happy hazard of things, which made any positive pretension or claimed importance a comparatively trifling question. We slid, in the steep little place, more or less down hill; we wished, stomachically, we had rather addressed ourselves to a tea-basket; we suffered importunity from unchidden infants who swarmed about our chairs and romped about our feet; we stayed no long time, and "went to see" nothing; yet we communicated to intensity, we lay at our ease in the bosom of the past, we practised intimacy, in short, an intimacy so much greater than the mere accidental and ostensible: the difficulty for the right and grateful expression of which makes the old, the familiar tax on the luxury of loving Italy.

1900-1909.

INDEX

References in italics are to illustrations

ACKNOWLEDGEMENTS

The front cover panel reproduces a detail from James Holland's "The Campanile and the Doge's Palace, with St. Mark's in the background" (Bridgeman Art Library). Drawings by Joseph Pennell from *Italian Hours* (1909 edition) appear on pages 3, 7, 35, 59, 87, 105, 121, 139, 153, 175, 187, 195 and 203. Acknowledgments for the other black and white drawings are due as follows: British Architectural Library, RIBA, London: pages 16, 90, 102, 104, 107, 108, 110, 115, 140, 156, 182, 191, 192, 196, 198, 210, 211 and 216 (Edward Anson); pages 56, 137, 164 and 172 (T.D. Atkinson); page 112 (J.M. Lockyer). Martyn Gregory Gallery, London: pages 37, 38, 66 and 69 (E.W. Cooke); page 45 (J. Holland); page 178 (W. Evans). Sotheby's, London: page 94. Christie's, London: page 152. Victoria & Albert Museum, London/Crown copyright: pages 9, 12, 22, 25, 26, 27, 41, 62, 74, 118, 142, 146, 155, 207, 212 (W. Boutcher); page 159 (T.H. Longfield); pages 30, 77, 81, 82, 84 and 193 (W.J.N. Millard); pages 15, 46, 48, 51, 52, 125, 128, 130 and 183 (T.C. Lewis); pages 60 and 73 (W. Hilton); pages 61, 72, 204 and 205 (E.L.T. Jenkinson); pages 13 and 33 (R.P. Spiers); page 44 (W.J. Muller); pages 53, 88, 95, 97, 99, 101, 134, 149, 177 and 201. Tate Gallery, London: pages 19 and 122.

Acknowledgment is due as follows for permission to reproduce colour paintings: Christie's, London: pages 2, 28, 47, 93 and 133. Fine Art Picture Library: pages 11, 17, 42, 100, 120, 129 and 208. Bridgeman Art Library: page 21 (Christopher Wood Gallery); pages 54 and 183 (private collections); page 79 (Gavin Graham Gallery); pages 109 and 117 (Louvre). Scala: pages 58, 67, 186 and 215 (Galleria d'Arte Moderna, Florence); page 70 (Galleria d'Arte Moderna, Genoa); pages 161, 171 and 174 (Coll. Casse di Risparmio).

The town plans on pages 39, 86, 166 and 179 are from *Baedeker's Italy* and the map on page 6 was drawn by Studio Briggs, after Baedeker.

Picture researcher: Mary Jane Gibson.

·DHF·